Black Literature for High School Students

Black Literature for High School Students

Barbara Dodds Stanford
Utica College of Syracuse University

Karima Amin
Buffalo City School District, New York

National Council of Teachers of English
1111 Kenyon Road, Urbana, Illinois 61801

Grateful acknowledgment is made for permission to reprint several poems in this book: "The New Integrationist" from *Black Pride* and "Black Woman" from *Don't Cry, Scream* by Haki R. Madhubuti (Don L. Lee), reprinted by permission of the author and Third World Press, 7524 South Cottage Grove, Chicago, Illinois 60619. "For Paul Laurence Dunbar" from *On These I Stand* by Countee Cullen. Copyright 1925 by Harper & Row, Publishers, Inc.; renewed 1953 by Ida M. Cullen. Reprinted by permission of the publisher.

Staff Editor: Diane Allen

Book Design: Tom Kovacs

NCTE Stock Number 03308

Library of Congress Cataloging in Publication Data

Stanford, Barbara Dodds.
Black literature for high school students.

Includes bibliographies and indexes.
1. American literature—Afro-American authors—Study and teaching (Secondary) 2. American literature—Afro-American authors—Bio-bibliography.
I. Amin, Karima, 1947- joint author. II. Title.
PS153.N5S7 810'.8'0896 78-16890
ISBN 0-8141-0330-8

Contents

Preface

Ten years ago, as a white graduate student and a second-year teacher, I wrote a book called *Negro Literature for High School Students*, one of the NCTE's first books on minority literature, and for several years one of its best sellers. With annotations on approximately 150 books, it was comprehensive, including almost every literary work by a black writer or with a black main character that was in print at the time. In addition, a depressingly large number of out-of-print books were included, for such classics as Gwendolyn Brooks' *The Bean Eaters* and *Maud Martha*, William Demby's *Beetlecreek*, Ann Petry's *The Street*, and Richard Wright's *Eight Men* were all unavailable in bookstores.

Ten years ago *Negro Literature for High School Students* was complete and up-to-date. The wealth of black literature published since that time has made a new edition necessary. A new book was desperately needed to direct teachers to the important new works now available from black writers. And in addition to new books, a new perspective was needed. As black literature has become more popular, new insights have emerged from both critics and teachers. We have now recognized more honestly the impact that cultural preconceptions have on a person's ability to evaluate and to analyze literature objectively. Many contemporary black writers claim that their works are so far from white traditions that white critics have no right to evaluate them, and this rejection is often extended to white teachers. When I first heard challenges to a white teacher's ability to interpret black literature, I was upset and angry, but I have since recognized the validity of the statement that white people do not interpret literature the same way black people do. It is now obvious to me that my reaction to the works of Imamu Amiri Baraka is very likely not the same as a black person's reaction, and is probably not the reaction that the author intended. I am not willing to quit reading and reacting and sharing my reactions, but I am now more eager to compare my reactions to those of others and to learn more about both literature and myself as a result.

Ten years ago, neither I nor what was then the NCTE Publications Committee questioned whether a young white teacher could adequately write a survey of black literature. So little had been written on the subject that any effort seemed valid. Now, however, we recognize that not only race but ethnic background, age, region of the country, and size of the community influence a person's reactions to literature and limit the validity of any single point of view. A black farm girl in Mississippi, a middle-class black suburbanite from New Jersey, a second-generation Italian immigrant from upstate New York, an Anglo-Saxon college-professor's daughter, and a Hawaiian of Chinese descent will all react differently to the more controversial black writers. Some will identify with the oppressed, others with the oppressor. The same scene will appear totally false to one reader, realistic to another, and naively positive to a third. Because of these differences in perception, this new edition is a collaborative effort which included the work of a black and a white author, as well as suggestions from six consultants representing different areas of the country, and extensive review by NCTE editorial staff and Editorial Board. Because we recognize the way that background and experience can influence perceptions, we have included the following information about ourselves.

I (Barbara Stanford) am a white midwesterner. I have taught in an all-black school in St. Louis, Missouri, and in an almost all-white school in Boulder, Colorado. I am now teaching in a predominantly white college in upstate New York.

Karima Amin is a black teacher from Buffalo, New York, who teaches in that city. For eight years she has taught English, including a course in literature by and about black writers, to both black and white high school and junior high school students.

Black Literature for High School Students contains ten chapters. I wrote the Historical Survey of Black Writers and the Biography chapters. Karima wrote the Adolescent Literature chapter and several teaching units for the classroom uses of black literature section. Each of us contributed material for the supplementary bibliographies. The introductory chapter contains ideas from both of us. Both of us reacted to each other's chapters; however, we did not try to reach consensus or to disguise our differences. We felt that it would be instructive for the reader to see the differences in our approaches and impressions.

To deal with different reactions from different parts of the country, we invited teachers from all regions to serve as consultants on the project. Six people volunteered to assist: Norma Register of New Mexico; Jack Busher of Colorado Springs; Grace Larkin of Oneonta, New York; Kay Kasberger and Sanford Phippen of Syracuse, New York; and B. Joyce Pettigrew of Rock Hill, South Carolina. Their comments on the teaching of black literature are included in Chapter 1, and their suggestions about specific titles were incorporated into the other chapters.

As we worked on the revision of this book, we were encouraged by the changes that have occurred in the past ten years. Even though the collaboration with a number of people required extra work, we feel that the final product was worth the effort. To some extent, the changes in the production of this book parallel the changes that have occurred in our society. The differences among us in race, region, and ethnic background are now being recognized and far more voices are being heard. The struggle for equality and respect for all Americans is not yet completed, however. We all sincerely hope that after another ten years another revision of this book will be needed, and that it will reflect both the appearance of many more new writers and additional growth in our society's ability to recognize and respect cultural differences.

Barbara Dodds Stanford
Utica College
of Syracuse University

I Black American Literature

"... At first, most of us assumed that black literature could and should be taught and interpreted in the same ways as white literature. [In the 1960s] the struggle was for integration, and both blacks and whites were trying to prove that we were all the same under the skin and that the happy ending was only a few more freedom marches away. Ten years later, we have been more open with ourselves and each other and are realizing that the experience of blacks and whites in this country is quite different and that the evils of three hundred years cannot be dissolved in one rousing chorus of 'We Shall Overcome.'"

Barbara Dodds Stanford

1 Teaching Black Literature in Today's High Schools

Barbara Dodds Stanford

Not many years ago segregation reigned in most of the United States. Whether by law or by custom, most cities in both the North and South had separate and unequal schools, separate and unequal hotels, separate and unequal restaurants, and separate and unequal neighborhoods. Most school curricula did not even allow blacks separate and unequal status. "Whites Only" could have been stamped on almost every literature series for high school students published before 1965. The fact that such a warning did not appear led insidiously to the conclusion that no black people had ever written anything worthy of inclusion with such notables as Sarah Eleanor Royce, Henry Timrod, Francis Hopkinson or Stanley Vestal in a survey of American literature. Until the late 1960s, a literature text that contained even a couple of spirituals or a biography of George Washington Carver was quite unusual. In 1966, a survey of thirty-seven literature textbooks showed that twenty did not have a single selection either by or about black people. A study by Nancy Larrick of five thousand children's books published in 1962, 1963, and 1964 revealed that only 349, or 7 percent, included any black characters, and of this 7 percent, almost 60 percent were set outside the United States or before World War II. Quite clearly, the books used in American schools were primarily by and about white, Anglo-Saxon middle-class people.

The "Discovery" of Black Literature

During the late 1960s, a change began to occur. As a result of the civil rights movement, more attention began to be focused on black Americans, and schools began to recognize the needs and interests of their black students. Publishing houses responded to the increased interest in black people and published a wide range of new authors as well as reprints of older works. Encouraged by the example of cities like Detroit, which refused to buy books for its school system that did not adequately represent minorities, textbook publishers began to prepare special inner-city texts and to integrate their more general texts. Many schools began offering black literature courses and mini-courses or incorporating black literature into traditional courses. In 1976, a quick survey of general and American literature texts displayed at the NCTE Convention revealed only one which did not include at least one black writer. Most of these textbooks contained between 8 and 20 percent black writers, with a liberal sprinkling of writers from other non-Caucasian backgrounds—Puerto Rican, Native American, Oriental, and others.

Trade books for children, roughly a decade after Nancy Larrick's study, also reflect change. A similar, recent study of a sample of children's books published from 1973 to 1975, conducted by Jeanne Chall at Harvard University, showed that 14.4 percent of such books depicted black characters. Chall was quoted in the *New York Times* as saying that the doubling of the percentage of books depicting blacks over the 11-year period "still leaves 86 percent of children's trade books in an 'all white world,' to borrow Larrick's phrase of 1965" ("Children's Books Depicting Blacks, While Rising, Are Still Only 1 in 7," by Edward Fiske, *New York Times*, Jan. 8, 1978).

At the present time, the teaching of black literature appears to be alive and thriving. However, a few disturbing signs are beginning to appear. Teachers make comments like these: "Black literature? Oh, that was the fad of the sixties. We're into the basics now." or "We've already done black literature." Unfortunately, some teachers seem to assume that black literature is something transient and faddish, rather than an enduring part of the literature curriculum which deserves study and analysis as intensive and as ongoing as the British Romantic poets or the transcendentalists receive.

During the past ten years, we have made remarkable strides in filling gaps in our literary tradition, but even that task is less complete than many people like to think. The six consultants for this project unanimously agreed that black literature is underrepresented in the curricula of their schools. Only two of the schools represented by the consultants offered a black literature course, and all but one consultant estimated that less than 5 percent of the literature in courses not labeled "black literature" was written by blacks. So while black literature is certainly taught more frequently now than it was a few years ago, it still receives little attention.

Black Literature and Today's Teachers

The quantity of black literature being taught is not the only criterion which should be considered. While many teachers are doing an excellent job of teaching black literature, the majority of English teachers have not had such thorough training in the analysis of black literature as they have had in other bodies of literature. Many more critical studies are now available, and there are now plenty of opportunities for teachers to acquire more thorough knowledge of black literature than there were a decade ago, but unfortunately, most people now teaching were trained more than ten years ago.

The experiences of the two authors of this book were probably typical of the experiences of most of today's teachers. Barbara Stanford graduated from the University of Illinois with a bachelor's degree in English in 1964, having studied only one selection by a black writer in her entire elementary, high school, and college career: James Weldon Johnson's "The Creation," which was included in the eleventh grade literature anthology. She began teaching in a predominantly black school and discovered that that same poem was the only selection by a black writer in the entire curriculum. At first, she was frequently warned by other teachers that departing from the curriculum could get one in trouble, though she later found the curriculum committee supportive of her interest in teaching black literature. A master's degree program at Columbia University did provide an opportunity to learn about black literature—through independent study.

Karima Amin found only slightly more opportunities for studying black literature; during her elementary, high school, and college years she was taught a couple of poems by Langston Hughes as well as "The Creation." In 1968, when she student-taught at an all-black school, she worked with a supervising teacher who sparked her interest in teaching literature by black writers by introducing Langston Hughes' Simple stories and Lorraine Hansberry's *A Raisin in the Sun*. When Karima taught black literature for the first time in 1971, she started with very little preparation, studying independently and keeping one step ahead of her students.

Untrained and unfamiliar with the material, many teachers during the late 1960s rose to the challenge and educated themselves as the authors of this book did. At first, most of us assumed that black literature could and should be taught and interpreted in the same ways as white literature. At that time the struggle was for integration, and both blacks and whites were trying to prove that we were all the same under the skin and that the happy ending was only a few more freedom marches away. Ten years later, we have been more open with ourselves and each other and are realizing that the experience of blacks and whites in this country is quite different and that the evils of three hundred years cannot be dissolved in one rousing chorus of "We Shall Overcome."

Teachers today are helped in introducing black literature by recent changes in concepts of what is appropriate reading for high school students. The old convention of keeping all literature incorporating sex, other adult themes, and street language taboo until college, regardless of the facts of students' real lives, has given way to a tendency to see adult reading as appropriate for high school students. A number of the consultants for this volume mentioned instances of censorship of books by black writers in high schools. Eldridge Cleaver's *Soul on Ice* was most frequently cited as the cause of conflicts with parents and school boards, though Dick Gregory's *Nigger* and Richard Wright's *Native Son* were also mentioned. A number of important works of black literature deal with adult themes and include street language. This fact is mentioned in the discussions of the individual books. Teachers will need to know the books they select for class use and consider their choices in the light of their experience with their communities and their individual students.

In the past ten years, black people's attitudes toward their own self-image have changed considerably. Not too many years ago, many middle-class Negroes wanted to be assimilated into white culture and therefore rejected any elements of their culture and heritage frowned upon in white society, straightening their hair, spurning watermelon and "chitlins," and either learning opera and ballet or taking pride in their inability to sing and dance. Now most black people are exhibiting a growing identification with their African heritage and enjoying without inhibition elements from both African and European cultures.

Prior to the militancy of the 1960s the terms "Negro" and even "Colored" were generally acceptable to most black people. Then the "new-think" of Black Power advocates prompted a reappraisal of these terms by many, who abandoned them in favor of "Afro-American" and "Black." Now, "Colored" is rarely used and is offensive to many, and "Negro" is widely regarded as a term which perpetuates a master-slave mentality. Today's black literature reflects a widespread preference among blacks for the terms "Afro-American," "Black American," "Black," and even "African."

Black Literature as a Separate Tradition

As black people have become more willing to recognize their African roots, they have taken a new look at black literature and are beginning to recognize that it is not just a subclass of American literature, but is also a descendant of African literary traditions, which are only now being explored by Americans. Likewise, those of us who had begun analyzing black literature with the same assumptions and tools we used with white literature started to see elements we were missing or misinterpreting.

Black literature has some different traditions and aesthetic values from literature descended from British traditions. Recent analysis of black language patterns, folklore, rhetorical devices, humor, and styles have demonstrated that contemporary black culture retains more elements of African culture than had previously been recognized. Although it is almost impossible to trace completely the complex origins of black American culture, it is evident that the sources include many African and several European and American Indian cultures, as well as new inventions needed for survival in the New World. The excitement generated by the 1977 television screening of Alex Haley's *Roots* showed how great Americans' curiosity about the African elements of their national heritage has become.

A large percentage of popular black American folktales can be found with minor variations in Africa. Harold Courlander's *A Treasury of Afro-American Folklore* (Crown, cloth & pap., 1976) contains a vast collection of folklore from black people throughout the Americas and shows its relationship to African as well as European folklore. The influence of complex African rhythms and dance steps on modern American music, both black and white, is well known, but the influence of these same rhythms on the poetry of writers such as Langston Hughes and Ted Joans is less obvious. A teacher who attempted to analyze a work like Hughes' *Montage of a Dream Deferred* by British-American rhythm schemes would probably reach quite inaccurate conclusions. There also appears to be some evidence that even though most black Americans accepted Christianity, they retained some aspects of African styles of worship, particularly ceremonies and rhetorical patterns which found their way into sermons and later influenced prose styles. Language, too, has had African influences. *The Black Book* by Middleton Harris et al. (Random, cloth & pap., 1973) lists the following words which may be descended from African words: "o.k." from "yaw kay," meaning all right; "hip" from "hipi" meaning aware; "guy" from "goy," meaning a young man of no standing; and "banjo" from "banzar," a musical instrument.

Black culture has also been influenced by African aesthetic ideals which differ from those of Europe. In most of Africa, art, literature, and music were utilitarian—used in community-wide ceremonies or everyday life, not segregated to concert halls. Songs and poems were used by all, not just professionals, and were shared by the whole community. Tales and stories were used to teach moral principles. Black music has traditionally served many of the same kinds of community functions in America as it did in Africa, and many modern black writers are trying to return to the communal sharing spirit with poetry and drama.

In addition to its African heritage, black American culture contains a number of other elements from the black experience in America not shared by most white Americans. Folk heroes such as Stagolee, historic figures such as Emmett Till and Rosa Parks, and enterprising black entrepreneurs such as Madame C. J. Walker (one of America's first woman millionaires) are often referred to in black literature and are known to most blacks, but unfamiliar to the average white. The passage of time in black novels is often marked by events in black history rather than events of white society. For example, in black literature the period after the Civil War is not the Gilded Age, but the Age of Reconstruction and later Jim Crow; after World War I came the Harlem Renaissance, not the Roaring Twenties.

Of course, black people in America have also been influenced by European literary traditions and have shared many experiences with all Americans. Some black writers have lived and written almost entirely in the European tradition, while others now use predominantly black and African elements. Many contemporary writers have rejected European influences and are trying to create a black aesthetic based on black American and African values and traditions. Literary allusions are made to black, African, and Moslem cultural heroes instead of to Greek or biblical characters. Language is manipulated to reflect black dialects and black rhythms. Poetry and drama are created for utilitarian, community-service purposes instead of being an end in themselves. Sophisticated students and teachers may find a study of the critical works of such writers as Imamu Amiri Baraka, Nikki Giovanni, Clarence Major, and Ishmael Reed a challenging and exciting way of gaining a new perspective on literary traditions. Even if these works and theories are not taught, teachers should at least be aware that black artists they are teaching may be using different traditions and different aesthetic principles from those commonly taught in American colleges.

Affective Aspects of Black Literature

Besides becoming aware of black literary traditions, the teacher of black literature needs to be sensitive to the effect of literature on the attitudes and values of students. While some teachers will argue that literature should be taught as art for art's sake, most secondary school teachers have at least some interest in the value of literature as a means of helping students understand themselves and other people better. Both of the authors and all of the consultants for this project agreed that in selecting appropriate literature to recommend for high school students, concern about the effect a work of literature will have on the social attitudes and values of their students is at least as important as the literary qualities of the book.

While no definitive research has been done on the effect of black literature on attitudes, a number of studies of attitude development show that concepts taught in school do have an impact on students' attitudes. R. D. Hess and J. V. Torney in *The Development of Political Attitudes in Children* (Irvington, 1967) report that the eighth-grade students they studied had political attitudes and opinions more similar to those of their teachers than to those of their parents. Several studies have found that the personal opinions of the teacher have more impact on students than ideas from textbooks, though most of the studies deal with textbooks rather than novels, which are more emotionally involving.

Most teachers who have worked with black literature feel that the subject is of some benefit in providing students insights about themselves and other people. Kay Kasberger of Syracuse, in responding to a question asked of the consultants to this project, stated, "I am hopeful any well-written book will inform the ignorant, deepen the awareness of the injustices blacks have endured in our society, increase understanding of the joys and griefs blacks, as whites, experience. Besides the differences, students may see all the similarities between individuals of different races. That is it, really; one sees a part of himself in a character and can feel, for a moment anyway, what we mean by brotherhood —a kinship." Norma Register, however, in responding to the same question, pointed out that there are limits to the insights that can be gained from literature. "I definitely feel it is helpful in improving relations between blacks and whites. But the amount of attitude improvement that can result from reading the literature of another people is limited. For one thing, one can't interact with literature. One gets no feedback. Also, non-verbal cues and impressions which one receives in face-to-face interaction can't be communicated through literature."

Although most teachers agree that black literature can have a positive effect on people's understanding and attitudes, black teachers and white teachers often differ widely in their opinions about what kinds of books have a beneficial effect. Whites tend to react favorably to books in which white people behave generously and kindly, and often do not notice when behavior is somewhat patronizing and fails to bring about meaningful change for black people. *To Kill a Mockingbird* by Harper Lee (Lippincott, 1960; pap., Popular Lib, 1975) is probably the best example of a book which many white teachers feel promotes positive interracial attitudes by showing Atticus' courage. Most black teachers, however, point out that Atticus, in fact, compromised and survived in a destructive social system, and that for the blacks in the novel, Atticus' "heroism" was a paternalistic insult. In a just system, Tom Robinson would never have needed defending—and Atticus would not have been a hero. Norma Register describes the results of teaching a novel with a similar "message."

> I once taught a science fiction novel (*Alas, Babylon* by Pat Frank) to an all-white suburban class. In the book, the Bomb had been accidentally detonated and most of the world's population had been destroyed. However, a well-to-do young bachelor and his family and friends and his loyal "Negro" neighbors whom he had employed had all been spared. Though the whites were kinder to the Blacks in some ways after the disaster (some [blacks] even rode in the front seat of the hero's truck), they still filled a subordinate role in the lives of the whites. The author managed to have them prefer to eat alone, and they still called the bachelor-hero "Mr. Randy." But my students failed to grasp what I am sure was an unintentional but salient message of the novel—that even a nuclear holocaust won't lead some people to question their racist customs.

While books which portray patronizing attitudes toward blacks anger black students and promote unhealthy attitudes among whites, many teachers also feel that books that frankly portray ghetto life and that use four-letter words cause some white students to react negatively toward black people. Jack Busher of

Colorado Springs noted that while studying Dick Gregory's *Nigger*, "some students got so hung-up on 'hate attitudes' that they couldn't empathize with Gregory. Others over-empathized, and lost their objectivity in the opposite direction."

Goals and Objectives for Black Literature Courses

Teachers who want to use literature to help their students understand themselves and other people better and to improve relationships between the races need to consider their goals and objectives as carefully as those who are interested in teaching literary forms. The following four goals seem to us to be the most appropriate aims for a teacher to attempt to achieve with high school students.

1. Developing Empathy

Students will recognize the basic human needs, desires and concerns felt by both blacks and whites and the ways that these are manifested in black culture. Students will be able to empathize with black characters in a variety of situations.

The ability to empathize with other people, to feel what they feel, and to understand what they believe and why they believe it, even if you disagree, is one of the most basic human relations skills. To some extent, empathy is based on the recognition of the underlying similarities among all people and the ways that the differences among people are differences of degree, not kind.

Exposure to literature by black writers may enhance the black student's self-image, particularly if selections which express black pride, such as *Roll of Thunder, Hear My Cry* and *Song of the Trees*, both by Mildred D. Taylor, are studied. Some students will discover through reading that some writers are "just like me." Others will appreciate reading selections by writers who "tell it like I *know* it is." Students who have doubts about their own potential may find their self-confidence rising after reading about people who are similar to them and who have been successful.

White students, too, will often recognize that a black writer is expressing their own experiences and feelings. But white readers, and some black readers, will also find that the experiences and ideas in some books are quite foreign to them. They may need help in recognizing the underlying human values and empathizing with the characters. For white students who have had no contact with blacks, or who come from areas where blacks are never mentioned in anything but a cruelly stereotyped manner, it may be helpful to begin with books about black people of a similar background, values, and social class. Such students, then, will not have to deal with their regional and class prejudices along with their racial bias. White middle-class students, even if they are from prejudiced backgrounds, should be able to empathize with the characters in *It's Good to Be Black*, *Mary McLeod Bethune*, and *My Life with Dr. Martin Luther King, Jr.* Working-class, urban white students may find that they can identify with Althea Gibson, Connie Hawkins, or Gordon Parks.

2. Understanding Black Culture

Students will recognize that black culture has ancient, meaningful, and significant traditions.

The achievements of black people in Africa, America and other parts of the world are not so completely ignored as they were a few years ago, but most students still know little about the development of black culture. All students will benefit from gaining knowledge about black traditions, for it is difficult to understand contemporary black literature without some knowledge of its "roots." A study of their heritage can instill pride in black students and enhance their self-image. Learning about the black heritage will probably help white students correct misconceptions, may increase their ability to relate to black people, and may help them better understand their own traditions.

Roots by Alex Haley is, of course, a very valuable book for achieving this objective. In addition, books about African culture such as *Things Fall Apart* by Chinua Achebe ([1959] pap., Fawcett World, 1976) or books showing the relationship of black African and black American cultures, such as Courlander's *A Treasury of Afro-American Folklore*, are useful. A historical survey of black literature, using books discussed in Chapter 2, or a selection of biographies of black leaders throughout American history can help students understand the black heritage. The course outline "From Africa to America" in Chapter 6 also provides a way of achieving this objective.

3. Understanding Effects of Racism

Students should have a thorough understanding of the treatment of blacks in America. They should know the historical and sociological facts about slavery, Jim Crow laws, and contemporary institutional racism.

It is easy to teach students the facts about racism; but dealing with the accompanying affective issues is much more complex. The natural result of learning about slavery, discrimination, lynching, and other forms of repression is rage, and since the proper targets of this rage are dead or distant, students may vent their anger against other students or teachers. Anger is basically a healthy emotion. For many black people, a healthy expression of anger has been the way of liberating themselves from more damaging emotions such as self-hatred, inferiority feelings, or self-pity. The problem with anger is that it hinders a person's ability to think rationally and is often directed against inappropriate targets.

Usually the best way to respond to student anger is to convey to students that anger is an appropriate reaction to the situation and that you are angry, too. At the same time, it is important to provide healthy outlets for the anger and to protect innocent victims. Sometimes open discussions of emotional reactions to books can help students to deal with their anger. Sometimes the energy from anger can be mobilized for a fight against injustice. A class or individuals might be encouraged to undertake a project fighting against a current injustice related to the injustice in the book.

In addition to anger, white students are likely to have other emotional reactions to books which show white people as oppressors and perpetrators of sadistic atrocities. It is difficult to effectively teach the history of the black in America without encouraging in white children the kind of self-hatred which has been so damaging to black children. White children do need to learn about the evil that their ancestors have committed, but while they are assimilating this painful information, they need to be able to feel that their teacher respects them and cares for them. A teacher who conveys the attitude that "I know you are prejudiced and I am going to make you admit it" is likely to cause students to reject any comments he or she makes. If white children are to deal effectively with the ugly facts of their history, they need to be able to discuss their feelings—their prejudices as well as their sorrow and frustration—without fear of reprisal.

Because of the strong emotions generated by books which focus on racism and hatred, it is usually best to alternate books of this type with books which show people combating racism or depict positive aspects of black culture. Teaching nothing but anger-producing books may cause students to be so overwhelmed that they begin to despair or to react negatively to black literature or even to black people.

Although this objective is a difficult one to teach, it is extremely important that both black and white students recognize the racism which has been inflicted on black Americans. This knowledge may help prevent such behavior in the future; it is essential for understanding and correcting the injustices that remain from the racism of past generations, for blacks still suffer in many ways from past as well as present injustices.

Racism in America is so pervasive that almost all books by black writers include some examples of it. Some of the most useful books are *Youngblood* by John Oliver Killens, *Black Boy* by Richard Wright, *The Autobiography of Miss Jane Pittman* by Ernest Gaines, *For Us, the Living* by Mrs. Medgar Evers, and *Captain Blackman* by John A. Williams. With students who are not yet convinced of the positive aspects of black culture, it may be best to use books which show the effects of discrimination on characters who are able to maintain a strong and loving family and personal dignity, rather than books in which family and pride have already been destroyed, such as *Native Son* or *Manchild in the Promised Land*. *Youngblood*, for example, while a less powerful book than *Black Boy*, portrays a family which all students can respect; there is no danger of anyone's feeling that the Youngbloods deserve the treatment they receive.

4. *Understanding Human Reactions to Racism*

All students should recognize the various reactions both black and white people have had to racism and should understand which reactions lead to positive change and which do not.

After students are aroused to anger through learning about the injustices faced by black people, they need to carefully analyze alternative ways of reacting to injustice. Many students will glibly suggest that characters should fight back, without considering the consequences of various ways of fighting. Others may prematurely decide that situations are hopeless and give up. One of the most valuable functions of literature is to help us analyze alternatives and their consequences without facing the consequences ourselves. We can learn from others' mistakes, as well as their successes.

The unit "Eye + Mind + Heart = Experience" in Chapter 6 is valuable for this objective. This course outline covers varied modes of both active and passive resistance to oppression that black people have used since slavery. Unit II, Part B of this outline, entitled "Constructive Reaction," delineates some mental attitudes which govern the way black people deal with dehumanization in this society. Also listed there are several poems which describe these mental processes at work. The literature suggested in Unit III of this outline, "Black Struggle for Survival," goes beyond the initial psychological reactions to what one contemporary black poet calls "survival action in motion." In this literature, survival tactics are explored, black people's reactions to oppression are dealt with, and the results of such reactions can be studied. While this study should lead to an understanding of which reactions result in positive change and which do not, the teacher's sensitivity to the black perspective is crucial. Also helpful would be some knowledge of the author's philosophy. Take a look at the following poem by Haki R. Madhubuti (Don L. Lee), a black poet who is well known for his accomplishments in the fight for black liberation.

The New Integrationist

I
seek
integration
of
negroes
with
black
people.

Obviously this poem concerns itself with integration, an important survival tactic. But this integration is not the black-white integration that we usually think of; this is the integration of varied black minds. Black integration into white society is supposedly a positive act with positive results, but all too often it is a superficial gesture loaded with negativity that many black people can attest to. The "new" integration, or black unity, on the other hand, has often been looked upon with fear and derision, yet it has been largely responsible for the emergence of black self-determination and positive change.

It is difficult but absolutely necessary that a teacher looking at reactions to oppression and the outcomes of such reactions devote more than surface consideration to the question of which reactions lead to positive change and which do not, which are realistic and which would work only in fiction. In many older junior novels, problems of discrimination are solved by "Good Samaritan" white people who help the hero or heroine, but leave the system intact and also damage the self-esteem of black people who have to depend on others.

A few of the many books which deal effectively with strategies for combating racism are *The King God Didn't Save* and *Sons of Darkness, Sons of Light* by John A. Williams, *A Woman Called*

Moses by Marcy Heidish, *Why We Can't Wait* and *Stride Toward Freedom* by Martin Luther King, Jr. and *Revolutionary Suicide* by Huey P. Newton.

Among the greatest benefits of teaching, and particularly of teaching black literature, are the opportunities the teacher has for learning and growth. As we study with our students, we are likely to learn more about ourselves, about our past with both its positive and its negative aspects, and about ways of working for the future we desire. Teaching black literature by itself will not eliminate racism. But for those of us who are English teachers, achieving the four objectives listed above, even with some of our students, can be a significant contribution.

2 A Historical Survey of Black American Writers

Barbara Dodds Stanford

The first published poem by a black American writer appeared in 1760, a date which marks not the beginning of black literary effort in America but rather, the first incorporation of the black literary tradition into the European tradition. For almost a century and a half before the appearance of Jupiter Hammon's eighty-eight-line broadside, "Salvation by Christ, with Penetential Cries," black poets and storytellers had been creating out of African oral literature, plantation experiences, and such elements of European traditions as they were able to pick up, a body of songs and folk tales remarkable for their emotional power, humor and vivid symbolism. For the modern reader, the few stark, concise lines of "Were You There?" or "I Got Shoes" convey far more powerful religious fervor than Jupiter Hammon's classical imagery.

For over three and a half centuries, black oral literature has flourished, in stories, ballads, songs, poems, and sermons "published" as in Africa through community-wide gatherings, shared and preserved in memory, not on paper, impinging only occasionally on the written literature of the European tradition, but refreshing it whenever the two interact. Unfortunately for us, a history of this literature is almost impossible to reconstruct, because it is a literature of the moment, a celebration of this particular birth, this death, this sorrow, or this escape to freedom, for the people present. It is a living part of a community, not a series of monuments to individuals. It lives today, not as unique pieces of writing preserved in an anthology, but in the images and symbols used by a six-year-old child or a James Baldwin, in the rhythms of the Temptations or of Langston Hughes, and in the songs sung in a small Baptist church. It does not crystallize into completed works but constantly evolves, expressing the same ideas in the new circumstances of each new generation.

Coming to the New World at about the same time as African

traditions were European literary traditions. The Europeans, too, had a strong oral literature with ballads, legends, poems, and songs. In the early days, when black slaves and white indentured servants toiled together, these traditions mingled. But the Europeans also had a written literature—a body of works kept locked and hidden from the blacks as long as possible, for it contained ideas about brotherhood, equality, freedom, and revolution which the whites did not want to share. The tool of literacy itself was a weapon which made a slave a free person. The Europeans knew this, for they had only recently broken the shackles of feudal church and king through the power of the printed word. So as slavery became more and more entrenched, the denial of books to blacks became solidified in law. Evidence that a black person could read, whether the slave had learned from a kind master, picked up the skill through careful observation, or brought it from Arabic-language Koran schools in Africa, was grounds for severe punishment.

Before the Civil War, black and white literary traditions generally remained separate. The few blacks who wrote poetry, autobiography, tracts, or sermons that were published lived in unusual, privileged circumstances. They, like early whites, wrote for a purpose, not for pleasure. As the white colonists sharpened their literary skills into weapons for the Revolution, black writers saw the pen as a weapon against slavery. Like early white American writers, early black writers derived their style from what was currently—or slightly earlier—in vogue in England. New at the business, and with their time occupied in countless other ways, they had neither the courage nor the energy to innovate in style, though many were quite radical in their ideas.

It was not until after the Civil War that black writers had the leisure to write for entertainment or the freedom to incorporate styles and ideas from the black oral tradition. During the late 1800s, Paul Laurence Dunbar and Charles Chesnutt used black oral literature in European forms, as Washington Irving and Nathaniel Hawthorne had earlier used colonial legends and superstitions in traditional European forms to create a unique American literature. Limited severely by the tastes of their white audiences and by their own privileged backgrounds, which restricted their exposure to folk material, these early writers still created some quite good stories. But not until the Harlem Renaissance of the 1920s were black writers affluent and unconstrained enough to freely manipulate both black and white literary forms.

It is with the Harlem Renaissance that the great black writers Langston Hughes, Claude McKay, and Jean Toomer appear. Since the 1920s, black writers have gained more and more freedom. They have adapted elements of white American realism, naturalism and romanticism, and have incorporated to varying degrees the black oral tradition. They range from writers like Frank Yerby, who use totally European themes and techniques, to writers like Ted Joans, who use very little that is European.

This brief survey of black writers provides a very quick overview of the history of black literature in America and more detailed descriptions of the writers and works most likely to be of use in high school English classes. The focus is primarily on novels, poems, short stories and plays. Historical, sociological and other nonfiction works are not included, and biographical and autobiographical works are described in Chapter 4. More comprehensive surveys of black literature are annotated in the final part of this chapter.

The books included here are generally of interest and benefit to older adolescents, particularly eleventh and twelfth graders. Some students, or their parents, may object to the language or content of some of these books. The teacher should read any book in this section before recommending it to students. For junior high school students and immature high school students, the books listed in the junior novel section are likely to be more appropriate.

How to Use This Survey

In the historical portions of this survey, writers are discussed in chronological order by date of birth. In the sections after the Harlem Renaissance, they are arranged alphabetically. The bibliographic information supplied in the text guides the reader to editions of the works, most of which are available in print at this writing. Where these differ from the original edition, the original publication date is also supplied. Paperback editions are cited whenever possible. A series of supplementary bibliographies (Chapter 5) give information for broadening and enriching the content of black literature courses, developing special units, and responding to individual students' interests. The bibliography of recordings ranges over the entire history of black American literature, enabling teachers to bring the authors' own voices into the classroom or take advantage of professional reading and performances. The Directory of Publishers at the back of the book is a key to publisher abbreviations in the text and supplies addresses for ordering.

Pre-Civil War Writers

Before the Civil War, most black literature was oral literature: songs, poems, and tales produced by slaves to help them cope with plantation life. In the repressive atmosphere of slavery, simple-sounding songs and tales often masked complex and revolutionary meanings. Songs like "Go Down, Moses" or "Steal Away to Jesus" might signal that Harriet Tubman or another conductor on the Underground Railroad was near, or might mean that a secret meeting was to be held in a swamp or graveyard. "Follow the Drinking Gourd" provided almost the only "map" the runaway slave had—the North Star in the tail of the drinking gourd, or Little Dipper. Even slaves who would not dream of running away could let their imaginations rebel with animal stories which only thinly disguised tales of slaves outwitting the master. Black oral literature from this and later periods is available from many sources. One of the best retellings of folktales for young readers is Julius Lester's *Black Folktales*, described in Chapter 3 of this book. A thorough, scholarly collection of tales, songs, poems, proverbs, and miscellaneous recollections from the Caribbean and South America as well as the United States is Harold Courlander's *A Treasury of Afro-American Folklore* (Crown, cloth & pap., 1976). Dudley Randall's *The Black Poets* (Bantam, pap., 1971) contains a good selection of oral poetry.

The written literature of the period before the Civil War is of much lower quality than the oral literature, and is notable more for historic than for literary reasons. While the poems, tracts, letters, and essays of such early writers as Phillis Wheatley, Lucy Terry, and Benjamin Banneker will probably not be read with relish by many contemporary adolescents, the writers themselves were fascinating people; more about them can be found in Chapter 4. They are an important reminder that from the earliest days of our country, black people have functioned in a wide variety of roles outside of slavery. The first known poem by a black writer is "Bar's Fight" (1746), Lucy Terry's account of an Indian raid on the New England frontier settlement where she lived. While her poetry was rather humorous doggerel, Ms. Terry was apparently a formidable orator, for she argued a land case before the Supreme Court and appeared before the Board of Trustees of Williams College to successfully persuade them to allow her son to enter the school.

While poetry and nonfiction were written by black people for almost a century before the Civil War, the first novel by a black writer did not appear until 1853. It was *Clotel; or The President's Daughter* by William Wells Brown, and told the story of the slave daughters of Thomas Jefferson (Arno, 1969; pap., Macmillan, 1970). Three other little-known novels were published in the 1850s, but not until almost forty years later did successful novels by black writers begin to appear.

Benjamin Banneker (1731–1806)

Benjamin Banneker was, according to one version, the descendant of a white woman, formerly an indentured servant, and an aristocratic African who had been captured as a slave, and whom she bought and freed. Banneker became an important inventor and astronomer during the period before and after the Revolutionary War. Among his many accomplishments were publishing an almanac, building one of the early clocks in the country, and serving on the survey team that laid out Washington, D.C. His writings include several significant letters and his almanac. Particularly interesting are his "Letter to the Secretary of State" and "A Plan of Peace-Office for the United States." The former is a plea for justice for his race and an excellent example of argumentative writing. My students enjoyed it very much, and in fact several nominated it as the best selection of the semester. Both of these selections can be found in Benjamin Brawley's *Early Negro American Writers* (Peter Smith, 1935). See also Chapter 4.

Phillis Wheatley (1753?–1784)

A slave in pre-Revolutionary Boston, Phillis Wheatley was educated by her owners and became known in literary circles in the Colonies and in England. Her poetry, which compares favorably with that of other poets of her time, is in the neoclassic tradition, with frequent mythological references. Often personal in its subject matter, it is largely imitative, with stilted vocabulary and frequent lapses into forced rhythm and rhyme.

Collected originally in a volume titled *Poems on Various Subjects, Religious and Moral,* Wheatley's poetry is available in a modern collection, *Poems of Phillis Wheatley,* edited by Julian D. Mason (U of NC Pr, 1966). A sample of her better work is the third stanza of "To the Right Honorable William, Earl of Dartmouth," which glorifies freedom and would satisfy most students' curiosity about her writing. Shirley Graham's biography of Phillis Wheatley is described in Chapter 4.

Frederick Douglass (1817?–1895)

Frederick Douglass, a slave in Maryland, learned to read and later escaped to become famous as an abolitionist orator. A number of his speeches merit study and can be found in Brawley's *Early Negro American Writers,* cited above. Douglass is best known for his autobiographical works, *The Life and Times of Frederick Douglass* and a shorter memoir, *Narrative of the Life of Frederick Douglass, an American Slave.* These are discussed in Chapter 4. (See also the suggested lesson plan for Chapter One of *Narrative*... under "Slave Narrative and Autobiography," Chapter 7, and "Black Literature for a Unit on Prose Nonfiction" in Chapter 8.)

Post-Civil War Writers

The Civil War removed the most oppressive restrictions upon black thought. Learning to read was no longer considered inappropriate for former slaves, and a black possessed of almost superhuman drive could get an education. But the black writer still faced many obstacles including the prejudice of publishers, restrictions upon subject matter, and the problem of making a living.

Much of the writing of this period is somewhat conservative, attempting to minimize the injustices suffered by black people and to reassure whites that blacks appreciated their kindness. Because of the unprecedented improvements in their life during Reconstruction, many blacks believed that they could become equal citizens as soon as they became educated. Booker T. Washington, whose autobiography, *Up from Slavery,* is discussed in Chapter 4, was the spokesman for this position. However, by the beginning of the twentieth century, blacks had become thoroughly disillusioned by the oppressive Jim Crow laws which were being passed, and a strong protest movement began to grow, led by W. E. B. Du Bois. A number of earlier writers had written protest novels, but many of them tended to be pleas for special treatment for the educated black person, not outcries against discrimination. Also, protest writers such as Sutton Griggs and William Wells Brown were unskilled writers.

Like many white authors of the period, some black writers attempted to use folk traditions of their people. James Weldon Johnson, Paul Laurence Dunbar, and Charles W. Chesnutt, who wrote a number of stories and novels, were quite successful. Other writers imitated the genteel tradition to show that middle-class blacks could be as refined as white people.

Charles Waddell Chesnutt (1858–1932)

An Ohioan by birth, Chesnutt began at fourteen to help support his family by teaching at Howard School in Fayetteville, North Carolina, while he continued his own studies. He became a teacher and later principal of the Fayetteville State Normal School. His study of law began after he taught himself stenography and moved North to become a legal stenographer. After passing the Ohio Bar and joining a Cleveland law firm, he continued to write and lecture, and worked for civil rights for blacks.

Chesnutt managed the rather difficult feat of meeting the requirements of white publishers of the late nineteenth century while effectively portraying some aspects of black life. Chesnutt's first collection of short stories (*The Conjure Woman* [1899] Scholarly, 1977; pap., U of Mich Pr, 1969), is a series of dialect tales similar to the Uncle Remus stories, supposedly told by Uncle Julius McAdoo to a narrator who appears to be a white northerner. Although the narrator is amused by these tales of "conjures" and ghosts, it soon becomes obvious that Uncle Julius is a more complex person than Uncle Remus and has plenty of interests besides entertaining white people. In both "The Goophered Grapevine" and "Po' Sandy," Uncle Julius tries to keep white people away from property that he is using by convincing them that it is haunted. "Mars Jeems's Nightmare" describes what can happen to a white man who mistreats blacks, and inspires the narrator's wife to rehire Uncle Julius' grandson, who has just been fired.

Chesnutt's second collection, *The Wife of His Youth* ([1899] Scholarly, 1977; pap., U of Mich Pr, 1968), pictures the lives of black people after the Civil War in a wide variety of circumstances. The title story is interesting from both a literary and a historical standpoint. It describes the society of the "Blue Veins," a group of highly educated people, most of them with more white than black ancestry. One of the most eligible bachelors in this elite society is about to be married when an old, decrepit black woman appears. She has been searching for twenty-five years for the husband who had been separated from her during slavery. The husband, of course, turns out to be the bachelor, and true love wins the day. Other stories describe some of the less happy circumstances in which other black people lived during Reconstruction and the tragic events in their lives. Chesnutt's stories are interesting and well written, though styles have changed and modern readers are likely to consider them a little stilted, sentimental, and improbable.

Chesnutt's three novels are interesting and well written, though their formal language and intricate plots based on chance reflect the popular taste of their time. *The House Behind the Cedars* ([1900] pap., Macmillan, 1969) describes the problems of a mulatto who can pass for white. In *The Marrow of Tradition* ([1901] Arno, 1969; pap., U of Mich Pr, 1969) the conflicts between two half-sisters, one white and one black, are described. Included is a terrible scene of an anti-black riot, in which the black sister's child is killed. Some readers may find the long-suffering goodness of the black doctor, who saves the life of the child of the fomenter of the riot even after his own child is killed, rather unrealistic. Chesnutt's last novel, *The Colonel's Dream* ([1905] Arno, n.d.; pap., Mnemosyne, n.d.) exposes the evils of the convict lease system in the South.

W. E. B. Du Bois (1868–1963)

Though grouped here with the post-Civil War writers, William Edward Burghardt Du Bois belongs in any of the following periods, for his almost century-long life included six decades of writing as well as significant contributions in publishing, teaching and political struggle. Descriptions of his autobiographies are included in Chapter 4.

Born in Massachusetts, Du Bois studied at Fisk University and was the first black to earn a Ph. D. from Harvard. A professor on several campuses, including Atlanta University, he took part in the founding of the NAACP in 1909. His stands on issues from black autonomy in the 1930s to nuclear weapons bans and communism in the 1950s made him a controversial figure throughout his long life. He died in Ghana, the country he had adopted as his home on the invitation of President Kwame Nkrumah.

One of Du Bois' best books for high school students is *The Souls of Black Folk: Essays and Sketches* ([1903] Reprints incl. WSP, pap., 1970), a collection of well-written prose exploring historical and sociological aspects of the race problem. Many of the essays are now of interest chiefly as reflections of the times in which they were written; others appear quite modern. Du Bois was famous for his opposition to Booker T. Washington's Atlanta Compromise, and in the selection, "Of Booker T. Washington," he gives a calm, reasoned, and powerful indictment of Washington's politics. The essay would make a good text for studying the techniques of argument, or a good work for comparison with *Up from Slavery.*

Two narratives from *The Souls of Black Folk* might be used. "Of the Meaning of Progress" is the poignant story of the backwoods community where Du Bois first taught school. It shows the tragedy but also the beauty and strength of people barely managing to subsist against nature. "Of the Coming of John" tells the tragedy of an educated black who refuses to accept segregation.

Du Bois wrote one outstanding poem that is included in most collections of black poetry. "A Litany at Atlanta" uses a series of supplications and responses with vivid imagery to dramatize the blacks' plea for freedom and justice.

As a writer Du Bois is best known for his scholarly historical and sociological works. In addition to books, he wrote hundreds of articles, founded and edited magazines titled *The Moon, The Horizon,* and *The Crisis* (the NAACP magazine), and wrote a weekly newspaper column, poetry, and pageants. His novels are *The Quest of the Silver Fleece* (Reprint of 1911 edition, Arno, 1970; pap., Mnemosyne, n.d.), *Dark Princess* ([1928] Kraus Repr, 1975), and *The Black Flame*; the latter, a trilogy showing black history since Reconstruction, consists of *The Ordeal of Mansart* (1957), *Mansart Builds a School* (1959), and *Worlds of Color* ([1961] All Kraus Repr, 1976).

James Weldon Johnson (1871–1938)

Born in Jacksonville, Florida, where he became principal of a black high school and practiced law, Johnson turned to writing as a career in 1901, collaborating with his brother in New York on a comic opera and Tin Pan Alley hit songs. After several years in the diplomatic service in Spanish-speaking countries, he served as national secretary of the NAACP, 1916–1930. Later, as a professor of creative literature at Fisk University, Johnson continued writing magazine articles and poetry.

His poem "The Creation" is probably the most popular poem by a black writer. It and other selections in *God's Trombones* (Viking Pr, 1927) retell Bible stories in vivid modern language in the style of a black preacher, but without dialect. The other poems include "Listen, Lord—A Prayer," "The Prodigal Son," "Go Down Death—A Funeral Sermon," "Noah Built the Ark," "The Crucifixion," "Let My People Go," and "The Judgment Day." Both white and black students enjoy reading these poems aloud, as choral readings or with action, and a good number enjoy memorizing "The Creation," though it is quite long.

More of Johnson's poems can be found in *Caroling Dusk*, a 1927 anthology edited by Countee Cullen (Har-Row, 1974). The best of these are "The Glory of the Day Was in Her Face" and "My City." These poems, as well as "Fifty Years," are about the fiftieth anniversary of the Emancipation Proclamation. "Since You Went Away," a dialect poem, and "Lift Every Voice and Sing," which was known for many years as the Negro national anthem, are in Hughes and Bontemps' *The Poetry of the Negro* (Doubleday, 1973).

Johnson's novel, *The Autobiography of an Ex-Coloured Man* ([1912] Knopf, 1933; pap., Hill & Wang, 1960), is about a very light-skinned man who as a child does not realize that he is a Negro. He is shattered when his school principal informs him of his race. After the death of his mother and loss of the money he had for college, he spends some time in a cigar factory in the South. Then he becomes a jazz musician and with the help of a millionaire, goes to Europe. He returns South to write Negro music, but forsakes his race after he witnesses a lynching. He finally passes for white and marries a white girl.

The literary quality of the book is high, the style interesting and not too difficult. The character development is strong. The theme is tragic—not because a man falls after achieving something significant, but because he never does live up to his potential. It concerns the loss of ideals, the conflict between social-financial success and other goals, in the struggle between cowardice and courage. The problems of race are discussed at length but too often in passages that are not related to the plot and slow the action. Much of the discussion seems outdated and compromising. This is the best early novel by a black writer, though it is not so good as many recent books.

Along This Way, Johnson's autobiography (Reprint of 1933 edition, Da Capo, 1973; pap., Penguin, 1968) shows the life of a middle-class black in Florida. The narrative is lengthy and tends to become bogged down in details that were of considerable significance to Johnson's immediate family but have little interest for outsiders. This tame, middle-class life is not so interesting as some of the other autobiographies. There are some excellent passages, however, especially those about his first job as a principal and his struggles to become a lawyer. Some students may enjoy it. (See suggested lesson plan in "Slave Narrative and Autobiography," Chapter 7.)

Paul Laurence Dunbar (1872–1906)

The most widely read of the early black writers, Paul Laurence Dunbar was the first to make his living by writing. In his short life, this prolific author completed several volumes of poetry, a number of collections of short stories, and four novels. Not all, however, are worth studying; Dunbar frequently sacrificed quality for popularity.

He began writing as a child in Dayton, Ohio, but, though he was an honors graduate from high school, he could not afford college. Until William Dean Howells reviewed his book of poetry, *Majors and Minors*, and brought him national recognition, Dunbar worked in hotels and struggled to publish with private help. He traveled in Europe and worked for the Library of Congress until his health failed. His short stories appeared in national magazines including the *Saturday Evening Post* and *Harper's Weekly.*

Dunbar's works are suitable for high school students because they are easy to understand but demonstrate good poetic technique. Dunbar's topics are those that appeal to teenagers—love, family life, humor, and inspirational subjects. His poems fall into two categories: dialect poems that tend to use folk humor and stereotype, and nondialect poems that frequently have no racial overtones.

High school students may have mixed reactions to dialect poetry. Some individuals may argue that it is degrading and helps perpetuate unfavorable stereotypes. But discussing Dunbar in connection with other dialect writers such as James Whitcomb Riley can make them feel less self-conscious about dialect. And critical analysis of the techniques used can show them that dialect writing is not necessarily of poor quality. Despite these reservations, most students tend to like Dunbar's writing, particularly if poems such as "Little Brown Baby" are read by a class member with some acting talent.

An interesting series of dialect poems for any level would be "Little Brown Baby," "Scamp," and "Wadin' in de Crick." There is a nice progression from the "Little Brown Baby," who is scared of the bogey man, to "Scamp," the tired toddler, to the schoolboy in "Wadin' in de Crick." *Little Brown Baby* (Dodd, 1940) is a collection of Dunbar's poetry for children.

Other humorous dialect poems deal with love and courtship. "Discovered" is about two false lovers. "The Rivals" is about two boys who fight over the same girl. "A Frolick" is also about boys chasing girls, and "The Old Front Gate" shows a father's view of courtship. Another humorous poem in a different vein is "The Lawyer's Ways," about a lawyer's tricks in describing one person two different ways.

An interesting variation in dialect poetry is the tragic poem, "Puttin' the Baby Away." Here the dialect expresses poignantly a father's grief at his child's death, and students can see how deep emotions can be expressed well in simple words.

Dunbar's nondialect poetry is good, but not so appealing. One group of poems in standard English that would be useful for students is his series about famous people: "Douglass," "Booker T. Washington," and "Lincoln."

Dunbar's short poems are also useful for high school because they are very carefully constructed with vivid imagery. Recommended poems are "Theology," "Resignation," "Love's Humility," "Distinction," "Dawn," "To a Captious Critic," and "We Wear the Mask."

Many of Dunbar's poems are romantic, with a slightly bitter edge. They tend to be short and end with a pithy comment (*Complete Poems of Paul Laurence Dunbar* [Dodd, 1913]).

Although Dunbar is best known for his poetry, he also wrote novels and short stories. The latter, generally humorous and spiced with local color, poke gentle fun at the foolishness of mankind. However, they often have a plantation setting and use the stereotype of the black as a childish person to be humored by kindhearted plantation owners. Particularly objectionable by today's standards are stories in his collection, *In Old Plantation Days*. In one of these, Brother Parker, a black minister, is a party to his young master's prank of frightening all the blacks away from a rival preacher's service. Another story tells of a slave woman who is given money by her master to buy a slave for him and does so without any thought of freeing him or buying her own freedom (Reprint of 1903 edition, Negro U Pr).

Another of Dunbar's collections, *Folks from Dixie* (Reprint of 1898 edition, Negro U Pr, n.d.) has some stories that might be suitable for students, though several still stereotype black people. "The Ordeal at Mt. Hope" is an interesting story of a well-educated black preacher who goes to a small village where the people have no goals or ideals. "At Shaft 11" is about black strikebreakers who fight and win a place for themselves at the mine.

The Strength of Gideon and Other Stories (Reprint of 1899 edition, Arno, n.d.) contains more variety than Dunbar's other collections and fewer stereotyped characters. The stories concern topics ranging from plantation life to political maneuvers. There are still some characters the old plantation owners would like, but in several stories, Dunbar makes a strong protest against discrimination and a plea for proper treatment of blacks. "The Tragedy at Three Forks" is a lynching story. A poor white girl sets fire to a house out of jealousy and then watches in horror as two blacks are lynched for the crime. Her own lover is killed in a fight ensuing from the lynching.

Among other stories in this collection that would be useful for high school students are "The Ingrate," "One Man's Fortune," and "A Council of State," which show some of the problems of blacks in getting ahead. "The Finish of Patsy Barnes" and "Johnsonham, Junior" are interesting stories with almost no racial identification.

The Heart of Happy Hollow (Reprint of 1904 edition, Negro U Pr, n.d.) is a collection of sentimental stories about a variety of intriguing characters who live in Little Africa. There is the political boss, Mr. Asbury, who in "The Scapegoat" gets revenge on political enemies who try to use him as a scapegoat. "The Race Question" pokes gentle fun at an old Baptist who believes that horse racing is wrong and tries to rationalize his enjoyment of it. A more serious story is "Old Abe's Conversion," in which an old preacher learns to understand his son's modern ways. In "The Lynching of Jube Benson," an old doctor tells sorrowfully of lynching a friend by mistake.

Dunbar's novels, written in the worst genteel tradition, are practically useless to teachers. Except for *The Sport of the Gods* (Reprint of 1902 edition, Arno, 1969; pap., Macmillan, 1970), they are all about white people, and the descriptions of blacks are frequently offensive by modern standards.

The Harlem Renaissance

The 1920s noisily brought in the Harlem Renaissance—the exciting period when outstanding black writers suddenly began to appear and to assert the values of black culture instead of middle-class white society. This was also a period when white writers became intrigued with blacks, and Harlem became the most exciting part of New York.

Several factors contributed to the blossoming of the Harlem Renaissance. By the 1920s, education for blacks, though still difficult, was not unusual, and a fairly large middle class and a small intelligentsia had developed. Harlem became a center for black culture, where writers and thinkers could meet to analyze their work and share the problems of writing.

By the 1920s black writers were able to assume a more mature attitude toward white culture. They had attained enough freedom to be themselves; however, they had also experienced enough discrimination to know that assimilation was not possible, so they turned in the other direction, toward self-assertion. Earlier black writings had attacked the cruelties of white society; the writers of the Renaissance revolted against the culture itself. The Harlem Renaissance affirms that the white culture is weak, possibly inferior to the black culture, and that the black person should refuse assimilation. White society encouraged this rejection, for this was the Roaring Twenties, and whites were themselves rejecting their Victorian past. Many came to Harlem seeking a new culture.

Writing flourished. The black writers of this period were skilled enough to stand on their own merits in competition with other American writers.

Claude McKay (1890–1948)

Claude McKay educated himself in his native Jamaica with the help of an elder brother and an English collector of folklore. He began to write while supporting his brothers and sisters as a cabinetmaker's apprentice and later as a member of the Jamaican Constabulary. Two early collections of his poetry were published and won him a scholarship, on which he came to the United States to study. He worked in hotels and on trains in the U.S., visited England, and, after gradually winning recognition for his writing, became associate editor of a magazine, *The Liberator*. McKay traveled and wrote in the Soviet Union and Europe in the twenties and thirties, then returned to Harlem.

McKay was one of the most outspoken of the Harlem Renaissance writers, openly embracing ideas generally considered repugnant. He pointed out the weaknesses of the white culture while predicting its downfall. He gloried in both the virtues and what others may consider the vices of blacks and advocated revolt against whites and their culture. Many of his ideas are now being popularized by contemporary writers.

McKay's poetry is mature and shows a careful artistry. His poetic technique is well developed, and his effects are often subtle. His poetry does not have the folksy appeal of Johnson's or Dunbar's and is generally more appropriate for advanced and intellectually able students. His works include very sensitive, nostalgic nature poems about his homeland, Jamaica, that are generally too subtle for high school students. Some of his protest poems are violently anti-white, and some of his romantic lyrics deal a little more openly and intimately with the sex act than most school boards might approve.

Selected Poems of Claude McKay ([1953] Twayne, 1971) contains a number of poems that are usable in high school. "Flame-Heart" is a long poem about memories of McKay's childhood in Jamaica. "Summer Morn in New Hampshire" is a delicate poem about night and dawn far away from love. "Baptism" combines the strength of character of his more violent protest poems with a less violent attitude. "If We Must Die" portrays vividly the militant spirit of the fight against oppression. "To the White Fiends" explains that blacks are better than whites because they show the light of humanity instead of trying to match the whites' cruelty. "Truth" might appeal to adolescents who are confused about the meaning of truth. "America" demonstrates the blacks' conflicting feelings about America—love for "this cultured hell that tests my youth" and rebellion against it.

"The Harlem Dancer" is a sympathetic picture of the falsely smiling face of a girl dancing for prostitutes and their customers. "The Wild Goat" compares the wild goat who languishes in captivity with the poet who wants freedom. "On Broadway" expresses loneliness amid the bright lights of the city. "A Song of the Moon" shows how moonlight loses its magic in the city and so must return to the country. "The Castaways" contrasts the beauties of nature with the dregs of humanity, which the poet cannot bear to see.

McKay's novels are inferior to his poems. All of them attempt to affirm the primitive black against decaying Western civilization. *Home to Harlem* (Reprint of 1928 edition, Chatham Bkseller, 1973) and its sequel, *Banjo* ([1929] pap., HarBraceJ, 1970), both follow the life of a free, primitive, vagabond black man as interpreted by Ray, a young intellectual who wants to be free. *Banjo* is a long series of slightly related incidents in the lives of the beach-bums of Marseilles. The characters are lively and human, but the plot is almost nonexistent. The style is generally vivid, but Ray has too many soliloquies expounding McKay's philosophy. McKay's third novel, *Banana Bottom* (Reprint of 1933 edition, Chatham Bkseller, 1971; pap., HarBraceJ, 1974), contrasts Jamaican folk culture with the stifling missionary culture.

McKay's novels in many ways are similar to Langston Hughes' Simple stories. Both affirm the folk black culture in contrast to refined white culture. Both are a series of slightly related incidents, and both have a folk character and an educated interpreter. McKay's novels are a little more radical, dealing with people on the ragged edges of society and developing the black versus white theme more thoroughly. Hughes, however, is more usable with high school students, for his works are shorter, more modern, and generally easier reading.

Jean Toomer (1894–1967)

After attending the University of Wisconsin and the City College of New York, Toomer began writing fiction, poetry and criticism for periodicals. His major work, *Cane* ([1923] Liveright, cloth & pap., 1975), grew out of experiences with Southern rural black people, gained while he was principal of a high school in Sparta, Georgia. Toomer traveled widely, maintained ties with many writers and artists, and, in his later years in Pennsylvania, became a Quaker.

Robert Bone in *The Negro Novel in America* says:

> *Cane* is an important American novel. By far the most impressive product of the Negro Renaissance, it ranks with Richard Wright's *Native Son* and Ralph Ellison's *Invisible Man* as a measure of the Negro novelist's highest achievement. Jean Toomer belongs to that first rank of writers who use words almost as a plastic medium shaping new meanings from an original and highly personal style. Since stylistic innovation requires great technical dexterity, Toomer displays a concern for technique which is fully two decades in advance of the period. While his contemporaries of the Harlem school were still experimenting with a crude literary realism, Toomer had progressed beyond the naturalistic novel to the "higher realism of the emotions," to symbol, and to myth (Rev. ed. [Yale U Pr, 1965], p. 81).

Cane is an unusual book, a series of vignettes and poems about life among blacks in the South. It creates an impression like a photograph album of a trip. Some of the pictures, like that of Robert, are only character sketches; "Kabnis" is almost a novelette; many are poems, and other selections vary in length. Subjects, too, vary from the tender story of lovely Fern, who could not find love with anyone, to the story of Bessie, the outcast white woman with two black children. Although Toomer's themes are often of violence and oppression, his characters are drawn with sympathy and understanding. Jean Toomer did not fulfill the promise of his remarkable work, but instead disappeared from the literary scene.

Arna Bontemps (1902–1973)

Bontemps' works span half a century from the Harlem Renaissance to the 1970s, and as wide a range of genres, including poetry, novels, critical works, children's books, biographies, short stories and anthologies. Born in Louisiana and reared in the Los Angeles area, he wrote during his years as a high school teacher and principal, 1924–41. He became head librarian and later public relations director at Fisk University and was an established author by the time he completed an M.A. at the University of Chicago in 1943.

Bontemps' best novel is *Black Thunder* ([1936] pap., Beacon Pr, 1968), a highly fictionalized account of one of the most successful slave rebellions, led by Gabriel Prosser in Virginia. Gabriel is the central character, but the action shifts through the thoughts and deeds of a number of minor characters, both black and white, who figure in the rebellion. With this panoramic technique, Bontemps successfully maintains suspense.

Black Thunder appeals on several levels to high school readers. Gabriel, though uneducated, is depicted as a wise and powerful leader who commanded respect. Revolt, adventure, escape, and just a touch of romance give the book a high interest rating for the average adolescent. For the more serious student, the book is a careful attempt to analyze the motives and problems behind an important historic event. The yearning for freedom is a theme all should respond to.

Bontemps wrote two other novels, *God Sends Sunday* (Harcourt Brace, 1931), about the sporting world of racetrack gamblers, and *Drums at Dusk* (Macmillan, 1939) about the Haitian slave rebellion of 1791–1804.

Selections from Bontemps' poetry are included in almost all anthologies of black literature and are also available in his collection, *Personals* ([1963] 2d ed., Broadside, 1974). His poems are concerned with history, with the injustices suffered by black people in the past, and the rather pessimistic possibilities of the future. Most of them use nature imagery, a rather restrained tone, and somewhat traditional forms. "A Black Man Talks of Reaping," one of his most popular poems, contends, "small wonder then my children glean in fields/ they have not sown, and feed on bitter fruit," since they have been denied the legitimate harvest of the crops they have sown.

One of Bontemps' finest works, and one which is quite effective with high school students, is the short story "A Summer Tragedy," in which two elderly people who no longer have any means of support lovingly commit suicide together. This and other stories are available in Bontemps' collection *The Old South: A Summer Tragedy and Other Stories of the Thirties* (Dodd, 1973).

In *Chariot in the Sky: A Story of the Jubilee Singers* ([1951] HR&W, 1971), Bontemps retells for young people the story of the group of black musicians who brought Negro spirituals to a wider audience after the Civil War. His narrative centers on one of the founding members of the Fisk Jubilee Singers, a young slave named Caleb. It follows Caleb as he attempts to escape, is apprenticed to a tailor, sold away from his family, and finally freed by the Civil War. In the frightening, dangerous years after the war, Caleb teaches school, replacing a friend who is shot by white-robed Klansmen, and struggles to keep up with classes at Fisk.

When the financially destitute school appears ready to close, Caleb and a few other singers go North with the school treasurer to try to raise money through concerts. At first, they are barely able to pay expenses, but when they begin to sing spirituals, they become tremendously successful, raising more than twenty thousand dollars to save the school.

While generally optimistic and hopeful, *Chariot in the Sky* also portrays the tragedies of slavery, the attempts to continue a slavery-like system after the Civil War, and the courage and strength of both blacks and whites who struggled for a new life. The fictionalized account is both well written and easy to read.

Bontemps is also the author of two excellent children's books, *Sad-Faced Boy* (HM, 1937) and *Lonesome Boy* (HM, 1955), and several biographies. Also of interest to students are his historical works: *The Story of the Negro* (Knopf, 1958) and *One Hundred Years of Negro Freedom* (Dodd, cloth & pap., 1961), as well as his anthologies: *Great Slave Narratives* (Beacon Pr, 1959), *Hold Fast to Dreams* (Follett, 1969), *Golden Slippers: An Anthology of Negro Poetry* (Har-Row, 1941), and *American Negro Poetry* (rev. ed., Hill & Wang, cloth & pap., 1974).

Langston Hughes (1902–1967)

"Hughes, perhaps more than any other author, knows and loves the Negro masses," wrote Robert Bone in *The Negro Novel in America* (Yale U Pr, 1965, p. 75). That is why Hughes appeals to the masses of high school students. Both verse and stories are easy to understand and written with skill. Hughes did not write about the cultured, intellectual elite, who are unpopular with students, nor did he glory in gory lynchings and sex perversions, which are unpopular with school boards. He wrote about poor, ordinary people with a strong sense of humor. When asked what black writers they like, students and teachers invariably list Hughes.

Hughes, who grew up in Cleveland, Ohio, once said he began writing poetry after being elected class poet in grammar school. He tells of his youth in *The Big Sea,* discussed below. Hughes spent much of his life in Harlem, and after becoming known as a poet, toured the country giving readings. He roamed Europe, and in 1933, wrote a film scenario in the Soviet Union. His works have been translated into a number of European and Oriental languages.

Langston Hughes is difficult to classify as a writer. He was among the leaders of the Harlem Renaissance, but he continued to write later than most others of this period. He wrote poetry, short stories, novels, essays, and edited many collections of black literature.

Hughes' short stories are collected in *Laughing to Keep from Crying* (Henry Holt, 1952), *Something in Common and Other Stories* (Hill & Wang, pap., 1963), and *The Ways of White Folks* (Knopf, 1934; pap., Random, 1971). Most of them are humorous, but one always knows that much of the laughing is a defense against bitterness. Topics vary from white tourists in Harlem to brothels in Cuba to standard problems of getting a job and family spats. Although many of the stories deal with prostitutes, drinking, and the seamy side of life, Hughes rarely uses four-letter words or explicit descriptions of sex.

Among the best of Hughes' stories for high school students is "Thank You, M'am," the tale of a young boy who tries to snatch a purse from a strong, motherly woman, who takes him home and feeds him (in *Something in Common*). "On the Road" is a powerful, symbolic story of a black who tries to tear off the door of a church that would not help him when he was freezing and starving. "The Big Meeting" tells of two black boys who come to a revival to laugh but are offended when whites make fun of their mothers. Both the whites and the boys are finally deeply affected by the sermon (both stories are in *Laughing to Keep from Crying*).

The Simple stories form another large body of Hughes' writing. They are collected in *Simple Speaks His Mind* (S&S, 1950), *Simple Takes a Wife* (S&S, 1953), *Simple Stakes a Claim* (Rinehart, 1957), *The Best of Simple* (Hill & Wang, pap., 1961), and *Simple's Uncle*

Sam (Hill & Wang, pap., 1965). All these collections give vignettes of Simple, an average, Alabama-born Harlem man who comments on current situations from a bar stool to his college-educated pal. Discussions range from the space race to Mississippi to Cousin Minnie, but always bring up the race problem in some way. The humor and interest in the Simple stories come from the variety of well developed characters including the wife, Joyce, who wants to move to the suburbs and enjoy culture; ugly Cousin Minnie, whom Simple had never heard of before she appears asking him for money; and Simple himself, one of the most original philosophers of our times. His discussions on race are presented with delightful humor that does not quite mask their depth of bitterness and injury.

Not Without Laughter ([1930] pap., Macmillan, 1969), Hughes' first novel, was written while he was still in college and still strongly influenced by the Harlem Renaissance. Though somewhat defective as a work of art, *Not Without Laughter* has possibilities for use with high school students. Not exactly autobiographical but based on Hughes' experiences as a child, the book tells of the problems of a poor boy growing up in Kansas. Poverty is the villain that separates his parents, sends his aunt into prostitution, causes his grandmother to die from overwork, and forces his successful aunt to cut all ties with her poor family. Sandy is sent around from one member of the family to another but, with a strong will and encouragement from all, manages to keep out of trouble.

There is not much excitement, and the plot is rather formless. The main interest of the book is in the characters, who are realistic, alive, and humorous: Jimboy, the fun-loving, roving father; Angee, the dreamless, stay-at-home wife; adventurous Harriett, who finally makes good on the stage; and Hagar, the long-suffering grandmother. *Not Without Laughter* deals very realistically with all the problems faced by a child growing up in poverty and finding the strength necessary to overcome it.

Hughes' second novel, *Tambourines to Glory* ([1958] Hill & Wang, 1970), is about Essie Belle Johnson, a deeply religious but not very intelligent woman who pairs up with Laura, a very clever but quite irreligious opportunist, to form a church. Starting as sidewalk preachers, they eventually work up to the biggest church in Harlem. Essie's main interest is in getting her lovely young daughter Marietta to come to New York, and Laura's main interest is her handsome hustler, Buddy. When Buddy proves unfaithful, Laura plots to get rid of both Buddy and Essie by killing Buddy and blaming it on Essie. But the scheme backfires, and it is Essie who eventually becomes the leader of the church.

The plot is contrived and not meant to be taken seriously. The characters, though verging on stereotypes, are quite well delineated and human. The scheming, unprincipled Laura is especially lively. The style is fairly humorous. Some students might find the book offensive because of the way it makes fun of both blacks and religion. Used improperly it could contribute to an unfavorable stereotype.

The Big Sea ([1940] Hill & Wang, cloth & pap., 1963) is Hughes' autobiography, and his life provides a fascinating subject. Shunted around from relative to relative, he seemed to learn something from each one. Pride from his grandmother, religion from Auntie Reed, and courage from his mother were his heritage. At seventeen, he went to Mexico to visit his father, whom he began to dislike, for his father was interested only in making money and was contemptuous of the poor, common people whom Langston loved.

After a year at Columbia University, Hughes began work as a sailor, and the next section of the book relates his adventures in Africa and Europe, where he was often stranded without money or food. By the time he returned to America, the traits that so enliven his writing were well established: a love of the common people, and a sense of humor that can laugh at the most serious problems. *The Big Sea* is an exciting book. It is likely to be interesting to adolescents because it deals with problems of becoming an adult and finding one's place in the world. Also, its anti-middle class values should give them something to think about.

Five Plays by Langston Hughes, edited by Webster Smalley (Ind U Pr, cloth & pap., 1963), has several selections appropriate for high school classes. *Simply Heavenly,* a play made from the Simple stories, might be the most entertaining. It is a comedy centering on Simple's attempts to marry Joyce and escape the clutches of his former wife, Isabel, and his former girlfriend, Zarita. Comedy develops around Simple's bar companions and Zarita's schemes to steal him from Joyce.

Little Ham is a funny play about numbers racketeers and fights over girlfriends. *Tambourines to Glory* is based on the novel of the same name. More serious is *Mulatto,* a bloody play about the mulatto son of a planter, who refuses to be a slave and eventually kills his father. *Soul Gone Home* is an ironic play about a mother who fakes sorrow for her dead son, who comes back to life to berate her hypocrisy. Only four pages long and requiring only two characters, this play could easily be presented in the classroom.

The Selected Poems of Langston Hughes (Knopf, 1959) is a treasure-find for English teachers. Hughes' poems are about things teenagers are concerned with, such as romance, dances, dreams, and jobs. And they are written the way teenagers talk, with modern jazz rhythms, everyday words, sometimes even slang. Furthermore, they are easy to understand—at least the surface meaning is simple. From the teacher's standpoint, they are perfect for illustrating the basic principles of poetry—compression and the connection between metrics and meaning.

Hughes has a number of very short poetic sketches which, haiku-like, capture a mood in a three- or four-line image. Among the poems of this type are "One," "Garden," "Troubled Woman," "Sea Calm," "Luck," "Ennui," "My People," and "Suicide's Note."

In *Montage of a Dream Deferred*, a book-length poem (1951. In *Selected Poems*), Hughes experiments with sketches of Harlem life in bop rhythm. Teachers can make use of the entire poem or short selections from it, notably "Freedom Train," "Boogie: 1 A.M.," "Deferred," and "Harlem."

The Dream Keeper and Other Poems (Knopf, 1932) is another short collection, an attractive book illustrated by Helen Sewell. Again, all of the poems are easily understood by high school students and deal with appropriate themes. Among the most effective are "The Dream Keeper" and "Dreams."

Lost dreams form a major theme of Hughes' writing. Unfulfilled promises and the ruined life are pictured in a number of poems which capture the tragedy of the black experience in America. "As I Grow Older" is a long poem which shows how a dream flees from color. "Dream Variations" expresses the poet's longing to express and enjoy his racial heritage. "Litany" is a haunting poem that accuses even Heaven of having no love. "Vagabonds," "Delinquent," and "Troubled Woman" depict people who have finally been destroyed. "To Be Somebody" again pictures the almost hopeless dream.

Hughes also wrote several poems about the American Dream: "Freedom's Plow," "I, Too, Sing America," and "Let America Be America Again." One of his most beautiful and moving poems, "The Negro Speaks of Rivers," tells the history of the black race in terms of the rivers it has lived near.

The Panther and the Lash (Knopf, 1967) is Hughes' last collection of poetry. Many of the poems deal with events in the civil rights struggle of the 1960s, both in the U. S. and around the world. Like all of his works, they assert the rights of black people to be themselves and to be proud of themselves, and they point out the absurdity, the foolishness and the cruelty of oppression and of the attitudes of oppressors. In "The Backlash Blues," he warns that there is a "Great big world, Mister Backlash,/ Big and bright and round—/ And it's full of folks like me who are/ Black, Yellow, Beige, and Brown," and that "I'm gonna leave you, Mister Backlash,/ Singing your mean old backlash blues" (*The Panther and the Lash*, p. 9).

Countee Cullen (1903–1946)

Countee Cullen (pronounced Coun-tay′) was one of the most significant writers of the Harlem Renaissance. He grew up in New York City, began writing in his teens and, in 1926, a year after graduating from New York University, became assistant editor of *Opportunity* magazine. After earning an M. A. from Harvard and studying in Paris on a Guggenheim Scholarship, he taught in the New York City Public Schools while continuing to write.

More middle class than McKay, Cullen wrote with pathos and understatement instead of violence and passion. *On These I Stand* (Har-Row, 1947) is his own selection of his best poems. The poems from *Color* (Reprint of 1925 edition, Arno, 1970) deal with the black's search for identity and the meaning of race. "Yet Do I Marvel," one of Cullen's most famous poems, asks how God could make a poet black and bid him sing. "The Shroud of Color" is a long poem that explores the meaning of color in a kind of mystical vision. "Heritage" contemplates blacks' relationship to their African heritage. Two other poems with milder racial undertones which should be useful with high school students are "Saturday's Child," about a child born into poverty, and "Tableau," about a white boy and a black walking together.

Cullen's "Epitaphs" are short, but convey much meaning in a few words. Among the most interesting are "For My Grandmother" and "For a Mouthy Woman." In a group of poems titled "Varia," "She of the Dancing Feet" and "The Wise" stand out.

"The Black Christ" (1929), a very long poem, is quite difficult. In it, Christ returns to substitute for a black boy who is to be lynched (*The Black Christ and Other Poems*. [Harper, 1929]).

Along with original poetry, Cullen composed a new version of Euripides' *Medea* in simple prose (*The Medea and Some Poems*

[Harper, 1935]). He also wrote a novel, *One Way to Heaven* (Reprint of 1932 edition, AMS Pr, n.d.). The story starts with Sam Lucas, a fake penitent, who puts on a demonstration for a Harlem congregation and converts Mattie Johnson, who falls in love with him. After the unregenerate old sinner marries Mattie, the scene switches to Mrs. Brandon, the head of the new black elite for whom Mattie works. Mrs. Brandon starts her social season by giving Mattie, her former maid, a fabulous wedding that ends with a speech by a rabid Southern segregationist. Among Mrs. Brandon's unusual guests are a number of writers and duchesses of the back-to-Africa campaign. The story finally returns to Sam, who has grown tired of Mattie but dies faking a deathbed conversion for her.

Cullen's style, humor, and excellent description make this book of higher quality than most black writing of the period. Characterization, though humorous, is excellent, and the portrayal of society is reminiscent of Henry James. While some students might resent Cullen's poking fun at blacks and his use of the stereotype of the religious fake, his humor is sympathetic enough that readers are unlikely to be seriously offended.

Past Becomes Present (1930–1950)

The Great Depression of the 1930s ended the Harlem Renaissance and caused a change in the focus of black writing. The economic problems of the Depression hit black people hardest, and writers became concerned simply with the problems of survival rather than with cultural expression. Instead of flocking to New York, writers lived and found their subject matter in the cities of the Midwest and the rural areas of the South, and they told more openly and more graphically about the suffering and frustration of poor black people confronted by vicious racism and overwhelming poverty. The poor in the writings of Richard Wright and William Attaway are not cute, quaint or exotic, as they were often portrayed in earlier writing. Like the poor in the writings of white naturalistic writers of the early part of the century, they are portrayed as helpless, almost mindless, victims of a violent, sordid environment.

Richard Wright easily dominates the two decades from 1930 to 1950. In fact, in the shadow of *Native Son* and *Black Boy* little else is visible. These two books brought Wright recognition as a major American writer and began a new direction in black American fiction. Wright's novels are tough and relentless. He said about *Native Son* that he wanted to create a novel which "would be so hard and deep that they [the white readers] would have to face it without the consolation of tears." Wright stripped away the "Laughing to Keep from Crying" facade adopted by so many of the post-Civil War and Harlem Renaissance writers to expose the brutal racism of American society and the hopeless agony suffered by America's blacks. Inspired by Wright's success with a naturalistic, vivid portrayal of evil, most black writers since Wright have been much less squeamish about describing the sordid details of their own experiences.

Despite the acclaim given to Richard Wright, little note was taken of other black writers during the period. Indeed it was a less productive period than those which preceded and followed it. Many of the authors of the Harlem Renaissance, particularly Langston Hughes, continued to write and produce important works, but few new writers achieved acclaim during the 1930s. During the 1940s four interesting new writers appeared: Ann Petry, Chester Himes, Frank Yerby and Willard Motley—interesting because all four departed in some way from black literary traditions. Petry, Yerby and Motley all chose white characters and settings for at least one of their major works, and Yerby and Himes both gained their greatest fame with popular fiction—Yerby with a steady stream of very popular historical romances and Himes with his Harlem detective novels. Versatile writers, all four produced successful works of several types, and Petry, Yerby and Himes are still writing today. Motley, who used naturalistic techniques similar to those of Richard Wright in his best known novel, *Knock on Any Door* (Appleton-Century-Crofts, 1947), died in 1965.

Three important poets began their careers during the 1940s: Gwendolyn Brooks, Margaret Walker, and Robert Hayden. All continue to write today, and Brooks and Hayden could well be classed with the most contemporary of writers.

William Attaway (1912–)

The son of a Mississippi physician who moved his family to Chicago, Attaway later used the theme of the disintegration of Southern black folk culture in the industrial North in his writing. His first novel, *Let Me Breathe Thunder* (Reprint of 1939 edition, Chatham Bkseller, 1969), published when he was twenty-five, dealt with two white migrant farm workers whose encounter with Hi Boy, a ten-year-old Mexican, gives their lives new meaning.

Blood on the Forge (Reprint of 1941 edition, Chatham Bkseller, 1969) the better of the two novels, was somewhat eclipsed by the sensation caused by Richard Wright's *Native Son*. It is the story of three brothers who flee the oppression of the South to an Allegheny Valley steel town and gradually disintegrate there. It depicts much sex and violence, but unlike most naturalistic novels, it has a profound theme and can be used with students who are mature enough to look for ideas and not just sensationalism.

"Not much is known of him, although part of Attaway's anonymity is undoubtedly of his own doing," Edward Margolies wrote in his introduction to a 1970 edition of *Blood on the Forge* (Collier. Macmillan). Attaway attended public schools in Chicago, and interrupted his college years at the University of Illinois for an interlude as a hobo, laborer, seaman, and actor. He subsequently wrote for radio and TV, developing the script for an hour-long special on black humor, screened in the late sixties. Recently, he has lived on the island of Barbados in the Caribbean with his wife and children.

Gwendolyn Brooks (1917–   )

Gwendolyn Brooks is the only black poet to win the Pulitzer Prize, and a contemporary poet who has definitely won a lasting place in American literature. She was born in Topeka, Kansas, and has lived most of her life in Chicago, where she attended junior college. Since she became established as a writer, she has lectured at colleges and universities.

Brooks' imagery is strong, multisensory. In a few lines, she can recreate a life and a scene, complete with smells and feelings. Her poems are powerful, but unfortunately are rather difficult for unsophisticated readers.

Her earliest collection, *A Street in Bronzeville* (Harper, 1945), includes some of her most memorable visions, such as "Kitchenette Building," in which the smells of onion fumes and garbage choke dreams; also, "A Song in the Front Yard," about the "good little girl's" envy of the "bad children"; and "The Preacher Ruminates Behind the Sermon" feeling sorry for God who has no one to slap Him on the shoulder or buy Him a beer.

Annie Allen (Reprint of 1949 edition, Greenwood, 1972) contains a collection of poems about womanhood. Particularly powerful, though fairly difficult for high school students, are the series of sonnets called "The Children of the Poor."

The Bean Eaters (Harper, 1960) encompasses a wider variety of subjects than the earlier collections. Some of the most appropriate poems are the following: "The Explorer," which tells of a youth searching for peace while confronted by all the choices he must make; "My Little 'Bout Town Girl," a sensitive poem about a cheap, painted girl; and "We Real Cool," a clever, "hip" poem about dropouts that would be appropriate for any reading level.

Several of the poems explore the feelings of white people which led to anti-black behavior. In "The Chicago Defender Sends a Man to Little Rock," the puzzled reporter cannot reconcile his perception that "they are like people everywhere" with images of these same people "hurling spittle, rock, garbage and fruit . . . " "The Lovers of the Poor" with their contradictory innocence and cruelty are shown in their fat offensiveness through the eyes of the "not-so-worthy-poor." "The Ballad of Rudolph Reed" is the story of a man whose family moves into a white neighborhood where they are so tormented that he attacks white people with a butcher knife until he is killed. The collection ends with "In Emanuel's Nightmare: Another Coming of Christ," which shows Christ coming "to clean the earth of the dirtiness of war," and returning in tears because "He found how much the people wanted war."

In the Mecca (Har-Row, 1968) is a long poem showing the reactions of the people in an apartment house to the search for a lost girl—and thereby showing the lives and attitudes of a black community. The book also contains several short poems, including a memorable description of Malcolm X.

Gwendolyn Brooks' novel is *Maud Martha* (Reprint of 1953 edition, AMS Pr, n.d.), the sort of sensitive, subtle piece of prose one might expect from a poet. *Maud Martha* is a series of episodes in the life of a black girl. Maud is not a pretty girl like her sister, and she worries about being unable to keep her handsome husband. Students may at first have trouble with the somewhat fragmented style; the episodes at first appear unrelated. However, the reader soon becomes accustomed to the technique. *Maud Martha* has little plot and little action except the birth of the baby, which is described in some detail. However, the characters are developed with great insight, and the vignettes are very human and occasionally humorous. *Maud Martha* would probably not be a popular book for young people but could be enjoyed by the more sensitive readers.

Gwendolyn Brooks is to some extent a forerunner of the modern black poets. The contemporary themes were all there ten or twenty years before the current poets began writing—the pride and appreciation for the ghetto black, the disillusionment and rejection of white culture, the honest vision of both good and evil. Gwendolyn Brooks, both as a poet and as a person, has been a major influence on contemporary poetry.

A Street in Bronzeville, Annie Allen, Maud Martha, The Bean Eaters, In the Mecca are all collected in *The World of Gwendolyn Brooks* (Har-Row, 1971).

Owen Dodson (1914-   )

After taking a master's degree in drama at Yale, Brooklyn-born Owen Dodson had a career in college theater which included heading the drama departments at Howard University and Atlanta University, directing summer theater and reading his poetry on various campuses. He has also written two operas, but is primarily known as a poet. His collection *Powerful Long Ladder* is difficult but good ([1946] FS&G, cloth & pap., 1970). His poetry can be found in most anthologies of black literature.

Dodson's novel *Boy at the Window* (Reprint of 1951 edition, Chatham Bkseller, 1972) tells with sensitivity the story of a young boy growing up in a poverty-stricken home. His mother, paralyzed from a stroke, eats cheap, inadequate food so her children can have something more substantial. The father struggles to provide enough money at his low-paying job, but loses his pride as he fails. The older brother gets into trouble, and the older sister is made to sacrifice marriage to help her family. The main events in Coin's life are his religious conversion, the death of his mother, and his trip to Washington to stay with his blind beggar uncle.

Boy at the Window, though written from a child's point of view, is an adult book. Its interest and effect come through the development of ideas with Coin's impressions. The character portraits, especially of people in the neighborhood and the church, are excellent. However, there is little action and not really much plot, so probably only the more sensitive and mature students will respond to this novel. It is a well-written book that could be valuable for adolescents, but one has the impression that Dodson is too much a poet trying to be a novelist.

Robert Hayden (1913-   )

Robert Hayden was born in Detroit and has drawn on the experiences of his youth in the city's slums for subjects for his poetry. He attended Wayne State University and the University of Michigan and taught English for over twenty years at Fisk University. Since 1969, he has been on the faculty of the University of Michigan. Among his many awards for poetry have been the Grand Prize for Poetry at the First World Festival of Negro Arts in Dakar, Senegal, 1965, and the 1975 Fellowship of the Academy of American Poets.

Hayden's careful artistry may be too difficult for many adolescents to appreciate, but his poems reward close study. Two of his best poems for high school students have historical themes: "Middle Passage" vividly describes the journey of a slave ship, and "Runagate Runagate" recaptures the frantic struggles of a runaway slave. Another popular poem, "Those Winter Sundays," is about Hayden's foster father. These works can be found in *Selected Poems* (2d ed., October, 1966).

Poetry collections by Hayden include *Heart-Shape in the Dust* (Falcon Pr, 1940), *The Lion and the Archer*, with Myron O'Higgins (Hemphill, 1948), *A Ballad of Remembrance* (Breman, 1962), *Night-Blooming Cereus* (2d ed., Broadside, 1972), and *Angle of Ascent: New and Selected Poems* (Liveright, cloth & pap., 1975). He also edited a popular anthology: *Kaleidoscope: Poems by American Negro Poets* (HarBraceJ, 1968).

Chester Himes (1909–)

Himes grew up in Augusta, Georgia; Pine Bluff, Arkansas; St. Louis, and Cleveland, and attended Ohio State University. He began publishing stories in magazines in the 1930s and novels in the late forties.

The Third Generation (Reprint of 1954 edition, Chatham Bkseller, 1973) probes the psychological problems of a middle-class black family. The mother is very light skinned and resents the fact that she must live with blacks. The father is very dark and, though he is a college professor, is never able to gain the respect of his wife. Tragedy seems to plague the family as one son, William, is blinded in an accident and the younger son, Charles, is injured at work.

A very well-written, cohesive novel, *The Third Generation* shows the deterioration of the family and Charles' attempt to build a new life. Like John A. Williams' *Sissie*, it develops the theme that the children must overcome the effects of their parents' problems on their lives.

Chester Himes is best known to many readers for his detective fiction, particularly *Cotton Comes to Harlem* (Reprint of 1965 edition, Chatham Bkseller, 1975), which will interest the large number of students who enjoy mysteries. Other works by Himes include *If He Hollers Let Him Go* (Reprint of 1945 edition, Chatham Bkseller, 1973; pap., NAL, 1971), *Lonely Crusade* (Reprint of 1947 edition, Chatham Bkseller, 1973), and *Cast the First Stone* (Reprint of 1952 edition, Chatham Bkseller, 1973; pap., NAL, 1972).

Zora Neale Hurston (1901?–1960)

Born in a village in central Florida, Zora Neale Hurston began to write while putting herself through school by working as a maid and a manicurist. She graduated from Barnard College on a scholarship and served as secretary to novelist Fannie Hurst while submitting her own work to magazines. Although her major works were published later, she was a key figure in the literary circles of the Harlem Renaissance. On private grants, she studied folklore and anthropology and did folklore research in the West Indies. Her later career included producing black folklore programs and writing for films.

Hurston is a writer whom many contemporary critics, particularly feminists, feel has not received adequate recognition for the quality of her work. Mary Helen Washington claims that *Their Eyes Were Watching God* (Reprint of 1937 edition, Negro U Pr, n.d.; pap., U of Ill Pr, 1978) is "probably the most beautiful love story of a black man and woman in literature." Whether or not that claim is true, the novel is very well written. It has a sensitivity of language that at times becomes poetic. Theme and character are developed well. From tender adolescent dreams, Janie is forced into a respectable but loveless marriage. She soon runs away with another man in a spirit of romance, but this relationship too becomes respectable, and she finds herself the mayor's wife, though still not in love. Finally, as a forty-year-old widow with a fortune, she throws over her respectable position for a young gambler who offers nothing but love. Although her two years with Tea Cake bring terrible suffering, Janie feels she has found fulfillment.

The novel is not only enjoyable reading, but also an excellent tool for the study of dialect, use of symbolic language, and imagery. Since Hurston symbolically recreates the Creation, the Fall, and the Flood, the book could also be used to study the influence of the Bible on literature.

Hurston's *Mules and Men* (Reprint of 1935 edition, Negro U Pr, n.d.), a collection of folklore, tales, music, and hoodoo rituals recorded within a framework of Southern black speech and social life, is the product of a year of research in rural Florida, New Orleans, and other parts of the South. Anthropologist Franz Boas, in his foreword to the book, says, "... it throws into relief also the peculiar amalgamation of African and European tradition which is so important for understanding historically the character of American Negro life, ..."

Ann Petry (1911–)

Ann Petry is a sensitive writer whose reputation has steadily increased since the publication of her novel *The Street* in 1946. After studying at the University of Connecticut, she worked as a pharmacist, advertising salesperson, reporter, woman's page editor, and teacher while establishing herself as a writer of fiction.

The Street (Pyramid Pubns, pap., 1969) portrays a black counterpart of Sister Carrie or Jennie Gerhardt. Like Jennie and Carrie, Lutie Johnson is trapped in an environment from which escape is impossible, and Lutie also has a young son whom she wants to see grow up right. Unlike Jennie and Carrie, she refuses to yield to the men who offer her escape. But for Lutie, virtue is not rewarded, as one of her spurned suitors vengefully tricks her son into crime. Finally she kills one of the men who have been molesting her.

The Street is strong reading for high school students, but students who consider poverty to be a result of personal weakness need to read such a book to give them a more balanced view.

Petry's next two novels, *Country Place* (Reprint of 1947 edition, Chatham Bkseller, 1971) and *The Narrows* (Reprint of 1953 edition, Chatham Bkseller, 1973), are both set in small New England towns, and both examine complex social relationships. *Country Place* shows the effects of World War II on the town, and *The Narrows* examines relationships within the black ghetto and between members of that community and the white community. In *The Narrows,* everyone is that mixture of the heroic and the ludicrous that we humans like to pretend we are not. Abbie Crump, the virtuous and respectable widow, honors the memory of her dead husband, but completely forgets her adopted son for several months. Mr. Powther, the polished butler, so loves his wife that he ignores her many lovers. Bill Hod, who appears to run all of the illegal and sinful establishments in the area, takes care of the forgotten eight-year-old. The action which affects all of these people concerns Link Williams, Abbie's adopted son, who falls in love with a white girl, not knowing that she is a wealthy heiress and married. Refusing to play the role of the rich girl's toy, Link breaks off the relationship, but as a result of the girl's revenge and several other slightly contrived circumstances, he is killed. *The Narrows* is an adult book, but one which will appeal to many adolescents.

Ann Petry is a skilled writer. David Littlejohn writes of her:

> There is, first, more intelligence in her novels, paragraph for paragraph, than in those of any other writer I have mentioned: solid, earned, tested intelligence. This woman is sharp. Her wisdom is more useful, even, more durable than the brilliant, diamond-edged acuteness of Gwendolyn Brooks.
>
> This wisdom, secondly, reveals itself in a prose that is rich and crisp, and suavely shot with the metallic threads of irony. It is a style of constant surprise and delight, alive and alight on the page. . . . And out of the female wisdom, the chewy style, grow characters of shape and dimension, people made out of love, with whole histories evoked in a page. There is not one writer in a thousand who owns so genuine and generous and undiscriminating a creative sympathy (David Littlejohn, *Black on White* [Penguin, pap., 1969], p. 155).

In addition to her novels, a number of Petry's short stories such as "The Winding Sheet" are useful with high school students.

J. Saunders Redding (1906–)

Born in Wilmington, Delaware, and educated at Brown University, Redding has taught on college campuses for most of his life and is currently Ernest I. White Professor of American Studies and Humane Letters at Cornell University. His *Stranger and Alone* (Harcourt Brace, 1950) is a tragic novel. It deals with the empty world of the "white man's nigger." The hero, or anti-hero, Shelton Howden, the son of a black woman and a white man, is born in isolation. Raised in an orphanage, Howden works his way through college up to a position as a professor. But because he was raised without love, he never develops the capacity to feel for other people. Instead, he learns the techniques of getting ahead in a white man's world—of playing dumb when asked to play dumb. Eventually he sells out his people, with almost no sympathy.

Stranger and Alone shows the destructive effects of racial discrimination from an unusual angle—from the viewpoint of the black who does manage to get ahead. It would make an interesting comparison with *Black Boy* or another book which shows the struggle from the bottom.

Stranger and Alone is not an outstanding novel. The characters tend toward caricature—they are exaggerated and seem to lack basic human feelings—though it might be argued that this is the point the book makes. Still, a person who can walk out of the room while his roommate is dying, who can marry one girl with no regrets while he is sexually involved with another, is less than believable. Dr. Posey, the sarcastic racist preacher; resident Wimbush, controller of all the blacks in the state, and his sex-crazed daughter also seem two-dimensional. Character development of Howden, however, is excellent. The progressive stages of his betrayal are very well handled.

Melvin B. Tolson (1900–1966)

A professor of English and speech who was educated at Fisk, Lincoln, and Columbia Universities, Tolson spent much of his teaching career at Wiley College and Langston University. He was for four terms mayor of Langston, Oklahoma, directed the Dust Bowl Theatre, and organized South Texas sharecroppers. Though his work was acclaimed by such writers as Karl Shapiro and Robert Frost, he received little attention from critics during his career.

His collection *Rendezvous with America* (Dodd, 1944) tells about the American dream of freedom and democracy through the history of the nation. The second group of poems, "Woodcuts for Americana," gives short sketches of various people around America, for example, an old farmer, Michael, who is trying to root the tares out of his field.

"Dark Symphony" uses a symphonic form to tell of the contribution of blacks to American history. It is a fairly difficult poem and would probably require explanation by the teacher, but it is significant and incorporates much black history. The other selections in the book: "Song for Myself," "Of Men and Cities," "The Idols of the Tribe," and "Tapestries of Time," could be used with high school students but are less interesting.

Libretto for the Republic of Liberia ([1953] Twayne, 1971; pap., Macmillan, 1970) is a lengthy, very difficult modernist poem which in jazzy, energy-charged rhythms celebrates black history and culture.

Harlem Gallery, Book I: The Curator ([1968] Twayne, 1971; pap., Macmillan, 1969) has received high praise from critics. Unfortunately, it is far too difficult for most high school students.

Margaret Walker (1915–   )

Margaret Walker, who grew up in Alabama, the daughter of a minister and a teacher of music, began planning a novel about her great-grandmother while studying at Northwestern University, but it was her poetry which first attracted national attention. After college, she worked in Chicago as a typist, reporter, and editor. Her poetry collection, *For My People* (Reprint of 1942 edition, Arno, 1969), was published in 1942 as a winner of the Yale Award for Younger Poets. Walker was then teaching at Livingstone College in North Carolina. It includes a number of poems of interest to high school students, among them "Molly Means," an eerie narrative about a conjure woman, and "For My People," a free-verse poem in which Walker prays for a new earth. A longer work, "Harriet Tubman," about the conductor of the Underground Railroad, is written in folk rhythm and makes an effective choral reading.

Walker has taught on several campuses, currently Jackson State College, Mississippi. She completed her long-planned novel, *Jubilee*, on a fellowship at the Creative Writers' Workshop at the University of Iowa. *Jubilee* (HM, 1966; pap., Bantam, 1975) recounts with pride the lives of Walker's ancestors under slavery. It is primarily the story of Vyry, a young woman with a strong and optimistic spirit, of her life on her master's plantation, and her attempts to build a home for her family after the slaves are emancipated by the Civil War. Though its length (nearly 500 pages) may discourage some students, *Jubilee* is fast moving and well written in a very readable style. Walker's account, *How I Wrote Jubilee* (Third World, pap., 1972) would be of interest to students who like literature and are interested in the "Roots" phenomenon.

Richard Wright (1908–1960)

Richard Wright is the first black to be recognized as an outstanding American novelist. The themes for his fiction center on the agonies of the black experience as he knew it during a painful youth in Mississippi. (See the discussion of *Black Boy*, below.) Wright's formal education ended with the ninth grade. After a series of unskilled jobs in Jackson, Memphis, and Chicago, he became a postal clerk and a publicity agent for the Federal Negro Theatre. During the thirties, Wright worked with the Federal Writers Project. The stage version of *Native Son*, on which he collaborated with Paul Green, was a success in New York in 1941. For the last fourteen years of his life, Wright lived abroad, writing and lecturing.

Native Son (Reprint of 1940 edition, Har-Row, 1969; pap., n.d.) is without doubt one of the important American novels of the period. It is also without question a book which teenagers can easily become involved with. However, it is also a very violent book which does not attempt to hide sex, rough language, or hate. Immature students might find it disturbing, but mature students with good guidance can profit from studying it. A classic of American naturalism, *Native Son* provides a thorough study of society's stranglehold on an individual. The book holds society responsible for Bigger Thomas' destruction just as clearly as society holds Bigger responsible for Mary's death. The communist characters provide excellent mouthpieces for Wright's denunciation of society, and the mobs demonstrate society's corruptness.

Native Son deals with the problems a black has attaining manhood in a society that conspires against him. The story begins by showing the difficulty of achieving normal human relations in the squalor of a Chicago slum. Bigger Thomas has what appears to be amazing luck when he gets a job as a chauffeur with a wealthy family. However, in fear and confusion, he accidentally kills the daughter. He tries to escape, but is caught and tried for murder. The events seem to be a long nightmare over which Bigger himself has little, if any, control.

Uncle Tom's Children (Reprint of 1936 edition, Har-Row, 1969; pap., 1965) consists of four horror stories about the plight of blacks in the South. "Fire and Cloud," which has possibilities for classroom use, is the story of a preacher who leads his people in a communist-inspired march. Although the situation involves violence, the story has good character development. The blacks in these stories, pressed by circumstances into crime, are punished by whites, who appear to be looking for blacks to torture. Of the eight major black characters, one is burned alive, four are shot, one is raped, and one is severely beaten.

Eight Men ([1961] pap., Pyramid Pubns, 1969) includes stories and novelettes, shorter than some of the stories in other collections and less emphasis on violence. "The Man Who Lived Underground" is a nightmarish story, strikingly similar in both mood and symbolism to *Invisible Man*. "The Man Who Saw the Flood" shows nature and whites conspiring to destroy the blacks' chances. "Man of All Work" is an exciting story about a man who is so desperate for work he dresses in women's clothes. The other stories in the collection are powerful literature, full of symbolism and imagination, but too harsh for many high school students.

Black Boy: A Record of Childhood and Youth (Reprint of 1945 edition, Har-Row, 1969; pap., n.d.) is one of the bleakest accounts in literature of the effects of poverty and prejudice on a child. Wright's vivid memories include burning the house down at the age of four, being beaten almost to the point of death by his parents, being a drunkard at the age of six, and always being hungry. From these revelations, it is easy to see how Wright developed his philosophy of suffering and fate. Everything in his environment conspired to keep him from his manhood. Not only did white people force him to be obsequious, but his own people, out of fear, begged him to endure insult and even kept him down themselves. Yet he maintained a remarkable integrity, refusing to compromise his own worth. This integrity and courage make *Black Boy* an outstanding challenge for teenagers.

Black Boy is one of the best books of any kind for use with high school students. It is so absorbing that even reluctant readers find it hard to put down. In terms of literary quality, both *Black Boy* and *Native Son* are among the best works by American authors. Wright's strengths as a writer, his vivid description of action, his effective creation of mood, and his memorable characters are qualities that high school readers appreciate as much as mature critics do. For the teacher concerned about teaching human relations, *Black Boy* is one of the most effective books possible for helping students understand and respect black anger, and for showing the value of literature as a means of liberating a person from psychological oppression.

Frank Yerby (1916–   )

While most black writers have probed their racial heritage for their subject matter, Frank Yerby has made his reputation and his fortune with white, European historical romances. He has written over twenty novels including *The Foxes of Harrow* (1946), *The Vixens* (1947), *The Golden Hawk* (1948), *A Woman Called Fancy* (1951), *Floodtide* (1967) and *Pride's Castle* ([1968] Reprints of all titles, Dell). Sales of Yerby's novels have totaled more than 21 million copies.

In *The Dahomean* ([1971] pap., Dell, 1972) Yerby finds that the African heritage also provides opportunity for romance and adventure. Nyasanu, the son of a chieftain, grows to adulthood, falling in love, enduring initiation rites and marrying his childhood sweetheart. Conscripted to fight in an unjust war, he becomes a hero, but begins to recognize and resent the despotic monarchy that rules Dahomey. As a result of his bravery and honor, Nyasanu rises high in the government and marries a princess, but eventually intrigue overthrows him and he is sold as a slave to America.

In the introduction, Yerby points out that the customs described in the book are based on anthropological research and portray both the positive and negative qualities of African society. "... truth," he says, "is an uncomfortable quality; ... neither the racist, the liberal, nor the advocates of Black Power and/or pride will find much support for their dearly held ... myths herein." While his portrayal of African society may be objective, the extreme stereotyping of homosexuals is a regrettable flaw.

The Dahomean is by no means a great work of literature, but it is an enjoyable and exciting book which is likely to appeal to the kind of student who finds Alex Haley's *Roots* too long and Chinua Achebe's *Things Fall Apart* too difficult.

Before his success on the best seller lists, Yerby published several short stories in the naturalistic tradition. One of the best, "The Homecoming," is in several anthologies, including John Henrik Clarke's *American Negro Short Stories* (Hill & Wang, cloth & pap., 1966). A Georgian, Yerby taught English and worked in industry until he became established as a writer. He has lived in Europe since the 1950s.

Contemporary Black Writers (1950–1965)

The period from 1950 to 1965 saw some of the most significant achievements by black American novelists. Although it is a period without a name and is often ignored in favor of the Harlem Renaissance or the new black poets, the 1950s and early 1960s saw a steady increase in significant works by blacks. Some of these are now recognized as modern classics.

Ralph Ellison's *Invisible Man*, judged in a 1965 *Book Week* poll of critics, authors, and editors as the "most distinguished single work" published in America between 1945 and 1965, has taken its place with such works as *Moby Dick*, *Huckleberry Finn*, and *The Great Gatsby* as one of the masterpieces of American literature. *Invisible Man* was followed the next year by the first novel of another of the major black novelists, James Baldwin's *Go Tell It on the Mountain*. While none of his individual works have been quite so highly praised as *Invisible Man,* Baldwin proved to be a more prolific writer, averaging a book every two years for the next decade, and he quickly dominated the field.

Ellison and Baldwin were highly visible, noted, acclaimed and discussed by the established white critics, causing other black writers whose works were largely ignored to complain that the press had room for only one black writer at a time. The complaint perhaps had some validity, for books that were ignored and even went out of print in the 1950s quickly became popular in the late 1960s, when black literature again became the vogue. So while their works did not become popular until the time of the new black poets, described in the next section, most of our contemporary novelists had already produced some significant work before that movement began. In addition to Ellison and Baldwin, the period from 1950 to 1965 introduced William Demby, Ernest Gaines, Kristin Hunter, William Melvin Kelley, Julian Mayfield, Paule Marshall, Herbert Simmons, and Margaret Walker, the latter already known for her poetry. Writers from earlier periods also produced significant novels during this time. W. E. B. Du Bois' trilogy *The Black Flame* was published from 1957 to 1961. Richard Wright published *The Outsider, The Long Dream,* and *Lawd Today.* Ann Petry, Chester Himes, and of course Frank Yerby continued to write.

While an extraordinary number of novels were published, there was no distinct literary movement in the 1950s and 1960s comparable to the Harlem Renaissance or the new black poets. The writers were individuals rather than a community, and while some, such as William Demby, experimented with new forms of the novel, there was no new aesthetic. Rather it seemed as if the writers were responding to their new freedom to openly explore violence and repression, as did Richard Wright, and to techniques for analyzing the subtle subconscious effects of racism, as demonstrated by Ellison. Freed from previous constraints on black writing, the younger writers explored a variety of themes and styles.

Although most of the important writing of the fifties and sixties was in the form of novels, one significant dramatist should be mentioned. Lorraine Hansberry's *A Raisin in the Sun* became a highly successful play and movie, achieving the longest run on Broadway of any play by a black playwright and winning the Critics' Circle Award. In theme, style, and content, it is not closely related to the new black theater, which followed it, but by demonstrating that a serious black drama could be a box office success, and by advertising the talents of a number of black actors, it helped to make this later movement successful.

Few new poets appeared during this era, but a number of important poetic works were published by the poets who began their careers during the 1940s. Melvin B. Tolson and Robert Hayden brought out new poetry collections, and Gwendolyn Brooks published a number of new works. Owen Dodson wrote both fiction and poetry, and the poems of Dudley Randall and James Emanuel began to appear in magazines. LeRoi Jones' *Preface to a Twenty Volume Suicide Note* appeared in 1961, but his works are discussed in the next section because of his important role in the movement which began in the late 1960s.

James Baldwin (1924–   )

James Baldwin is without doubt one of the most significant modern American novelists and has few challengers as the leading contemporary black novelist. Unfortunately, his writings possess several qualities which make them less than ideal for the average high school reader. First, most of his works, except *If Beale Street Could Talk* and *The Amen Corner,* are rather difficult. The beautifully constructed sentences and the deep psychological insights which delight the mature reader tend to confuse and bore the unskilled reader. Also his delightfully vivid descriptions of sexual acts and his blunt handling of controversial themes disturb some parents and school boards. However, for those students who are mature readers, Baldwin's works are highly rewarding. His works have a remarkable honesty and integrity. His power lies in his ability and willingness to penetrate the masks of hypocrisy which all people wear and which keep them from facing themselves. Baldwin's characters experience painful, progressive self-revelation, and his writing is so powerful that it forces readers to identify with these characters and recognize hidden and sometimes taboo emotions as their own.

James Baldwin has said, "I began plotting novels at about the time I learned to read" ("Autobiographical Notes," *Notes of a Native Son,* [1955] pap., Bantam, 1971). As a boy in Harlem, he helped look after numerous brothers and sisters while reading widely. After preaching several years during his teens at his father's urging, he turned to various jobs, including waiting tables in Greenwich Village and writing book reviews. Early novels yielded fellowships but did not attract publishers. Finally, Baldwin went to France, where he completed *Go Tell It on the Mountain.* He lived in Europe for a number of years.

Of all Baldwin's works, the most suitable for high school students is *If Beale Street Could Talk* (Dial, 1974; pap., NAL, 1975). A beautiful love story about two teenagers, the novel is narrated by the girl and is shorter and simpler in style than his other works. Tish and Fonny grow up together and gradually fall deeply in love. They plan to be married and are looking for an apartment in the Village where Fonny will have room to work on his sculpture. But then, Fonny is arrested and falsely accused of raping a Puerto Rican woman. Although both Tish and another friend were with him at the time of the crime and the rest of the evidence is very weak, he is jailed. And Tish discovers that she is pregnant. Tish and her family work hard and sacrifice to try to get Fonny released and to provide a home for the unborn child, but the system seems determined to crush young, spirited, black males. And although at the end it appears that Fonny will be released, it is apparent that he will never be allowed to be completely free.

If Beale Street Could Talk is a beautiful and powerful book about proud and determined people who refuse to give in to destructive forces. This is an excellent novel for high school students.

A second Baldwin work appropriate for younger readers is *The Amen Corner* (Dial, 1968), Baldwin's first play, and the simple, moving story of Margaret, the dedicated pastor of a holiness church; Luke, her jazz trombonist ex-husband; and her son David, who is torn between the church and the world. The conflict between Luke, David, and Margaret is compounded by the arguments of the not-always-so-holy church members, who depose Margaret as she finally realizes that loving others, no matter what the cost, is what faith is really all about.

Several of Baldwin's books are suitable in content for high school use, though in style they are so difficult that only fairly advanced students will be able to read them without difficulty.

Go Tell It on the Mountain (Dial, 1953; pap., Dell, 1965) is Baldwin's first novel. In this story, John, an adolescent boy, is torn between his desire to be saved and his desire to be a regular teenager. Compounding his problem are his resentment against his self-righteous father and his dislike of his obviously favored brother. His inner struggles are further dramatized by flashbacks into the lives of his aunt, Florence; his father, Gabriel; and his mother, Elizabeth. As their soul-searchings go on, the reader gains insight into John, who is not actually Gabriel's son, but the son of Richard, who died before he could marry Elizabeth. Gabriel also falls from his holiness and fathers an illegitimate child, who later dies. John finally leaves the church, hoping to lead a life of holiness but aware of the suffering that must be borne by the black person.

The character development is excellent. The technique of using flashbacks to show each character's history and thoughts during the emotion-packed church service is very successful. The interest level is high, for there is continual action and a good build-up of suspense. However, poor readers may have trouble following the story and keeping the characters straight. The content is very worthwhile for teenagers, showing an adolescent's struggle to find himself and deal with family, religion, and society.

Nobody Knows My Name (Dial, 1961; pap., Dell, n.d.) is a collection of essays on topics including the thoughts of an American Negro expatriate, life in the Harlem ghetto, and segregation in North and South. There are also essays on William Faulkner, Ingmar Bergman, Richard Wright, and Norman Mailer.

The style is sensitive and vivid. Baldwin's honesty about himself brings us a penetrating understanding of people. Baldwin lays bare the human psyche in all of its contradictions. At the heart of the essays is every person's search for identity—a search which mature students can identify with. The essays fall into several groups: "The Discovery of What It Means to Be an American" and "Princes and Powers" are both on a high intellectual level. "Fifth Avenue Uptown," "East River Downtown," "A Fly in the Buttermilk," "Notes for a Hypothetical Novel," and "Nobody Knows My Name" are more readable narrative essays about segregation.

A second nonfiction work, *The Fire Next Time* (Dial, 1963; pap., Dell, 1970), contains a letter on the one-hundredth anniversary of Emancipation and a long, somewhat autobiographical piece concerned primarily with Baldwin's experiences with and thoughts on Christianity and the Nation of Islam. Baldwin powerfully indicts white American racism and warns that the Black Muslims may be correct in predicting the fulfillment of the biblical prophecy as expressed in a spiritual: "God gave Noah the rainbow sign,/ No more water, the fire next time." In addition to being worthwhile reading in its own right, the essay could provide interesting material for an analysis of the way an author weaves his own experiences and ideas into a novel. *The Amen Corner, Go Tell It on the Mountain* and *Another Country* are closely related to the themes from this essay.

An additional essay collection, *Notes of a Native Son* ([1957] pap., Bantam, 1971), and a short story collection, *Going to Meet the*

Man (Dial, 1965), might be useful with some students.

Baldwin's other works have little place in high school curricula. *Tell Me How Long the Train's Been Gone* (Dial, 1968; pap., Dell, 1975), a novel about an actor's search for identity, would probably be more meaningful to middle-aged people than to adolescents. *Blues for Mister Charlie* (Dial, 1964; pap., Dell, 1964), a play about a lynching, and *Giovanni's Room* (Dial, 1956), a novel about a homosexual love affair, are better appreciated by mature readers. *Another Country* (Dial, 1962; pap., Dell, 1970) would probably be too disturbing for many adolescents.

Eldridge Cleaver (1935–)

The Arkansas-born son of laboring parents, Cleaver continued his education in California prisons while serving time. His writing career began at Folsom, where he was imprisoned for assault with intent to commit murder and assault with a deadly weapon. Paroled in 1966, he became senior editor and a contributing writer for *Ramparts* magazine, which had campaigned for his release. His involvement with the Black Panther Party for Self-Defense in Oakland, California, led to further confrontations with the law. Due to enter prison in 1968 as a result of a gun battle, he fled the country and lived in Cuba and Algiers before returning in 1976 to await trial.

Cleaver's *Soul on Ice* (McGraw, 1968; pap., Dell, 1970) is one of the most popular, but also one of the most controversial, books by a black author currently used in high schools. A collection of essays written while Cleaver was in prison, *Soul on Ice* analyzes the mental and emotional colonization of the minds of black people by white society—a theme that was startlingly new to most readers in the late 1960s, but which is almost commonplace today. Although a few of Cleaver's themes have gained wide acceptance, and despite the fact that Cleaver and society have changed a lot in the last ten years, the book is still a powerful, honest tribute to human potential for growth, even in the most unlikely situations. While critics often revile it as full of hate, its message is really one of personal growth and love in spite of a hate-filled world. Cleaver himself sums up his philosophy: "The price of hating other human beings is loving oneself less" (*Soul on Ice*, p. 28).

William Demby (1922–)

Demby, who was born in Pittsburgh, wrote for *Stars and Stripes* during his Army service in Europe in World War II. He studied at West Virginia State College, Fisk University, and the University of Rome. Besides performing as a jazz musician, he has been a screen writer for Roberto Rossellini in Rome, has taught, and has worked in advertising.

His novel *Beetlecreek* ([1950] pap., Avon, 1967) is one of the best books by a black author for mature high school students. The story revolves around three characters. Johnny is a young boy from Pittsburgh who struggles with conflicting desires—to be a part of the gang and to do right. Johnny's uncle, Diggs, feels trapped in Beetlecreek and wants to escape to the North. Bill Trapp, an old white man who has been a hermit for fifteen years, finally decides he wants human companionship. When Bill, attempting to become part of the community, invites some little girls of both races to his house for a picnic, he is accused of molesting them. But neither Johnny nor Diggs, who have been his friends, stand up for him. Johnny gives in to his desire to be a part of the gang and burns the old man's house. Diggs deserts the village for Detroit and leaves his wife for an old college sweetheart.

Beetlecreek is a unified book. Characters, action, style, and symbol all develop the tragedy of men who lack the courage to be. Like Baldwin, Demby forces his readers to face honestly the weakness within themselves.

The Catacombs (Pantheon, 1965) is a significant experimental novel, but because of its extremely difficult style, it is not suitable for most high school students. Set in Italy, it is an unusual mixture of fantasy, newspaper reports, and true experience mixed in what the author calls cubistic time. Reading it is almost a psychedelic experience.

Ralph Ellison (1914-)

The author of *Invisible Man,* one of the greatest novels by a black author, was born in Oklahoma, studied music at Tuskegee Institute, worked in the thirties with the New York City Federal Writers Project, and served in the Merchant Marine during World War II. Since the publication of *Invisible Man* (Random, 1951; pap., 1972), he has taught literature and writing on campuses including Bard College and Rutgers University and has published literary criticism.

Invisible Man, like *Moby Dick,* is a nightmarish novel of a man trying to comprehend the confusion of myth, experience, and inner reactions that control his life. The symbols of oppression—

invisibleness, the forbidden white woman, the leering note that says "keep that Nigger-boy running," and loss of manhood—appear and reappear as in a nightmare. The bizarre plot of this novel, which seems half real, half dream, creates a deep sense of disillusionment.

Invisible Man unmasks the various kinds of escape the black might seek, to keep from dealing honestly with his heritage. Escape into the middle class proves to be fraudulent in the protagonist's experiences at the Negro college. Later in the book, escape into communism proves just as hopeless. Throughout the book there is a groping for meaning, for a way of becoming visible.

Despite its importance as literature, *Invisible Man* is not appropriate for most high school students. The language is earthy, and several scenes are very raw, especially a rape scene and the castration dream at the end. An even more serious drawback for the high school student is that the book is very difficult. *Invisible Man* calls for the same ability to comprehend symbolism and myth that Faulkner or T. S. Eliot requires, and not all high school students have this ability. However, the few outstanding students who can read it will find it an extremely valuable book, both for its literary qualities and for its sociological and psychological insights. This is probably one of the four or five greatest works of American literature, but like *Moby Dick*, it should be college reading for most students.

Ellison's other major work is a collection of critical essays, interviews, and book reviews entitled *Shadow and Act* ([1964] pap., Random, 1972). He has also published a number of short stories, available in many anthologies. The best of these are "Flying Home" and "King of the Bingo Game."

Ernest J. Gaines (1933-   )

Rural Louisiana, which figures in his fiction, was Ernest Gaines' birthplace. He studied at San Francisco State College, did graduate work at Stanford, and now lives and writes in San Francisco. One of the most artistically skillful of contemporary black writers, Gaines has written works that both delight the literary critic and interest the adolescent reader. Most of his fiction is set in the rural South and combines a deep sensitivity to the culture of the people with the theme of desire to maintain one's humanity.

The Autobiography of Miss Jane Pittman (Dial, 1971; pap., Bantam, 1972) has become justifiably popular, with interest encouraged by a very fine television special based on it. Supposedly the recollections of a black woman whose life spanned the century from the Civil War to the civil rights campaign of the 1960s, the novel tells the story of an ordinary woman who endures tragedy and oppression throughout her century-long life, but who remains indomitable and full of spirit.

Born in slavery on a Louisiana plantation, Jane is freed at the end of the Civil War. From the first chapter, when she offers a drink of water to a Yankee soldier, until the end, when she goes to demonstrate for the right to drink from the water fountain in the courthouse, Jane retains her dignity. With candor, compassion, wisdom, and a sense of humor, Miss Jane tells her story and the stories of slave masters, heroes, cowards, lovers, murderers, martyrs, ordinary men and women, blacks and whites who have touched her life. She has seen it all, and her recollections provide the reader with a deeper insight not only into the history of black people but into the history of America. In addition to Miss Jane's pride and dignity, the reader will remember the white chauvinism of the plantation owner Mr. Bone, the determination of Ned, who wants to build a school for blacks though he knows it will mean his own death, the death of Joe Pittman and his love for Jane, the cold-bloodedness of the murderer Albert Cluveau, and the youthful, freedom-fighting militancy of Jimmy, whom Jane knows is the *One*.

In Miss Jane, young readers will find a character deeply human and believable. The authenticity that Gaines brings to this work may make separating fiction from nonfiction difficult. The genre of autobiographical novel may confuse some young readers and should be explained by the teacher.

For young people, one of the great values of Gaines' works, particularly *The Autobiography*, is the sense of perspective they offer. The book could have been four short stories about men who worked for change and died tragically in the attempt, apparently in vain. But through Miss Jane's eyes, we see that their work was continued by the unheroic and the uneducated who, like Miss Jane, appear not to resist or even oppose change but, in the end, are the inexorable force that eventually brings it about.

Bloodline ([1963] pap., Norton, 1976) is a collection of five long short stories set in the rural South. The first two stories, "A Long Day in November" and "The Sky Is Gray," frequently anthologized, are narrated by young boys seeking to survive, understand, and grow into strong men in a troubling, confusing world. The theme of the search for manhood in a world that encourages subservience from black males is strongest in the next two stories:

"Three Men," in which a young man in prison tries to decide whether to ask a white man to help him get out or to take whatever punishment is meted out to the ungrateful; and "Bloodline," in which the black nephew of the last member of a wealthy white family returns to demand his birthright. The final story, "Just Like a Tree," describes an old black woman who refuses to leave her home. She is seen through the eyes of all of the people attending her going-away party, which turns out to be a funeral. The skillfully and subtly developed characters, the imaginative use of point of view and the carefully revealed themes will delight sophisticated readers but may go unnoticed by the less mature, who may find that only "Bloodline" has enough plot and suspense to hold their interest.

In *Interviews with Black Writers,* Gaines describes the theme of his works:

> You must understand that in this country the black man has been pushed into the position where he is not supposed to be a man.... As Joe Pittman says in *Miss Jane Pittman,* a man must do something, no matter what it is, he must do something and he must do that something well. My heroes just try to be men; but because the white man has tried everything from the time of slavery to deny the black this chance, his attempts to be a man will lead toward danger.... In the case of Tee Bob and Jackson [in Gaines' novel *Catherine Carmier*], they were victims of the past. They tried their best to escape the influence of the past, and I think their attempt to do this can lead to someone else picking up where they left off. This is the kind of thing I am doing in all of my work.... to break away from the past, from one philosophy to another, is a burden that one person cannot endure alone. Someone else must pick up from there and go on (John O'Brien, ed., *Interviews with Black Writers* [Liveright, 1973], pp. 85, 84).

Gaines' two other novels may also be of interest to some readers. *Catherine Carmier* (Reprint of 1964 edition, Chatham Bkseller, 1972) is the story of a young man who returns South after studying in the North and finds he cannot readjust. In *Of Love and Dust* (Dial, 1967) a young man revolts against the plantation system and is killed.

Alex Haley (1921–)

Haley, who was born in Ithaca, New York, and studied at Elizabeth City Teachers College, North Carolina, began his career in journalism in the U.S. Coast Guard, in which he served 1939–49.

His national reputation began with the publication of *The Autobiography of Malcolm X* (Grove, pap., 1965), written jointly with Malcolm X.

Haley's name became a household word with the 1977 screening on television of *Roots: The Saga of an American Family,* a twelve-hour film based on his book about his search for his ancestors. The TV special was viewed by the largest audience in the history of television and changed many people's consciousness of American history.

The story of the writing of *Roots,* which the author expects to publish in the near future, is perhaps even more exciting than the book itself. For in a twelve-year search, Alex Haley managed to piece together his family history and the oral histories of an African village, tracing his ancestry not only back to Africa but for many generations further.

Roots (Doubleday, 1976; pap., Dell, 1977) begins in 1750 in the village of Juffure in The Gambia, with the birth of Kunta Kinte, son of Omoro, son of Kairaba Kunta Kinte, a holy man from Mauritania. Kunta's boyhood in Africa is described in loving detail: his education in the work and ritual of his people and his own passing on of this knowledge to his little brother, his travels to surrounding areas, his initiation into manhood, and finally, his capture by slavers.

The gruesome Middle Passage and the arrival in America are described through the eyes of the proud, devout Muslim. We see the relentless efforts to deprive him of his culture: he is forbidden to use his language, to play drums, or to practice his religion except in secret. Even his name is taken from him. Although disoriented, unfamiliar with the terrain, and kept in ignorance, Kunta continually tries to run away. But with dogs, patrollers, horses, and guns, he is caught each time. Each time he is beaten almost to death, and the last time his foot is cut off.

The story continues as Kunta, now known as Toby, unwillingly adjusts to plantation life, marries, and desperately tries to pass on to his daughter, Kizzy, something of his history and culture. When Kizzy is sold away and raped by her white master, she maintains her own dignity by telling her son the story of his ancestors. Kizzy is a field hand; her son Chicken George makes his master's fortune through his skill as a cockfighter. But when his master (and father) loses a huge bet, he gives George to the winner and sells his wife and children. Eventually, Emancipation comes and George goes West with his grown children, who find that the end of slavery has not necessarily brought freedom. From there the story is quickly summarized through the three generations until the author traces the story back to Africa.

Roots is a powerful story. Like no other book, it documents the history of black Americans. It is a monumental work. Many students may find its 587 pages much too long, especially since the first one hundred pages, which describe Kunta Kinte's life in Africa, are fascinating descriptions of a culture, but rather uneventful. I would not hesitate to direct less able readers to the condensed version published in *Reader's Digest*, or the serialized version which appeared in many newspapers. Students should not, however, assume that if they saw the television version, they do not need to read the book. The television version did not follow the book closely. The book presents a much more detailed and more accurate version of American history.

Roots deserves the audience it has reached, and is an excellent book for both English teachers and social studies teachers to recommend. Judged by purely literary standards, it is of uneven quality and not quite so well written as *Jubilee* or *The Autobiography of Miss Jane Pittman*, but *Roots* contains far more history and human experience than either.

Lorraine Hansberry (1930–1965)

A Chicagoan, Lorraine Hansberry was the daughter of a real estate broker who challenged a white neighborhood's right to bar him because of race in a case that was eventually won in the U.S. Supreme Court. She studied painting at the Art Institute of Chicago and in Mexico. After further work at the University of Wisconsin and the New School for Social Research, she lived in New York City and supported herself with various jobs while writing plays and short stories. *A Raisin in the Sun*, which won the New York Drama Critics' Circle Award for 1958–59, was the first Broadway play to be written by a black woman and marked the first time a black director had worked on Broadway since 1907.

In two years, my students wore out at least fifteen copies of *A Raisin in the Sun* (Random, 1969; pap., NAL, 1961). I have used it to entice reluctant readers and have not found one who did not like it. Memories of the movie often kindle their interest, but students are soon enthralled by what for many is their first encounter with literature about modern urban blacks.

Here are characters that black students can identify with, and all of them are magnificently strong and alive. Walter, the husband and son, is fighting for his manhood against a mother who still treats him as a child, a wife who does not believe in him, a community that still calls him a boy, and black friends who are ready to hustle him out of his money. Mama is a strong, proud pioneer woman who has held the family together, but sees it crumbling around her. Ruth, Walter's wife, is just a woman who wants to raise her children right, and Beneatha, Walter's sister, is a young intellectual who wants to escape by becoming a doctor or marrying an African.

A Raisin in the Sun is one of the better modern Broadway plays and probably the best work about blacks available for high school students. Both white and black students should find it an enlightening experience. Few books for adolescents are so full of life.

Another of Lorraine Hansberry's works, *To Be Young, Gifted and Black: Lorraine Hansberry in Her Own Words,* edited by Robert Nemiroff (P-H, 1969; pap., NAL, 1970), also has a strong impact on adolescent readers. A collage of her public and private writing put together and produced for the stage after her untimely death, this autobiographical work conveys a portrait of a proud, courageous human being. Hansberry's second full-length play, *The Sign in Sidney Brustein's Window* ([1965] pap., NAL, n.d.) deals primarily with white characters and with themes more distant from the concerns of most adolescents (anthologized in John Gassner and Clive Barnes, eds., *Best American Plays,* 6th Series [Crown, 1971]).

Kristin Hunter (1931–   )

A successful writer of both adult and adolescent fiction, Kristin Hunter, a Philadelphian, also teaches at the University of Pennsylvania. Her novel *God Bless the Child* (Scribner, 1964) deserves to be better known than it is. I found it to be one of the most successful books I ever taught to high school students. It has most of the elements which have made Hunter's adolescent novel *The Soul Brothers and Sister Lou* so popular: a lively plot and vibrant characters that the reader can love and worry about. *God Bless the Child* is an adult book, much better written, though not quite so easy to read.

The title comes from a blues song with lines like "Money, You've got lots of friends," and "God bless the child that got his own," and it tells, perhaps as convincingly as any book, the hopelessness of the black ghetto. Rosie is a girl with a dream, strong and tough, willing to work, fight, and risk to get the wealth her grandmother describes in the white home she works for, only to find that by the time she can afford such a home, termites and roaches have beaten her to the neighborhood. In the end, she and her friends discover that neither education, nor hard work, nor even the underworld provide the ticket to the dream, which itself turns out to be empty and unreal.

While *God Bless the Child* is a tragedy, *The Landlord* ([1966] pap., Avon, 1970) is a comedy, the humorous story of a rich white boy who buys an apartment building for fun and ends up finding himself and rebuilding the whole neighborhood. It is an enjoyable book, though the fairy-tale ending still shows the white man as the savior of blacks. On another level, however, beneath the comedy and stereotypes, it shows a number of confused human beings escaping from the masks and roles they have assumed and finding themselves.

William Melvin Kelley (1937–)

Kelley, the author of five novels and a number of magazine pieces, was born in New York City and educated at Harvard. He has taught at the New School for Social Research and, at this writing, is author in residence at the State University of New York at Geneseo.

A Drop of Patience (Reprint of 1965 edition, Chatham Bkseller, 1973) is a portrait of a blind musician. The novel begins when the boy is six years old and continues into his adulthood, showing his search for identity in his music, his marriage, and his love affairs; the story concludes with a nervous breakdown. Kelley effectively conveys the experience of blindness through brilliant aural and tactile imagery.

Dancers on the Shore (Reprint of 1964 edition, Chatham Bkseller, 1973) is a collection of short stories that cluster around a middle-class doctor's family. The book can be studied as one loosely connected narrative, or the stories can be taken individually. The following are the most significant for high school students: "Enemy Territory"—a small boy learns to stand up for himself after he hears a story about his grandfather; "A Visit to Grandmother"—the little boy observes his father returning to the home of his grandmother, whom he has neglected since he became well-to-do; "Connie"—a pregnant daughter struggles with her conscience and her family's pride; "Brother Carlyle"—a lower-class family's sibling rivalries are acted out, in this case by trying to burn the younger child alive; and "The Life You Save"—Peter, from the middle-class family, tries to help Mance, from the lower-class family, but is successful only when he gives up his middle-class values.

A Different Drummer ([1962] pap., Doubleday, 1969) tells how one day all of the black people in a mythical Southern state repudiate their society and leave. Tucker Caliban, descendant of an African who broke away from slavery, starts the exodus by quietly putting salt on his land, burning his house, and leaving. Behind him is a village of confused white people, many of whom think they are his friends. To six of them, and to one Northern black, Tucker's leaving is especially significant; the book explores their struggle to find meaning in his action and thus to understand more of themselves. Ultimately, Tucker's courage frees them to be human beings. However, another group, unable to understand, lynches the only black person remaining in the city.

A Different Drummer is a remarkable, thought-provoking novel. The writing is of very high quality, and character development is particularly outstanding. Unfortunately, many high school students find the shifting point of view confusing, so it is most effective with good readers.

dem (Doubleday, 1967) explores the disintegrating relationship of a white suburban couple and the effect on them of the birth of twins, one white and one black, the result of the wife's affair with a black man immediately after relations with her husband. The book raises significant and disturbing questions about the weaknesses of white middle-class culture, but the problems explored are those of middle-adulthood. Kelley's other three books are much more likely to be of interest and value to high school students.

John Oliver Killens (1916–   )

Killens, a Georgian, attended law school and studied at Columbia and New York Universities. He has worked with the National Labor Relations Board in Washington and directed the Harlem Writers' Workshop. His novels combine features of the earlier naturalistic novels with contemporary militant writing. His books portray in relentless detail the traps in which black people are held by white America.

Youngblood ([1954] Trident, n.d.) is his best work. It is the story of two generations of the Youngblood family from Crossroads, Georgia, and describes both the small and large humiliations and cruelties that deprive the members of the family of their dreams. The characters, with their strivings and disappointments and their love, are real and sympathetically drawn. Many of the chapters are self-contained episodes that could be used individually. The Youngblood family shows people coping the best way possible with destructive pressures. Sometimes they give in; Laura is forced to beat her son to save him from a reformatory. But at other times they are able to stand up for their rights; when Rob is accused of raping a white girl, Laura refuses to accept the "compromise" she is offered. They are leaders in the struggle to form a union and a chapter of the NAACP. Even when Joe Youngblood is killed for standing up for his rights, the family continues the struggle.

Youngblood is an excellent book for high school students. It is long but not difficult, with a lot of action and very well developed characters.

And Then We Heard the Thunder (Knopf, 1963) tells the story of a black man who becomes progressively disillusioned with white society. Saunders begins as a young man who plans to get ahead by entering the Army during World War II. However, he soon finds that the price for success was too much sacrifice of his manhood and self-respect and begins to assert himself more and more. The plot is exciting, with war, fights, and love affairs, but it is also violent and bitter.

Paule Marshall (1929–)

Brooklyn-born Paule Marshall became a magazine staff writer after studying at Brooklyn and Hunter Colleges. She has contributed articles to magazines and has lectured on black literature in the United States, England, and France.

In *Brown Girl, Brownstones* (Reprint of 1959 edition, Chatham Bkseller, 1972) Marshall shows some of the special problems of black immigrants from Barbados. The adolescent's search for identity is especially difficult for Selina Boyce for many reasons. There is a family conflict between her pleasure-loving father and her business-minded mother, as well as the normal problems of adolescence—development of friendships, acceptance of sex, and finding a career.

Brown Girl, Brownstones is a well-written novel, and its characters are its strongest asset. Selina herself is a very complex young woman, and her progress toward self-understanding, particularly the understanding of her relationship to her mother, is sensitively and realistically pictured. But even the minor characters—Suggie, the voluptuous worshipper of the body; Miss Mary, the old white woman who refuses to move or to die; the mother, who gains her property but loses the trust of her daughter; and Deighton, the father, who dreams instead of facing reality—are lively and exciting. Less mature students may not find the novel appealing because it does not have a lot of action. However, more mature and sensitive students should find that the book deals with a number of significant and relevant problems—the race situation, middle-class vs. lower-class values, immigrant problems, development of moral standards, and intra-family conflicts.

This is an excellent book for class discussions. Detailed teaching suggestions for this book are available in *Theory and Practice in the Teaching of Literature by Afro-Americans* by Darwin T. Turner and Barbara Dodds Stanford (NCTE, pap., 1971).

Paule Marshall's collection of short stories, *Soul Clap Hands and Sing* (Reprint of 1961 edition, Chatham Bkseller, 1971) might appeal to older, more sensitive and sophisticated students. One of the stories, "Reena," tells of disappointment in love and is frequently anthologized. All of these stories are rather subtle.

Marshall's novel *The Chosen Place, the Timeless People* ([1969] pap., Avon, 1976) is a monumental study of the relationships between white Americans, a folk black people, and westernized black people on an imaginary Caribbean island. However, the psychological insights are likely to be too complex for most adolescents, and the conflicts of the middle-aged characters are likely to have less interest for them than those in *Brown Girl, Brownstones*.

Julian Mayfield (1928–   )

Julian Mayfield is not only a successful novelist but also a political writer, actor, producer, and founding editor of *The African Review*, published in Ghana. He was an aide to President Kwame Nkrumah of Ghana in the sixties, and has recently been living in Guyana.

His novel *The Long Night* (Vanguard, 1958) tells of a long, frightening night spent by a little boy in New York City. It reveals the tensions, loss of dreams, and fears a child must face in the ghetto. The father, Paul, tries to instill pride in his sons but fails to show strength and manliness. The mother, Mae, wants love and a good home and is impatient with Paul, who wants to study law. The disintegration of the family and of Paul and Mae individually is shown in Steely's memories as he travels around the city trying to get back the twenty-seven dollars that has been stolen from him.

This is a powerful portrayal of family life in the ghetto showing both strength and tragedy. The style reflects the simplicity of a ten-year-old boy, but the depth of a mature artist. In *The Long Night*, as in *A Raisin in the Sun*, the laboring love, the dead dreams, and the desperate struggle of a black family signify the universal problems of all people. The characters are men and women struggling for life and handicapped by white supremacy. *The Long Night* is not a great book for those who can respond to deeper literary works, but it is an outstanding novel for most adolescents.

The Hit (Vanguard, 1957) is the story of a black building superintendent in Harlem who dreams of winning big at the numbers game. But when he finally "hits," the numbers man disappears, and his dream is destroyed.

After he wrote these two novels, Mayfield's interests became more political. *The Grand Parade* (Vanguard, 1961) describes how an ambitious politician tries to bring reform to a Southern town while still getting ahead himself. His efforts end with his assassination and a race riot. This book would probably be of less interest to high school students than Mayfield's other novels.

Herbert Simmons (1930–)

Simmons' better-known novel, *Corner Boy* (HM, 1957), a Houghton Mifflin Literary Fellowship Award winner, centers on Jake Adams, who has become top cat on the corner. He has the fanciest car, the sharpest clothes, and the prettiest girls in his section of Chicago, and nobody knows that he gets his money by pushing dope. He tries to make a successful life, even by following his girlfriend to college, but he refuses to give up the easy money of the rackets. Eventually it seems as if everyone he touches ends in tragedy; finally he goes to jail himself. But he knows no other way of life and plans to return to the corner when he is released.

Written in the language of the streets, *Corner Boy* is sometimes a little difficult for a "square" to translate. The action is rapid and there is plenty of excitement. Characters are fairly well developed. The contrast between Jake the hustler and his father is well drawn. There is some depth in the development of this conflict. The plot is well constructed, as Jake gets himself deeper and deeper into trouble, still thinking he is on top. The atmosphere and color of street life are portrayed well.

Herbert Simmons is also author of *Man Walking on Egg Shells* (HM, 1962). He was born in St. Louis, studied at Lincoln and

Washington Universities, and did graduate work at the University of Iowa. He edited *Spliv*, a literary experiment, and produced "Portraits in Rhythm," a mixture of poetry, prose, and jazz, for coffeehouses.

John A. Williams (1925–   )

John A. Williams is one of the most prolific contemporary black writers, with seven novels, three nonfiction books, and a number of articles to his credit. Born in Jackson, Mississippi, he was educated at Syracuse University and has worked in broadcasting, publishing, and reporting. He has been European correspondent for *Ebony* and *Jet* magazines and has covered assignments in Africa for *Newsweek*. Most of Williams' works explore attempts by his characters to find psychological, philosophical and/or political solutions to the problem of living in a racist society. Except for *Captain Blackman* and *The Man Who Cried I Am*, Williams' works are not difficult, but their themes make them more suitable for mature readers.

Williams' early novels generally explore psychological solutions to personal dilemmas. In *The Angry Ones* ([1960] Reprint titled *One for New York*, Chatham Bkseller, 1975) his protagonist seeks success through traditional American goals—getting a good job and getting married. In *Sissie* (Reprint of 1963 edition, Chatham Bkseller, 1975) the characters are already successful, but must work to overcome the psychological damage inherited from childhood poverty. The book opens as Sissie's two children, Iris and Ralph, speed toward her deathbed. Iris has become a successful entertainer, but her private life is empty. She has never been given much love, because her mother pretended that she was another man's child to spite her father. Ralph, who has become a successful playwright, has gone through psychiatric treatment to try to overcome the pain left by his parents' violent quarrels. Both understand themselves better as they discover the terrible struggles which Sissie had to face in order to survive.

Sissie is of better-than-average literary quality. The character analysis, as Iris and Ralph explore their past to explain the present, is quite effective. Switches of scene and changing points of view are sometimes confusing, but they finally form a pattern, as the characters themselves put together the pieces of their background in preparation for a new life.

Williams' later novels have characters who reject the solution of escaping individually from oppression and recognize the necessity of working to change the oppressive system. *The Man Who Cried I Am* (Little, 1967; pap., NAL, 1972) has received the most critical attention and is generally considered his best literary effort. The novel takes place in Europe, where two American authors come to the realization that they must do more than write; they must take political action. While *The Man Who Cried I Am* is one of Williams' best works, it is likely to be one of the least popular with adolescents, because it is quite long and rather depressing, beginning with the hero suffering from terminal cancer.

In *Interviews with Black Writers* edited by John O'Brien (Liveright, 1973), Williams states that he is least satisfied with *Sons of Darkness, Sons of Light* (Little, 1969) because it is a "'straight ahead' novel. You start at A and wind up at Z." However, because it is simple and straightforward, it is likely to appeal to young readers. In this book, Williams explores what might happen if black people attempted a violent revolution. His hero, Browning, hires a Mafia hit man (a former Israeli commando) to assassinate a white policeman who had killed a black person, a move which starts a chain of violent revolutionary actions. It is an excellent book for young people who are glibly committed to either violence or nonviolence, and is a good example of the way a hypothesis can be tested through a novel. While it is a good book for teenagers who need practice in thinking through the consequences of their ideas, it is not a good handbook for a serious revolutionary. Williams admits in *Interviews with Black Writers*, "In that book I was dealing with nine tunnels and bridges leading into Manhattan. Well, hell, since last spring when the bridge-and-tunnel workers had a strike, I discovered that there were something like thirty-four bridge-tunnel approaches to Manhattan. A hell of a revolutionary I'd make!" (p. 242).

In *Captain Blackman* (Doubleday, 1972), Williams has created one of the most powerful indictments of white American racism and one of the most effective arguments for revolution yet written. Captain Blackman is wounded in Vietnam and while unconscious, relives the history of the black soldier, fighting in the Revolution, the Civil War, Indian Wars, and the World Wars, continually sacrificing for his country, and continually facing humiliation and physical hurt from the U.S. Army and Government. The book ends with a rather surrealistic vision of Blackman preparing a world revolution of black people. *Captain Blackman* is a valuable work both for the historic insights it provides and for the literary techniques it uses. Immature readers, however, may need help in sorting out the many different Captain Blackmans, the modern character and his historic counterparts in the dream.

Two other works by Williams are described in Chapter 4: *The Most Native of Sons: A Biography of Richard Wright* and *The King God Didn't Save*, a study of Martin Luther King, Jr.

The New Black Writers (1965–Present)

Suddenly in the late 1960s the markets were flooded with black literature. Books like *The Street* and *Boy at the Window*, which had been out of print a few years earlier, appeared on drugstore paperback racks. Publishers fought each other to discover new black talent or to reprint books which had disappeared decades ago, and black publishing houses printed poets who did not want to try to appeal to white readers.

The late 1960s were a time of excitement for black writers equal to or even greater than the Harlem Renaissance, for the interest in literature was nationwide. A writer did not have to go to Harlem to meet other writers and critics; writers' and dramatists' workshops sprang up in Watts, Newark, Chicago, East St. Louis, and hundreds of other communities. As riots focused attention on the ghettos, writers tried to tell their new audience about the realities of ghetto life and their ideas and programs for changing the oppressive system that produced them.

Many exciting new works were produced in the late 1960s, but the new black renaissance was as much a publishing phenomenon as a genuine increase in volume. Many of the newly discovered writers had been writing since the 1940s and 1950s with little reward or encouragement. The flood of new books and rediscovered old books was stimulated by the suddenly awakened interest in black people and their ideas.

But the late 1960s were not just a time of an increased quantity of black writing; a totally new form of writing evolved out of the new political situation, using the language, experience, values, and ideas that are unique to black people and are not shared by other Americans. After a decade of dedicated nonviolent struggle, many black people became disillusioned with nonviolent techniques and with their white allies. The techniques that had been successful against the legal segregation of the South seemed of little use against the far more powerful economic barriers in the North. After ten years of marching, turning the other cheek, and singing

"We Shall Overcome," blacks in Northern ghettos found themselves poorer and more hopeless than ever. People like Malcolm X, Stokely Carmichael, and Huey P. Newton seemed to make more sense as they called on black people to quit trying to persuade whites to give them rights for moral reasons, but to gain the power to take their rights, by force if necessary.

In addition to encouraging black people to use more militant methods of fighting for their rights, the new leaders emphasized that black people should be proud of themselves, recognize their own beauty, learn their own culture, and contribute to their own community instead of trying to move to the suburbs and act like white people. The excitement of militant activity, the number of new heroes and events to celebrate, and the emphasis on the beauties of black culture stimulated a lot of people to pick up their pens and get out their typewriters. A new black poetry and a new black drama sprang up from the streets, providing the revolutionaries with powerful new tools for spreading their ideas. The new voices sang the beauties of blackness, chided the reactionaries, encouraged the revolutionaries, and envisioned the glories of a new society.

In addition, the new black writers used poetry and drama to explore their own feelings as they searched for a meaningful identity in a nation they now admitted was hostile, and as they struggled with the conflicts their new ideas provoked. Many, like Carolyn Rodgers, explored the conflict between members of their generation and those of their parents' age, who rejected their militancy.

Other writers, like Ishmael Reed, looked back many generations in search of a tradition and a culture not corrupted by white oppression. African themes, images, languages, and poetic forms were studied and used. Many came to agree with Elijah Muhammad that black people should not bear names that originally belonged to white slaveholders, and took African names instead.

With the appearance earlier of poet Gwendolyn Brooks and novelist Paule Marshall, a trend had begun which increased as the women's movement took hold in the United States. New black writers, among them novelist Toni Morrison and poet-novelist Alice Walker, explored in their works the problems and strengths of black women seeking their own identity, rather than deriving their significance from their impact on husbands and sons.

Publishing their works themselves or through new small black publishing houses in inexpensive editions, and producing their plays in the black community, often in schools, churches or outdoors, the new black writers reached a new audience, an audience that had always responded to poetry in song but rarely before in printed form. Black teenagers who had previously found literature meaningless and irrelevant discovered poems that expressed in powerful and memorable phrases the ideas that they themselves had been thinking. Literary forms and techniques began to make sense to black students, who heard allusions to people and places they recognized, figures of speech with connotations that they felt, and rhythms and patterns they were familiar with. As a result of this different attitude toward poetry, high school students were encouraged to develop their poetic talents, and some produced very good work. Through the motivation offered by black writers' workshops throughout the country, many young writers, even while still in high school, have begun to see their works in print. Young readers have begun to realize that poetry is something that they can do, too.

But the new black writers have done more than find a new audience for poetry and drama. They have developed a new aesthetic with new elements and new rules. Stephen Henderson in "Survival Motion: A Study of the Black Writer and the Black Revolution in America" says:

> This baptism in blackness comprises two distinct elements which especially animate the recent pattern of black writing, although they were crystallized in many works of the Harlem Renaissance. They are (1) the rejection of white middle-class cultural values and (2) the affirmation of black selfhood, or, depending on the intensity of the writer's involvement, (a) the destruction of anything that stands in the way of selfhood and (b) a celebration of blackness (Mercer Cook and Stephen E. Henderson, *The Militant Black Writer in Africa and the United States* [U of Wis Pr, 1969], p. 72).

The new aesthetic of modern black writers looks, then, to black culture for its inspiration; the writers look to black people for their audience. They borrow rhythms and forms from black music and make allusions to voodoo, African myths, and black American folk heroes. In addition, the new black writers see the purposes of literature differently from most contemporary white writers. The new black literature tends to be functional and didactic. Its goals include creating a new self-image for black Americans, developing a sense of unity in the black community, and fighting against all of the systems—intellectual, economic and political—that have enslaved and oppressed blacks. Contemporary black writers often see themselves as people with a mission, and tend to be more interested in writing works with an immediate impact than in aiming at some distant immortality.

The aesthetic of the new black poets preaches that poetry is something useful and ordinary. Like soul music, it is something that anyone can sing or listen to just about any time. This aesthetic does not demand that a poem survive years of criticism to be considered valid. If a few people learn something from it or enjoy it or share the feelings it expresses, it has fulfilled its purpose.

These standards clash violently with contemporary white literary standards. While in other times European and American literature has been political and didactic, the contemporary style is to reject these as legitimate roles for literature and to label them as propaganda. Black writers in turn tend to reject white critics, with fairly good reason. White readers who are not thoroughly familiar with black culture are likely to miss a large percentage of the literary devices that are used. In addition, the subject matter of many works is quite anti-white. A white person who claims to be able to evaluate the poetic qualities of "Nigger, Can You Kill?" objectively is to some black writers the perfect confirmation of the contemporary stereotype of whites as repressed zombies with no emotions.

This is not to say that white teachers should not attempt to teach contemporary black poets. Contemporary black literature has a potential for awakening a lot of new ideas for both blacks and whites in both art and teaching. It can stimulate the development of new teaching methods by encouraging an integrated arts approach rather than sterile analysis. It can provide the opportunity for a more honest exchange of views than literature on which the teacher is clearly the expert. And it can encourage students to develop their own literary potential, as they recognize that poetry is not something just done by "the immortals" and read by English teachers, but can be an everyday way of expressing love, rage, and joy.

In addition, this literature can teach white teachers and critics important lessons about their own perspective on literature. Whites who read this new literature are likely to find themselves facing the same kinds of barriers that black students have faced for so long, when they have been forced to read white classics. Whites may find the language incomprehensible, the content so remote from their experience as to be boring or frightening, and the portrayal of whites so negative that they find it offensive. This reaction is one of the strongest reasons why white teachers should read some of this literature. The teacher who finds that he or she can't quite get carried away by the victory of the "Brothers" over the "Devils" in Imamu Amiri Baraka's drama *Bloodrites* may have a little more sympathy for the black student who cannot enjoy Tom Sawyer's "harmless" pranks against Jim. And the teacher who resents Captain Blackman's unrelenting hatred of whites, even after reading about the experiences that created that hate, may better understand why so many black students are unable to see the characters of *To Kill a Mockingbird* as nice people who just happen to be prejudiced. White people who seriously study the new black literature are likely to realize that white American literature is not nearly so universal as they had previously assumed.

The new black aesthetic is most obvious in poetry and drama. The new black poets, a term used to describe people such as Sonia Sanchez, June Jordan, Don L. Lee, Etheridge Knight, and Nikki Giovanni, among others, write for black audiences, often use black language and revolutionary themes, and generally try to embody the ideals of the new black aesthetic in their writing.

Dramatists, too, have turned away from aiming their work at Broadway and white audiences, rejecting that tradition's limitations on subject matter and language. Woodie King and Ron Milner in their introduction to *Black Drama Anthology* describe the new black theater as "the ritualized reflection and projection of a unique and particular way of being, born of the unique and particular conditioning of black people leasing time on this planet which is controlled by white men; it has something to do with the breaking of that 'leasing-syndrome.'" As King and Milner point out, the new black theater like the new black poetry is an attempt by black people to control their own art and culture, free from the influence and criticism of whites. Writers such as Imamu Amiri Baraka, Ed Bullins, Lonne Elder, and Douglas Turner Ward write with the goal of building and preserving the culture of black people, rather than of breaking into white culture.

The new aesthetic has found expression in the short story; examples can be found in magazines such as *Black World* or *Freedomways* by writers such as Sonia Sanchez and Toni Cade Bambara, but are not so readily available as drama and poetry. The modern novel, however, reflects the new aesthetic less than other genres, perhaps because it does not fit into the community values of the new aesthetic so well as drama and poetry, but instead sets up interaction between two individuals, the writer and the reader.

Few of the new writers have turned to the novel as a means of expression, at least until this point in their careers, though important new novels continue to come from writers who began their careers in the 1940s, '50s and '60s. Several of the older writers such as Ernest Gaines, and two new writers, Toni Morrison and Alice Walker, include elements of the new black aesthetic as they explore new ways of expressing the black experience through fiction.

Because many of the writers who have appeared since 1965 are still in the early stages of their careers and only a few have produced a large volume of work that is easily accessible, anthologies are very useful for teaching their works. Here, therefore, is a survey of available anthologies specializing in the writing of the new black poets and the current dramatists. This is followed by discussions of a representative sampling of the better known writers of the seventies whose works are particularly appropriate for high school students and available in individual editions. (Anthologies of broader scope are discussed in the following section, "Anthologies and Criticism.")

New Poetry in Anthologies

Black Out Loud: An Anthology of Modern Poems by Black Americans, edited by Arnold Adoff (Macmillan, 1970; pap., Dell, 1975), is the best introduction to contemporary black poets for younger students and those less interested in literature. With works by Don L. Lee (Haki R. Madhubuti), Imamu Amiri Baraka, Nikki Giovanni, Ted Joans, Mari Evans, Gwendolyn Brooks, Conrad Kent Rivers, Sonia Sanchez, and many others, it is a representative collection of the writers of the 1960s and 1970s who are not included in the older anthologies. Selected for use by young people in schools, the poems are chosen for their simplicity and for the lack of obvious red flags for censors. However, they deal honestly and vibrantly with the current themes of blackness, memories of leaders such as Martin Luther King and Malcolm X, rejection of white American culture, childhood, love, and the role of poetry.

This book captures one of the most exciting messages of the new black poetry. Poetry is for everybody and it is for real. It is fun, natural, and good for your health. You can use it to express love or outrage, to hold a treasured memory or to change your images of yourself. This is the kind of poetry that inspires more poetry. It sounds easy—almost like the popular songs that beat out "Come on and dance with me!"

More advanced collections focusing on the new black poets are:

19 Necromancers from Now. Edited by Ishmael Reed. Anch. Doubleday, 1970.

The New Black Poetry. Edited by Clarence Major. Intl Pub Co, cloth & pap., 1969.

Soulscript: Afro-American Poetry. Edited by June Jordan. Doubleday, pap., 1970.

Black Fire: An Anthology of Afro-American Writing. Edited by LeRoi Jones and Roy Neal. Morrow, pap., 1968.

Dices or Black Bones: Black Voices of the Seventies. Edited by Adam D. Miller. HM, pap., 1970.

There are many other collections by individual poets which contain poems useful for high school classes. A few of these are:

De Mayor of Harlem by David Henderson. Dutton, 1970.

Dear John, Dear Coltrane by Michael S. Harper. U of Pittsburgh Pr, pap., 1970.

Twenty-Six Ways of Looking at a Black Man by Raymond R. Patterson. Univ Pub & Dist, 1969.

Other important contemporary black writers whose works are frequently anthologized are Mari Evans, Clarence Major, Dudley Randall, Conrad Kent Rivers, and James Emanuel. All began publishing before the new black poets but are in some ways similar to them. Two contemporary poets, Naomi Long Madgett and Lucille Clifton, use more traditional poetic forms to explore the experiences of black women.

New Drama in Anthologies

Contemporary Black Drama: Raisin in the Sun, Purlie Victorious, Funnyhouse of a Negro, Dutchman, Blues for Mister Charlie, Day of Absence, Happy Ending, The Gentleman Caller, No Place to Be Somebody, edited by Stephanie Sills and Clinton F. Oliver (Scribner, pap., 1971) provides a good sampling of contemporary black theater. All of the plays in the collection would be useful for classroom study. Discussions of *A Raisin in the Sun* by Lorraine Hansberry, *Dutchman* by Imamu Amiri Baraka, and *Blues for Mister Charlie* by James Baldwin can be found in this book under their individual authors. *Purlie Victorious* by Ossie Davis is a comedy which satirizes every stereotype of Southern segregation. Two short, symbolic, avant-garde plays, Adrienne Kennedy's *Funnyhouse of a Negro* and Ed Bullins' *The Gentleman Caller*, from *A Black Quartet*, are included. Douglas Turner Ward's two successful comedies, *Happy Ending* and *Day of Absence*, both describe through bitter humor the parasitical relationship of whites and blacks. Charles Gordoné's *No Place to Be Somebody* was the first off-Broadway production and the first play by a black playwright to win a Pulitzer Prize.

Black Drama Anthology, edited by Woodie King and Ron Milner (Columbia U Pr, 1972), provides a more in-depth study of the new black theater. It includes authors such as Imamu Amiri Baraka, Ed Bullins, Ron Milner, Lonne Elder, Douglas Turner Ward, Langston Hughes, Elaine Jackson, and many others. The twenty-three dramas include short one-act plays and full-length plays, plays in highly experimental dramatic styles and plays that follow traditional formats. Many are very bitter, explosive, and some are homicidal.

A Black Quartet by Ed Bullins et al. (NAL, pap., 1970) offers a briefer introduction to contemporary dramatists. Included are a group of four one-act plays by Ben Caldwell, Ronald Milner, Ed Bullins, and LeRoi Jones (Baraka).

Black Scenes, edited by Alice Childress (Doubleday, cloth & pap., 1971), is a collection of scenes from black plays requiring two to five actors and suitable for practice material or for classroom use.

Imamu Amiri Baraka (LeRoi Jones, 1934–   )

Imamu Amiri Baraka, poet, politician, playwright, revolutionary, teacher, and perhaps novelist, is a central figure among the younger, radical black writers. Born in Newark, New Jersey, he was educated at Howard University, did graduate work at the New School for Social Research and Columbia University, and has taught poetry and drama on various campuses. He founded the Black Community Development and Defense Organization in 1968.

Although Baraka has had an extremely important influence on both contemporary poetry and contemporary drama, many of his works are not suitable for most classrooms. Much of his writing is quite difficult and bloodthirsty. However, as an author, he is significant enough that his works should be represented in any serious study of black literature.

Baraka has published collections of poetry, including *Preface to a Twenty Volume Suicide Note* (Corinth Bks, pap., 1961), *The Dead Lecturer* ([1964] pap., Grove, 1976), *Black Art* (Jihad, 1969), and *It's Nation Time* (Third World, pap., 1970). Among his poems most likely to be appreciated by high school students are "Preface to a Twenty Volume Suicide Note," a poem of existential despair, "A Poem for Black Hearts," an eloquent eulogy to Malcolm X, "Each Morning," a search for ancestry, and "Jitterbugs," an ironic poem which effectively compresses into a few lines the frustration of being imprisoned on a planet where there is no escape from white domination.

Frustration in the search for the meaning of life in a world of oppression is a major theme in Baraka's early poetry. Later poems explore the meanings of black consciousness and revolution, or just revenge.

Baraka's most significant work has been in the theater. *Dutchman,* winner of the 1964 off-Broadway Obie Award, is his best-known play and is usable with mature high school students. The setting is a subway train. Lulu, a white woman, sits next to a middle-class black man. She begins by trying to seduce him, but gradually she becomes insulting and demeaning, goading him to fury. When he responds in anger, she "defends" herself by stabbing him. As the subway passengers help her get rid of the body, and as Lulu sits back down and begins the act with a second black man who enters the car, the audience recognizes that this subway drama symbolizes the destruction of black manhood by a society which scoffs at black achievement and murders black rebels. (*Dutchman.* In Sills and Oliver, eds., *Contemporary Black Drama* [Scribner, pap., 1971]).

Almost as important as his own writing has been Baraka's encouragement and inspiration of the new black dramatists. In 1965, Baraka founded the Black Arts Repertory Theater and School in Harlem, where he produced black plays for black audiences. He later moved to Newark, where he founded the Spirit House Movers and Players. Baraka's vision of the theater as a way of inspiring revolutionary beliefs and actions has been followed by many of the younger playwrights.

Baraka's prose writings include *The System of Dante's Hell* ([1965] pap., Grove, 1976), part autobiography, part novel, part random collection of images and events. Most readers find it both confusing and brilliant.

Other important works by Baraka are his books and articles on jazz, particularly *Blues People: Negro Music in White America* (Morrow, cloth & pap., 1963).

Lucille Clifton (1936-)

Lucille Clifton, who lives in Baltimore, has published several poetry collections and a number of books for children. Her short collection of easy-to-read poems, *An Ordinary Woman* (Random, pap., 1974) deals with the complexities of love, of strength, and of the black heritage. Clifton's poems do not have the depth and subtlety of Gwendolyn Brooks' works nor the violence and obscenity of Ted Joans'. Most of them would be appropriate for high school students, though they are not the most powerful poetry available.

Nikki Giovanni (1943-)

One of the most popular of the contemporary poets among young people is Nikki Giovanni. Easy to read, honest, tactless, her poems express the things all adolescents feel and are taught not to say. Some are adolescent and transient, while others meet all of the criteria for major writers. Some, such as "The True Import of Present Dialogue, Black vs. Negro," better known by its first lines, "Nigger/Can you kill?" are angry and homicidal. Others express love, loneliness, and other feelings that have no racial boundaries.

Giovanni's most recent collection, *The Women and the Men* (Morrow, 1975), was one of only two collections of poetry selected by high school students participating in the University of Iowa Books for Young Adults Poll, 1975–1978 (*English Journal*, January 1975, 1976, 1977, 1978). Other collections, *Black Feeling Black Talk/Black Judgement* (Morrow, pap., 1970) and *Re: Creation* (Broadside, pap., 1970) contain some of her best known poems. "Nikki-Rosa" points out that black childhood is often happy, contrary to the images white people have. The brief poem "The Funeral of Martin Luther King, Jr." eloquently expresses the attitudes of contemporary militants who seek "the construction of a world/Where Martin Luther King could have lived and preached non-violence." "For Saundra" shows clearly why Nikki Giovanni does not write traditional poems.

Giovanni, who teaches English at Livingston College of Rutgers University, founded a chapter of SNCC while a student at Fisk in 1964, and a publishing cooperative in 1970. Her popular autobiographical work, *Gemini*, is described in Chapter 4.

Ted Joans (1928-)

A painter and jazzman as well as a poet, Ted Joans was born in

Cairo, Illinois, and educated at Indiana University and (in his words) in "the streets of Harlem/Greenwich Village/Europe and Africa . . . " His poetry, collected in *Black Pow-Wow: Jazz Poems* (Hill & Wang, cloth & pap., 1969), needs to be read aloud for its full impact. The poems are simple, playing with rhythm, words, type styles, and format. They lack the sophistication and careful artistry of poems by writers like June Jordan, but their immediate impact may make them more interesting to young readers.

June Jordan (1936-)

Harlem-born June Jordan is a versatile writer, author of a book of poetry, *Some Changes* (1971); a history book, *Dry Victories* (1972), told through dialogue and pictures; and a novel, *His Own Where* (1971. See Chapter 3.) She studied at Barnard College and the University of Chicago, has worked as a research associate and writer, taught college English, and helped found and direct the Creative Writing Workshop for Children in Brooklyn.

June Jordan's poems are short and look deceptively simple, but they have the tightness and complexity of haiku; like haiku, they often use the juxtaposition of images to create a subtle effect that is expressed by implication rather than stated directly. Some of the poems, such as "Maybe the Birds," capture a moment. Others, such as "The Reception," "The Wedding" and "For Christopher," are brief biographies. There are expressions of love, of romance, and of despair, rage, and anger. "What Would I Do White?" describes the concept of whiteness—"like wintertime, acquiring and empty." Comments on events such as "Uhuru in the O.R.," about the successful heart transplant of a black heart into a white South African, and "Solidarity Day, 1968," which describes the lost hopes of the poor people's march on Washington, show an artistically controlled outrage. These poems can be found in *Some Changes* (Dutton, pap., 1971).

Who Look at Me (T Y Crowell, 1969) is a poem about the image of blacks in America combined with paintings of blacks by both black and white artists. It makes a provocative comment on black identity, showing the past that has shaped it and the reactions of whites that still rankle today. It is both a bitter and a loving book. Designed for younger readers, it also has appeal for adults.

Dry Victories ([1972] pap., Avon, 1975) tells the story of Reconstruction and the civil rights struggle in a dialogue between two teenage boys and in a collection of pictures. June Jordan describes the goal of the book this way: "History is the business of choose and show. I have chosen two times, Reconstruction and Civil Rights, when Black folks were supposed to win, when we were supposed to have a victory and be victors, freed from various enslavements. And I have shown, both times, how we were prevented from real victory, and how what we won was not nearly enough. Both times, we were denied the economic bases of freedom. And if you don't have the land or the job or the money, Brother, you don't have nothing much, at all" (*Dry Victories*, author's note).

Etheridge Knight (1931-)

Knight began his career as a poet with *Poems from Prison* (Broadside, pap., 1968), published while he was an inmate in the Indiana State Prison. One of his most remarkable accomplishments is a group of haiku written about prison, which find wonder even in that barren place. Other popular poems are "It Was a Funky Deal," on the death of Malcolm X, and "The Idea of Ancestry," a poem on family history.

Born in Corinth, Mississippi, Knight was educated through the eighth grade in Paducah, Kentucky. He has adopted the name Imamu E—K— Soa.

Naomi Long Madgett (1923-)

Born in Virginia, Naomi Long Madgett is an associate professor of English at Eastern Michigan University, specializing in Afro-American literature and creative writing. She also initiated courses in those subjects while teaching in public high schools.

Madgett uses both traditional poetic forms with rhyme and rhythm patterns and the free verse that is popular with modern poets. Many of the poems in her first collection, *Star by Star* ([1965] 3d ed., Lotus, pap., 1970) are brief comments on love and everyday life, similar in form to the quiet, carefully structured poems of Countee Cullen. Most of her poems do not fit the tradition of the new black poets, and in fact, her poem "Newblack" satirizes their style.

Haki R. Madhubuti (Don L. Lee, 1931-)

Madhubuti's collection, *Think Black* (3d ed., Broadside, pap., 1967), is a good introduction to understanding black consciousness: what it is, and why there is a need for it. The volume contains excellent poems for class discussion. *Don't Cry, Scream* (Broadside, cloth & pap., 1969) contains more good poems for discussion. Black awareness is again held up for examination and suggested as a means of black survival in a white world. *We Walk the Way of the New World* (Broadside, cloth & pap., 1970) contains powerful poems with between-the-lines subtlety. The author describes them as "louder, but softer."

Madhubuti has taught on several campuses including Cornell University and the University of Illinois, and was poet in residence at Howard University, 1970–77. He is one of the founders and editor of the Third World Press, and director of the Institute of Positive Education in Chicago. His political and literary essays have been published in magazines and newspapers, and he is an active lecturer, community worker, and organizer. Since 1969, he has taken part in several festivals in Africa, and, at this writing, is on the Board of Directors of the North American Zone of the Second World Black and Afrikan Festival of Arts and Culture.

Toni Morrison (1931-   )

An Ohioan, Toni Morrison studied at Howard and Cornell Universities and taught college English before becoming an editor at Random House. Her first novel, *The Bluest Eye* (HR&W, 1970), portrays the devastating effect of the images of white beauty—Shirley Temple, golden-haired dolls, and the movies—on a black girl, who becomes so convinced of her own ugliness that she trades her sanity for a pair of blue eyes that only she can see. The mocking words of the "Dick and Jane" story echo nightmarishly through the reality with which each of the people in Pecola's life must live. Her mother, Pauline, lives almost the same story, trying to escape from ugliness through the movies; eventually, she escapes into a dream world of the white family she works for—her own form of "blue-eyed" madness. Cholly, Pecola's father, is thrown away by his mother and raised by a maiden aunt. His dream of freedom also dies, and in his drunkenness he rapes his daughter.

The survivors fight back. Claudia, who tells the story, and Frieda, her sister, systematically destroy the blond-haired, blue-eyed dolls they are given. They taunt and reject Maureen Peal, the "high-yellow dream child" who is adored by the rest of the town. And when they hear the gossips of the town clucking about Pecola being pregnant with her father's child, they pray for the universally hated black baby to live—"just to counteract the universal love of white baby dolls, Shirley Temples, and Maureen Peals." In their childish attempts at magic they plant seeds, hoping to sell marigolds and buy a bicycle. But the marigolds fail to sprout and the baby is born dead.

The Bluest Eye is a beautifully written, powerful demonstration of the devastating effects of the more subtle forms of racism. Morrison writes with considerable literary skill, in a style that is almost poetic in its simplicity.

Sula (Knopf, 1973), Toni Morrison's second novel, is a more sophisticated book, perhaps too subtle for high school readers. In structure it is similar to *The Bluest Eye*. A woman, strange and outcast, is the focus and mingles with the stories of the lives of those related to her. The device is effective, but in both books, the shifting point of view and the changing time and setting may be confusing to immature readers. Sula, like Pecola, is mangled by forces around her, but unlike Pecola, who destroys herself, Sula maintains her selfhood by destroying others. The book is full of memorable characters, among them Sula herself and Eva, her grandmother, who according to rumor sacrificed her leg in a train wreck to earn the insurance settlement that would feed her family.

Morrison's latest work, *Song of Solomon* (Knopf, 1977), like her earlier novels, is peopled with characters who are both bizarre and intensely human. The protagonist, Milkman Dead, leaves his suffocating, money-obsessed father to search for his ancestors, eventually discovering Solomon the African, who according to legend flew back to Africa. While Milkman is undertaking his personal search for his own roots and meaning, his friend Guitar has joined a secret band determined to liberate the race by avenging the death of every black person murdered by whites. This is a powerful book, sometimes frightening, sometimes uplifting, filled with mystery and brilliance.

All of Toni Morrison's works show a mastery of the European literary tradition, but they also convey a sense of the depths of evil and intricacies of the relationships between good and evil, and an almost animistic image of nature that links Morrison to modern African writers such as Ama Ata Aidoo and Bessie Head.

Ishmael Reed (1938–)

Ishmael Reed has put together a collage of American pop culture, ancient Egyptian mythology, and voodoo ideals which becomes, in the reader's mind, either an incomprehensible mess or hilarious satire. Reed's message is a very critical challenge to white Western culture. He describes one of his books as "artistic guerilla warfare against the Historical Establishment" (John O'Brien, ed., *Interviews with Black Writers* [Liveright, 1973], p. 179).

Reed, who was born in Chattanooga and now lives in Berkeley, California, describes himself as largely self-taught. He has lectured at universities, helped found a publishing company, and operates a communications center for writers and artists.

Conjure: Selected Poems, 1963–1970 (U of Mass Pr, cloth & pap., 1972) expresses his philosophy clearly. In one of his most significant poems, "Neo-HooDoo Manifesto," Reed claims that "Neo-HooDoo" is the "Lost American Church," a black religion opposed to Christianity, and that Jeho-vah is "a party-pooper and hater of dance" (*Conjure*, p. 24). Neo-HooDoo, according to Reed, affirms "that every man is an artist and every artist a priest" (*Conjure*, p. 21). This is a powerful book that turns almost every Western cultural concept upside down. It is a good test for a teacher trying to understand the new black aesthetic, but it is probably too sophisticated and possibly too disturbing for most students.

Yellow Back Radio Broke-Down (Reprint of 1969 edition, Chatham Bkseller, 1975; pap., Avon, 1977) is a novel about a black, voo-doo cowboy, Loop Garoo, and his exciting adventures with Chief Showcase and his helicopter, Zozo Labrique and a circus, and the town of Yellow Back Radio, in which the children have chased all adults out of the town. It is a satire on the western, and on the American values that made the western popular.

The Free-Lance Pallbearers (Reprint of 1967 edition, Chatham Bkseller, 1975; pap., Avon, n.d.) satirizes the entire country. The novel begins: "I live in HARRY SAM. HARRY SAM is something else. A big not-to-be-believed out-of-sight, sometimes referred to as O-BOP-SHE-BANG or KLANG-A-LANG-A DING-DONG. SAM has not been seen since the day thirty years ago when he disappeared into the John with a weird ravaging illness." It is a unique book with unlimited potential for class discussion.

Carolyn M. Rodgers

Carolyn M. Rodgers' collection, *how i got ovah: New and Selected Poems* (Doubleday, 1975; pap., 1976) is a book full of sass and strength, warmth, love, and humor. Revolution, religion, and human relations are the topics of her poems. Among the most powerful are "Portrait," about her mother's sacrifices for her children's education; "IT IS DEEP (don't never forget the bridge that you crossed over on)," which conveys her respect for her mother even during a major generation gap crisis; and "For Our Fathers," a poem about black love. Other poems react bitterly to injustice. "Esther, as Lead" describes a tiny news item about the death of a child from lead poisoning.

Sonia Sanchez (Laila Mannan) (1934-   )

Sonia Sanchez's poetry collection, *We a BaddDDD People* (Broadside, cloth & pap., 1970) contains hard-hitting poems about life, love, and progress. The nuances of living in an oppressive society are dealt with in Section I: "Survival Poems." Section II: "Love/Songs/Chants" includes lyrical evocations of the many shades and degrees of love. The "TCB/EN (takin' care of business)" poems in Section III deal with black people's movement forward in spite of the odds.

A Blues Book for Blue-Black Magical Women (Broadside, cloth & pap., 1973) includes sensitive and subtle poems that celebrate the black woman. This book is best for the mature student.

Sanchez was born in Birmingham, Alabama, and educated at Hunter College. Since 1973, she has been an associate professor of literature and creative writing at Amherst College.

Alice Walker (1944-   )

"For me, black women are the most fascinating creations in the world. Next to them, I place the old people—male and female—who persist in their beauty in spite of everything. How do they do this, knowing what they do? Having lived what they have lived? It is a mystery, and so it lures me into their lives," states Alice Walker in *Interviews with Black Writers* (John O'Brien, ed. [Liveright, 1973], p. 192).

Walker, who grew up in a small Georgia town, studied at Sarah Lawrence College under poet Muriel Rukeyser. She began to publish when she was twenty-four, after taking part in civil rights demonstrations and traveling in Africa.

Revolutionary Petunias and Other Poems (HarBraceJ, pap., 1973) begins with biographical poems about ancestors, recalling, Walker says, "that we are not the first to suffer, rebel, fight, love and die." The poems following "are about Revolutionaries and Lovers; and about the loss of compassion, trust, and the ability to expand in love that marks the end of hopeful strategy. Whether in love or revolution. They are also about (and for) those few embattled souls who remain painfully committed to beauty and to love even while facing the firing squad" (Foreword, *Revolutionary Petunias*).

Alice Walker has lived many of the experiences some of the young black poets dream about. Her travels in Africa, her experiences in the civil rights campaigns as well as an abortion and a planned suicide are the experiences from which the poems in *Once: Poems* (HarBraceJ, pap., 1976) were written. The book contains a wealth of poems, many short, simple, and significant enough to appeal to adolescents. "The Enemy" contrasts the impulses of children with a nation's impulses to war. "Once" is a collection of fourteen tiny vignettes which capture the conflicts and anguish of people, both black and white, who worked for integration. "Johann" questions whether a black and a German have too much war and enmity in their history to make love.

In Love and Trouble: Stories of Black Women (HarBraceJ, 1973; pap., 1974) contains sensitive stories about the feelings and thoughts of mature women and their bittersweet experiences with love. One of the most effective is "Everyday Use," in which a mother mediates a conflict between her sophisticated daughter, who comes home from the city, and her shy sister, who has remained at home.

A novel, *The Third Life of Grange Copeland* (HarBraceJ, 1970; pap., 1977), describes the lives of black Southern women through their interaction with a boy and his father. The main character, a victim of cruel circumstances, grows and changes through his experiences.

Alice Walker's latest novel, *Meridian* (HarBraceJ, 1976; pap., PB, 1977) is a study of a modern woman who, after deadening experiences as a wife and mother, exciting but short-lived work in the civil rights movement, and distressing interaction with the revolutionary movement, seeks to work out a way of life that will permit her own growth and will allow her to stimulate growth in others. Meridian's own pilgrimage is paralleled by the struggles of the black man she loves and the white woman he marries to free themselves from past conflicts. Meridian must go through an illness of the body and the mind before she becomes whole, but even while she is still struggling, she is a source of strength to others. Even Lynn, her former rival, draws courage and renewal from Meridian as she grieves over the death of her child and her marriage. In addition, Meridian learns to combine the political activism of contemporary blacks with the sense of community and concern of older generations. Eventually she becomes a model for others to follow in a quest for meaning and self-understanding.

Meridian is a sensitive, sophisticated book that is more meaningful for people who, like the main character, have suffered through several periods of life. Most adolescents, therefore, probably will not understand all of its ideas, but may still find it valuable reading. As the book suggests, there are probably no shortcuts to maturity, but young readers may still find the model encouraging and reassuring.

Anthologies and Criticism of Black Literature

The number of collections of black writing now available makes the anthology a useful tool for studying black literature. Anthologies range over the whole of American literary history. Several writers not mentioned earlier are described in this section because their works are most accessible in anthologies. See also the collections of contemporary poetry and drama discussed in the preceding section. In the following lists, anthologies and critical works are arranged alphabetically by author.

Anthologies

Adams, William, Peter Conn, and Barry Slepian, eds. *Afro-American Literature*. 4 vols. HM, pap., 1970.

This series includes four paperback volumes subtitled by genre: *Fiction*, *Drama*, *Poetry*, and *Nonfiction*. The emphasis is on modern literature, although a few early writers are included.

Adoff, Arnold, ed. *I Am the Darker Brother: An Anthology of Modern Poems by Negro Americans*. Macmillan, cloth & pap., 1968.

An attractive, thematically arranged volume of poems ranging from the Harlem Renaissance to the early 1960s. Poems are selected for their appeal to high school students and attractively arranged to create an especially useful anthology for high school teachers.

Chapman, Abraham, ed. *Black Voices: An Anthology of Afro-American Literature*. NAL, pap., 1968.

Probably the best buy among general anthologies, this moderately-priced 700-page paperback contains poetry, short stories, autobiography, and literary criticism. Besides excerpts from the best known black writers of the past, it includes examples of the work of contemporary writers such as Mari Evans, Gwendolyn Brooks, LeRoi Jones (I. A. Baraka), and Robert Hayden.

Cullen, Countee, ed. *Caroling Dusk: An Anthology of Verse by Negro Poets.* [1927] Har-Row, 1974.

A thorough anthology of early black poets through the Harlem Renaissance. In addition to major poets mentioned in this historical survey, it includes lesser-known, but significant poets such as Sterling Brown, Jessie Fauset, and Georgia Johnson.

Emanuel, James A., and Theodore L. Gross, eds. *Dark Symphony: Negro Literature in America.* Free Pr, cloth & pap., 1968.

A scholarly anthology, this volume contains extensive background information on authors and literary periods. It is suitable for advanced high school students as well as for college use, and is highly recommended as a reference book for teachers. It places more emphasis on short stories than the Chapman anthology.

Hill, Herbert, ed. *Soon, One Morning: New Writings by American Negroes 1940–1962.* Knopf, 1963.

This collection of writings by black authors includes essays, fiction, and poetry. Most of the fiction selections are from novels discussed in this book. Most of the poetry is well known and frequently anthologized. One clever short story is "Rat Joiner Routs the Klan" by Ted Poston, a humorous tale of a black community's attempt to stop the town theater from showing *Birth of a Nation.* The humor never masks the tragedy of segregation.

Hughes, Langston, ed. *The Best Short Stories by Negro Writers.* Little, cloth & pap., 1967.

This anthology includes forty selections representing all of the well-known black writers from Chesnutt and Dunbar to James Baldwin and William Melvin Kelley, and would therefore be an excellent introduction to black literature. All of the works are of excellent quality, but they are adult and somewhat intellectual. The stories are of the quality that would be found in the *New Yorker* rather than in a high school collection, and many are a little too subtle for the average high school student. Since many deal with adult problems, the teacher would probably want to read most of them before assigning them.

The following stories might be enjoyed by younger high school students. "The Revolt of the Evil Fairies" by Ted

Poston deals with color discrimination among blacks. It is the clever, humorous account of a little boy who is too dark to be the good prince in the school pageant, but who plays the evil fairy to the hilt. "Almos' a Man" is a tragic story of a boy who wants a gun, and when he gets it, accidentally shoots a mule. "The Pocketbook Game" by Alice Childress tells of a black woman who turns the tables on her suspicious white employer. "The Blues Begins" by Sylvester Leaks shows how a poverty-stricken boy tries to help his family by stealing, but is reprimanded by his mother and eventually ends up in trouble with the law. "A Long Day in November," from *Bloodline* by Ernest J. Gaines, is a long story about a boy's family problems with his parents, whose marriage seems to be breaking up. "Junkie Joe Had Some Money" is a frightening story by Ronald Milner about a boy who finds out about a murder and lives in mortal fear of the murderers.

More mature students might be interested in the following stories. "Marijuana and a Pistol" by Chester B. Himes is a strange, dreamlike narrative of a man under the influence of marijuana, who accidentally kills a man. "The Almost White Boy" by Willard Motley is the tragic story of a mulatto who falls in love with a white girl and is cruelly rejected. "Flying Home" by Ralph Ellison is about a black flyer, one of the first to break through the race barriers, who is stranded in a Southern white area and in grave danger. "This Morning, This Evening, So Soon" by James Baldwin tells of a black man who is returning to the United States from Paris with a white wife and son, and of his fears for them.

"See How They Run" is an inspiring story of a black schoolteacher who insists on trying to help her students and is not discouraged by her cynical fellow workers. "An Interesting Social Study" shows a black girl passing for white in a resort town. "The Only Man on Liberty Street" by William Melvin Kelley tells of a white man who tries to buck social opinion and live with his black concubine and child. "Red Bonnet" by Lindsay Patterson is about a stubborn old grandmother whose refusal to cooperate with her daughter or white people finally leads to her death. "Direct Action" by Mike Thelwell is a very funny story about an interracial college group who are forced to get into the civil rights action by integrating the restrooms at a small department store.

Hughes, Langston. *New Negro Poets: U.S.A.* Ind U Pr, 1964.
This anthology was compiled before most of the writers known as the new black poets began publishing, and thus is useful only for examples of the work of earlier modern poets.

Hughes, Langston, and Arna Bontemps, eds. *The Poetry of the Negro: 1746–1970.* Doubleday, 1970.
Called "a definitive anthology," this collection is quite thorough, and if a teacher is limited to only one book, this one offers the most complete selection. An earlier edition ended with 1949. This new edition contains a broad selection of modern poets, omitting only a few very recent writers. Most of the poets are represented by only a few works.

Two poets not discussed elsewhere in this book are worth mentioning, because they have poems in this anthology which are appropriate for high school classes. Georgia Douglas Johnson's "Interracial" is an optimistic poem pleading for racial understanding. "My Little Dreams," a sentimental poem about failed dreams, has appeal for slower readers.

Frank Horne's "On Seeing Two Brown Boys in a Catholic Church" compares the suffering of black children with the suffering of Christ. "Kid Stuff" mocks Christmas, but pleads for a return to childlike simplicity. "Toast" offers congratulations to a person who is complete and beautiful—except for soul.

Murray, Alma, and Robert Thomas, eds. *Scholastic Black Literature Series.* Schol Bk Serv, pap., 1971.
This series consists of six thematically organized paperbacks titled *The Journey, The Scene, The Search, The Black Hero, Major Black Writers,* and *Black Perspectives.* They are designed to be used as supplementary texts in grades 9–12. A valuable feature of the series is the accompanying set of teacher's guides, which contain background essays and detailed teaching plans.

Randall, Dudley, ed. *The Black Poets.* Bantam, pap., 1971.
This particularly valuable anthology offers not only an excellent selection of works by contemporary poets but also a historical survey of both literary and folk poetry. Almost all poets of each period who have attained recognition are represented, most of them by enough poems to show the range of their work. The anthology also includes useful reference

material such as a list of publishers of black poetry, periodicals publishing black poetry, disc and tape recordings, videotapes, and films. The poets range from Phillis Wheatley and James Weldon Johnson to June Jordan, Sonia Sanchez, Don L. Lee, Nikki Giovanni, and Naomi Madgett.

Stanford, Barbara Dodds, ed. *I, Too, Sing America: Black Voices in American Literature.* Hayden, cloth & pap., 1971.

A historical survey of black writers, with literature selected for its appeal to students. Arranged chronologically, it contains background material on each period.

Turner, Darwin T., ed. *Black American Literature: Essays, Poetry, Fiction.* Merrill, pap., 1969.

A three-volume scholarly work suitable for college, advanced high school students, or teachers' research.

Turner, Darwin T., Jean M. Bright, and Richard Wright, eds. *Voices from the Black Experience: Afro-American and African Literature.* Ginn, pap., 1972.

A text for secondary school students with accompanying teacher's guide.

Washington, Mary Helen, ed. *Black-Eyed Susans: Classic Stories by and about Black Women.* Doubleday, pap., 1975.

A collection of very fine stories that explore in depth the problems, conflicts, and strengths of black women. One of the best features of this anthology is the introduction, a good essay on black womanhood which offers some of the best critical comments available on contemporary black female writers. This thin volume, containing stories and excerpts from novels by Jean Wheeler Smith, Toni Morrison, Gwendolyn Brooks, Louise Meriweather, Toni Cade Bambara, Alice Walker, and Paule Marshall, is an excellent introduction to some of the best work by contemporary black writers.

Weisman, Leon, and Elfreda S. Wright, eds. *Black Poetry for All Americans.* Globe, pap., 1971.

A poetry collection designed for classroom use, this book is suitable for both junior and senior high. It is illustrated with many photographs by students, interpreting the themes of the poems. Each poem is reviewed in a section at the back of the book, which includes a glossary for vocabulary enrichment and questions for comprehension and appreciation.

Critical Studies

Abramson, Doris E. *Negro Playwrights in the American Theater.* [1967] Columbia U Pr, cloth & pap., 1969.

Critical essays on black theater in the United States from the 1920s, when segregation dictated a separate tradition of black theater. After sketching the earlier history of black drama, the author traces the effect of federal arts programs which involved blacks and the changes that occurred through the mid-sixties, when blacks entered the mainstream of Broadway. Individual plays and playwrights are discussed in depth.

Cook, Mercer, and Stephen E. Henderson. *The Militant Black Writer in Africa and the United States.* U of Wis Pr, pap., 1969.

Contains two long essays. One, by Cook, analyzes modern African protest writing; the other, by Henderson, is a good analysis of contemporary revolutionary black literature in America.

Cooke, Michael G., ed. *Modern Black Novelists.* P-H, cloth & pap., 1971.

An analysis of the work of contemporary black novelists in the United States and other countries.

Davis, Arthur P. *From the Dark Tower: Afro-American Writers from 1900 to 1960.* Howard U Pr, 1974.

Biographical and critical essays on twenty-eight major writers from W. E. B. Du Bois to James Baldwin, with pictures. This book is particularly useful for writers of the Harlem Renaissance and Depression periods, and includes detailed information on lesser-known but important writers such as Sterling Brown and Zora Neale Hurston.

Major, Clarence. *The Dark and Feeling.* Third Pr, 1974.

Critical essays on such modern writers as Richard Wright, John A. Williams, and Eldridge Cleaver, as well as June Jordan, Ishmael Reed, and Ernest Gaines. Also included are general essays on the new black writers and on Clarence Major's own work.

Margolies, Edward. *Native Sons: A Critical Study of Twentieth Century Negro-American Authors.* Reprint of 1968 edition, Lippincott, 1969.

Provides detailed analysis of the works of selected writers ranging from Charles Chesnutt to LeRoi Jones (I. A. Baraka).

O'Brien, John, ed. *Interviews with Black Writers*. Liveright, cloth & pap., 1973.

Seventeen black novelists and poets, from Arna Bontemps to Ishmael Reed, discuss their diverse styles, themes, and influences in a collection of recorded interviews that counteracts the widespread impression that black literature is a single monolithic tradition.

Turner, Darwin T. *In a Minor Chord: Three Afro-American Writers and Their Search for Identity.* S Ill U Pr, 1971.

Explores the writings of Jean Toomer, Countee Cullen, and Zora Neale Hurston.

Whitlow, Roger. *Black American Literature: A Critical History.* Nelson-Hall, 1973; pap., Littlefield, 1974.

A useful and detailed annotated bibliography of major works from all periods.

3 Adolescent Literature by and about Black People

Karima Amin

Literature for high school students has undergone some very significant changes within the past ten years, especially in dealing with racial topics. Most novels on black themes that fell into young hands, prior to the militancy of the mid-sixties, dealt primarily with middle-class blacks in integrated situations. These books, often written by white authors, seldom considered the realities of the ghetto and rarely dealt with adolescent problems beyond the scope of dating, choosing a career, and participating in high school activities. In their handling of racial topics, these junior novels tended to be optimistic, frequently sacrificing realism for a happy ending. In addition, the authors of these books showed us that black people have "problems" *because they are black*; black people must strive for "acceptance" by whites *because they are black*; and above all, black people must always remember to stay in "their place" *because they are black*. The same books were filled to overflowing with "kind" white characters who "helped" the lowly blacks because they could not help themselves, and who "learned" to accept Rastus because "we're all the same under the skin." These books may have acknowledged the existence of prejudice in specific incidents, but they completely ignored the pervasive presence of racism. The white power structure was seldom pictured as responsible for perpetuating racism; it usually seemed that the black characters were somehow to blame for the oppression they experienced. These junior novels may have encouraged white youths to stop discriminating, but they did very little to enhance the black youths' images of themselves. The characteristic deceit inherent in these books damaged the psyches of the black readers (perhaps, irrevocably), and by the same token, young white readers suffered, for they derived an inflated perception of themselves.

The authors of today's junior novels are handling racial themes with more sensitivity, but the junior novel that sanctions racism, by omission or commission, is still with us. Racism may appear as an overt monster that leaps out at the reader from every page or as an equally dangerous, covert demon that hides between the lines. An awareness of this must guide parents, teachers, and librarians in their selection of books for young people.

Some generalizations about the junior novel that were made ten or twelve years ago are still applicable. Literature for the high school student is generally easier to read than that created for an adult audience, although the incidence of black English may pose some difficulty for the uninitiated. In general, the junior novel has more emphasis on plot than on psychological problems, so that the cumulative psychological effects of prejudice are not described. The "happy ending" may still be listed as a characteristic of the junior novel, but today it may realistically conclude a story that mentions sexual intercourse or that has episodes of violence, topics that the junior novel of ten or more years ago unrealistically avoided.

This chapter is divided into three parts. The first includes reviews of junior novels by black writers; the second briefly summarizes six short story collections by black authors; the third reviews novels on black themes by white writers.

To guide the teacher in selecting books, an evaluation is given after each annotation. Reading levels are defined as follows:

Easy: for ninth and tenth graders reading below the ninth grade level

Average: for ninth and tenth graders reading on level, and for eleventh and twelfth graders who are poor readers

Advanced: for students who are capable of handling difficult reading and who have a certain appreciation of literary skill

The second part of the evaluation (poor/good/very good/excellent) is this writer's estimate of the book's literary merit as compared with other titles discussed.

Junior Novels by Black Writers

The books listed here as junior novels are representative of a meaningful development in literature: black literature with direct appeal to adolescents. No book listed in this section was published before 1966. Each is a quality product by a black writer, characterized by the kind of black awareness that flourished during the "Harlem Renaissance" of the 1920s. Unlike novels by black writers which were written in the fifties and early sixties, dealing primarily with young blacks trying to "make it" in a white world, literature of the "New Renaissance" is peopled with black characters growing into a positive sense of black-self—rediscovering and redefining their past, looking into themselves, and exercising some degree of self-determination as they look to the future. One might be inclined to think that such books would fail to appeal to white students, but classroom experience has shown this to be far from the truth. In dealing with the "black experience" as a subject, each of these novels deals in fact with the human experience. A goodly portion of black literature depicts people in search of their identities, and every adolescent, regardless of race, is engaged in some aspect of this search. "Who am I?" "Where did I come from?" and "Where am I going?" are questions that every one of us can relate to. In black literature, these questions are frequently thematic. In the lives of young people these questions are crucial considerations.

Brown, Margery W. *The Second Stone*. Putnam, 1974.

Henry Wilson is growing up. He is fifteen and lives in a middle-income housing project with his brother Dan, Dan's wife Jeannie, and their young daughter, Patty. Henry is doing reasonably well in school, has a part-time counseling job at the Boys' Club, and his family life is happy, although having a big brother who just happens to be a police detective, assigned to the area where they live, makes for some friction as the story progresses.

As the novel opens, the reader quickly discovers that the neighborhood where Henry lives is turning into a place of fear and suspicion. A gang of youths is terrorizing the community, attacking and robbing some of its citizenry. A dozen trained policemen, including Dan, cannot get a lead and the criminal activity persists. Although his reasoning is flimsy, Dan suspects that Ric Martinez, Henry's best friend, may be involved. Henry resents Dan's accusations, and a bitter tension grows between them. The action that follows quickly leads to solving the crimes, Ric's death, and Henry's dramatic entrance into manhood.

The Second Stone is a fast-paced, easy-to-read, powerful story of a young boy trying to make some sense of his loyalty and relationship to family and friends. This would be a good novel to use in the classroom in connection with the study of urban crime or peer allegiance.

Reading level: easy. Literary quality: good.

Childress, Alice. *A Hero Ain't Nothin' But a Sandwich.* Coward, 1973; pap., Avon, 1974.

This novel tells the story of thirteen-year-old Benjie Johnson, who is on the verge of becoming permanently hooked on heroin. His story is told from varied viewpoints, including Benjie's own. Through street-wise Benjie, we learn of his introductions to marijuana, skin-popping, and finally, mainlining. We are told of his mixed feelings about school, his love for his mother and grandmother, his conflicting feelings for his "stepfather," and his feelings of alienation from Jimmy-Lee, a best friend. Most importantly, Benjie tells us how he feels about himself, with a toughness that belies his vulnerability.

As the other characters speak, they not only describe Benjie's situation, but inspect their own feelings about the quality of life and reasons for living. The social implications of Benjie's problem are described by two of his teachers, Nigeria Greene and Bernard Cohen, and the school principal, who is looking forward to "the haven of retirement." Miss Emma Dudley, a neighbor, tells the reader that finding a husband is more important than Benjie's trouble. Jimmy-Lee wants to be a real friend but finds Benjie shutting him out. Walter, the pusher, who has no sympathy for junkies, explains that he is simply trying to make a living. At first Benjie's mother, grandmother and "stepfather" do not know how to deal with him, but they finally come to realize that it is not only the *quantity* but the *quality* of love and support that counts.

Brilliant characterization and an honest approach to a difficult subject make this novel one that should be read by both young and old. No easy solutions are offered, but the reader will certainly be moved to care about Benjie and others like him.

Reading level: easy to average. Literary quality: excellent.

Fair, Ronald L. *Cornbread, Earl and Me.* [1966] pap., Bantam, 1975. Previously published as *Hog Butcher.*

We learn immediately that Cornbread is a neighborhood "Star," a college-bound, talented athlete who is loved and respected by all who know him. The "me" who tells this story is ten-year-old, fatherless Wilford Robinson, who dreams of being just like Cornbread someday—tall, athletic, well-liked and "cool." Earl Carter, Wilford's best friend, shares this dream. They play, argue and grow up together, and Chicago's South Side is their world.

The novel moves swiftly from introducing "Cornbread," "Earl," and "me" to a shocking incident that sparks the novel's action and reveals the anger, fear, and bitterness in this community: Wilford and Earl witness the death of Cornbread. Their hero is fatally shot in the back by policemen, one black and one white, who mistakenly assume that he is a thief running away from the scene of a crime. The story that follows is about a ten-year-old boy who must grow up fast, understanding at an early age how society and circumstances force his mother to stay on welfare, force a "sometime-father" to live a life of lies and contradictions, and force scared black people to accept the consequences of political corruption as they succumb to the white officialdom that makes their lives a living hell. Yet, there is hope and Wilford represents that hope. He knows that he must not allow officialdom to triumph. He knows that he must testify at the coroner's inquest and allow truth to destroy the cover-up that intimidates would-be witnesses and seeks to discredit Cornbread's good name.

Cornbread, Earl and Me is well written and wastes no words, moving from the killing, to the trial, to Wilford's all-important decision. Fair's descriptions of Chicago that appear between chapters of the story proper provide vivid pictures of Chicago's black population: their arrival in Chicago after migrating from the South, the black-on-black discrimination spawned by self-hate and fear, the ghetto's vitality and positive vibrations coupled with its despair and frustration, and the oppression carefully nurtured by the immorality of those in power. These descriptions invite the reader to understand the origin of the fear and racism that appear as essential elements in the telling of this story.

Reading level: easy. Literary quality: excellent.

Two other books by Ronald Fair, while not quite as popular as *Cornbread, Earl and Me,* also deserve mention. *Many Thousand Gone: An American Fable* (Reprint of 1965 edition, Chatham Bkseller, 1973) is about an isolated region in an imaginary Mississippi county which has maintained slavery to the present. A short, powerful and frightening fable, it is easily read, but contains much to think about. *World of Nothing* (Chatham Bkseller, 1970) consists of two strange, symbolic novellas.

Guy, Rosa. *The Friends*. HR&W, 1973. *Ruby*. Viking Pr, 1976.
The Friends and *Ruby* are discussed together because the latter is a sequel. Both are tender, moving studies of teenage girls in search of friendship, love and self-knowledge. *The Friends* revolves around the problems of fourteen-year-old Phyllisia; the story of her older sister, Ruby, is told in the second book. Character development in both novels is so well-rounded that the reader comes to know both Phyllisia and Ruby as personal acquaintances, for the author details their likes and dislikes, their fears and strengths, their difficulties and achievements. Emotions and mental complexities are convincingly laid bare and then explored with a sensitivity and depth that invite the reader to share each girl's experience.

Both novels probe deeply into adolescent struggling but *Ruby* is a more mature treatment. In *The Friends*, Phyllisia finds herself to be the target of abuse in school, having moved to Harlem from the West Indies. Her classmates perceive her to be too different to be one of them. Her need for a friend is desperate. The elder sister's story in *Ruby* is similar in that Ruby is also not accepted by her peers. She incurs their contempt for her willingness to help an elderly, crippled teacher who despises them all.

Phyllisia reasons that having a friend will help her to survive, so she selfishly cultivates the friendship of shabby, tough, fifteen-year-old Edith. At first Phyllisia nurtures the friendship for her own protection but, by the novel's end, the friendship has developed into a genuinely warm relationship of understanding and sincere concern. The abuse that Ruby experiences in school in the sequel leaves her feeling alone and confused. She wants to feel that someone cares for and loves her, and it seems that her family can offer no respite for her ailing spirit. Her mother has died of cancer a year earlier. Her younger sister has adjusted to life in Harlem and takes only a superficial interest in Ruby's problems. Her proud father, tall, handsome Calvin Cathy, allows the success of his restaurant business to consume so much of his time and attention that he has little to give to his daughters. He truly loves them both, and fears that he may lose them, but he can express his love only in a domineering manner. In *The Friends*, Calvin is opposed to Phyllisia's friendship with Edith. In *Ruby*, he tries to stop his elder daughter from seeing Daphne, a girl in whom Ruby believes she has found solace and love.

The relationships that Phyllisia and Ruby have with Edith and Daphne respectively lead to an undeniable self-awareness. Ruby's revelation is more explosive, however, for she nearly commits suicide before coming to the realization that *she* must assume responsibility for the quality of her life. Dependence, lack of confidence, and extreme self-absorption almost destroy her.

(*Ruby* will be of interest to many adolescents, but it is a more adult novel than *The Friends*. Allusions to Ruby's lesbian affair with Daphne are minimally detailed but may be unsuitable for some young readers.)

The Friends: reading level—average; literary quality—very good. *Ruby*: reading level—average; literary quality—excellent.

Hamilton, Virginia. *M. C. Higgins, the Great.* Macmillan, 1974; pap., Dell, 1976.

When the story opens, Mayo Cornelius Higgins is perched atop his cherished forty-foot pole, looking across the hills and valleys that surround his family's land on Sarah's Mountain. He is pretending that the strip mine spoil heap behind him and the burial ground below him do not exist, and imagining he is M. C. Higgins the Great, master of all he surveys. But he knows that in reality, the spoil heap is slowly moving down the mountain, threatening life and property, and that the pole rising from the burial ground is a bizarre but fitting monument to his family heritage. Personal desires and commitment to family clash as M. C. struggles to establish his identity and make some sense of his future.

Through two outsiders who come to Sarah's Mountain, he achieves a clearer understanding of who he is and where he is going. One is Mr. James K. Lewis, a wandering "dude" who is collecting authentic folk music on tape and records M. C.'s mother's songs. M. C. imagines that Lewis will make his mother a star in Nashville, so the family can escape the spoil heap, although the "dude" has no such plans. The other outsider is Lurhetta Outlaw, who appears briefly and mysteriously to challenge M. C.'s physical strength and pride and show him he has the power to shape his own destiny. In a striking climax, M. C. decides not to flee, because what is important to him is "Not just living on the mountain. But *me* living on the mountain" (p. 273).

Reading level: average. Literary quality: excellent.

Hamilton, Virginia. *The Planet of Junior Brown.* Macmillan, 1971; pap., 1974.

The originality of this story and its unusual central characters should capture the imagination of every reader. This novel has been described as "a story of tomorrow," and in it, fantasy and reality go hand-in-hand.

Junior Brown and his best friend Buddy Clark are unforgettable. Junior is a 262-pound musical genius who feels "an awful ugliness about himself." Buddy is a highly intelligent, street-wise boy who has no family. Eighth grade has nothing to offer them, so they are truants who spend most of their days in the school cellar. There, the janitor, Mr. Pool (a former teacher), has made a model of the solar system in a secret room behind a bogus wall. In the semi-darkness, the planets orbit and glow, and Junior, Buddy, and Mr. Pool share a peace that can be found neither in the classroom nor in the streets. Buddy creates a new planet called "Junior Brown," which he and Mr. Pool add to the system in an attempt to draw Junior out of his shyness.

But Junior's problems are deep, and the new planet fails to prompt the boy to talk about his frustrations. Junior mistakenly assumes that Buddy's concern for him is pity. The climax comes when the truants are caught by an assistant principal and Mr. Pool is reprimanded for being a part-time janitor with full-time responsibilities. The pressures of having a sick and overprotective mother, an absentee father, and a neurotic music teacher combine with the strain of playing hookey and lead to Junior's nervous breakdown. Buddy and Mr. Pool are his mainstay, and they plan to nurse him back to health in a condemned building which Buddy calls "The Planet of Junior Brown."

Most young people will probably enjoy seeing how Buddy and Junior try to create for themselves a world divorced from societal demands—a special place, a "planet" where rules are not adult creations and the only law is that "people live for each other."

Reading level: easy. Literary quality: excellent.

Two earlier junior novels by Virginia Hamilton centering on black characters are *The House of Dies Drear* (Macmillan, 1968; pap., 1970) and *Zeely* (Macmillan, 1967; pap., n.d.).

Hunter, Kristin. *The Soul Brothers and Sister Lou.* Scribner, 1968; pap., Avon, 1976.

Fourteen-year-old Louretta Hawkins lives in a small apartment with her mother, seven sisters and brothers, and a nine-month-old niece. Lou wants and needs a place of her own: "... someplace to go between school and suppertime. Someplace where she could talk, and have fun, and be with her friends." In a novel that is chock-full of coincidences, Lou and her friends manage to get just such a place. The clubhouse becomes a place for rapping, pursuing personal hobbies, and printing a newsletter that deals with community issues. Louretta's big brother, William; two interested teachers, Miss Hodges and Mr. Lucitanno; and Blind Eddie Bell, a shabby old man who knows all about music, help Lou and her friends get their program off the ground, but not without some setbacks and trouble from the police. At a clubhouse dance, Lou's friend Jethro is shot by a policeman. The boy dies, and at his funeral Louretta sings "Lament for Jethro," which was written by Fess, the group's black militant character. At the funeral, Lou comes to know the meaning of "soul" and to realize how the power of music can soothe anger, bitterness, and frustration.

In the second-to-last chapter, things move too quickly, cramming too many coincidences into too few pages. At this point the novel loses a good deal of its realism, as Lou and her friends are skyrocketed into fame and fortune by Jewel Records. In the final chapter, we learn that six months have passed quickly. "The Soul Brothers and Sister Lou" have cut a hit record, made some money, and are no longer kids. In growing up, Louretta has experienced life's joy and pain in a short span of time, and she must now face some serious questions about her identity, her needs, and her purpose in life.

The Soul Brothers and Sister Lou is well written until the final chapters. Here the action is not smooth; there is too much superficiality—too many underdeveloped and incidental details. As a result, some of the final matter is unrealistic and appears to develop illogically compared to the earlier chapters.

Reading level: average. Literary quality: poor to good.

Jackson, Jesse. *The Fourteenth Cadillac.* Doubleday, 1972.

Nostalgia, humor, and sadness combine to make *The Fourteenth Cadillac* a touching story of adolescent self-realization. The year is 1925 and the place is Columbus, Ohio. The central character is seventeen-year-old Stonewall ("Stoney") Jackson, a high school dropout, in search of the elusive and magical "wisdom and understanding."

Nothing seems to be moving in the right direction for Stonewall. His prospects for finishing high school appear hopeless. His girlfriend Talitha rejects him. His brother Moses, a paragon of virtue, constantly assaults him with belittling remarks. His neighbors insist that he join the church like everyone else on Seventeenth Street. The walls are closing in on Stoney, the pressures of life are mounting, and his father issues an ultimatum: "Either you work or go to school."

His search for a job is in vain. He cannot get an interview at the Cadillac Company where his Uncle Ernie works. He encounters prejudice at a printing company where a delivery boy is needed. He is rejected at the Neil House Hotel because he is too small for the bellhop uniform. His visit to the employment office is a gross disappointment. Stonewall's prospects are looking mighty dim, and he is having serious doubts about ever finding "wisdom and understanding," when his good buddy Steeple comes to the rescue by helping him to get a job on a nearby horse farm. Steeple tells him, "You your own man now," encouraging Stoney to leave home, be a man, and be free.

Author Jackson, not to be confused with the Reverend Jesse Jackson, portrays the clumsy but lovable Stonewall in a way that moves the reader to share his problems and his victories. His references to some important figures in black history—Marcus Garvey, W. E. B. Du Bois and Booker T. Washington—may inspire some readers to learn more about the Afro-American past. Boys and girls alike will identify with the central character's botched-up search for manhood, which the author handles with humor and compassion.

Reading level: easy. Literary quality: good.

Jordan, June. *His Own Where*. T Y Crowell, 1971; pap., Dell, 1973.

This novel, as lyrical as the poetry that June Jordan writes, is an emotional story and a stirring tribute to life and love. *His Own Where* is the story of Buddy Rivers, sixteen, and Angela Figueroa, fourteen, who create "their own where," away from distressing and embittered family relationships and the lethargic atmosphere of school.

Buddy's mother has abandoned him, leaving him with his father. After years of trying to build a new life and creating a new home for them, Buddy's father is hospitalized, having been hit by a car. He is dying, and the only thing that Buddy can do is to see him every evening. Silently sitting next to his father's bed, the boy feels a strong sense of guilt, for his thoughts are turned primarily toward someone else. This important someone is Angela, whose young life has been turned into a struggle for survival because of her brutally punitive parents. The deep love between him and Angela leads Buddy into a determined fight for their liberation. He saves himself and rescues Angela from the perils of a life that would destroy them. He takes her to "his own where," where they can make love and be happy, creating a new world with new values where love may grow.

Black idiom and poetic license may make this difficult reading for some, but the plot is simple enough to follow, even if some of the nuances of language are unclear. *His Own Where* is a novel for readers who believe that dreams can sometimes come true.

Reading level: average to advanced. Literary quality: excellent.

Mathis, Sharon Bell. *Listen for the Fig Tree*. Viking Pr, 1974; pap., Avon, 1975.

Listen for the Fig Tree is a novel about the strength and beauty of black children that says, "Let's celebrate blackness." Marvina ("Muffin") Johnson, a blind sixteen-year-old, does just that as she learns to cope with adolescence and family problems. Mr. Dale, Muffin's friend and neighbor, advises her to listen carefully for her "growing-up time," which he says is quiet and not far away. Muffin denies wanting to grow up, but it happens anyway and she comes to realize a time of "knowing," a time of understanding. Muffin's journey into womanhood and her ensuing transformation are handled realistically and objectively without the avoidance of pain and unpleasantness.

When the story opens, it is five days before Christmas and Marvina Johnson is looking forward to Kwanza, a seven-day Afro-American celebration that begins immediately after Christmas Day. She wants to envelop herself in the joy and excitement of the season, but the torment of her mother's problems intrudes. Leola Johnson, Muffin's mother, is mourning the death of her husband, who was killed a year ago on Christmas Day. Leola is unable to deal with her loss and tries to drown her misery in alcohol. She scorns the sympathy and aid of family friends, Mr. Dale, Mr. Willie Williams, and Miss Geneva, and the help of her daughter and Ernie Braithewaite, Muffin's boyfriend, whom Mr. Dale calls "Black Jesus."

In an effort not to dampen the spirit of Kwanza, after Leola rejects her help, Muffin pretends that her mother is really all right and that everything is just fine. She must finish making her Kwanza dress and the only thing that matters is the forthcoming celebration at the Black Museum. Ernie tells her that she is "riding a horse backwards," trying to ignore facts that cannot be denied. He tells her that Kwanza is all about "knowing," facing reality and evaluating priorities. Muffin insists that she can walk away from her problems.

On the evening before Christmas Eve, Muffin is attacked in a hallway of her apartment building. The author treats the brutality of the assault and Muffin's terror with an admirable frankness that draws the reader into the experience, without the sensationalism of lurid detail.

With the help of Mr. Dale and Ernie, Muffin is able to pull herself together and make some sense of her life. At the Kwanza ceremony, Muffin comes into her "growing-up time," and returns home with the insight and strength needed to meet the challenges of life.

Although some adolescent boys are not inclined to relate to stories which feature a girl as the protagonist, *Listen for the Fig Tree* is an exception, because the portrayal of Ernie is so strong and central to the telling of this story. Boys will identify with his "cool," his militancy, and his calm, proficient manner in the face of life's difficulties. Details about Kwanza in the novel will probably spark an interest in all readers to learn more about this celebration, which is rapidly spreading throughout black America. (For information about Kwanza, write to: The East, Distribution and Publication, 1310 Atlantic Avenue, Brooklyn, N.Y. 11216.)

Reading level: average. Literary quality: very good.

Mathis, Sharon Bell. *Teacup Full of Roses.* Viking Pr, 1972; pap., Avon, 1973.

Teacup Full of Roses is a novel about the kind of love, loyalty, and sacrifice in a family that enable black children to survive, even when their parents may have become physically or emotionally exhausted.

Joe Brooks is seventeen. For two years he has worked at full-time jobs, attending high school at night. When the story opens, his graduation is just a few days away. Joe has his sights set on a diploma, college, success, security, and marriage to his girlfriend Ellie. But dreams of a bright future begin to fade when Joe's older brother Paul, a talented artist and heroin addict, returns home. Joe refuses to abandon his dreams for *what can be,* but he knows that he has many decisions to make on the basis of *what is.*

Joe lives with his father, Isaac, who is unemployed because of a bad heart; his mother, Mattie, whose sole concern is Paul; his younger brother Davey, an A-student and basketball whiz, who has only Joe to look out for him; and his Aunt Lou, an old woman to whom the spirits speak and tell her, "Trouble coming hard to this house." Joe listens to Aunt Lou and believes, because she is never wrong.

Paul returns, insisting that his drug addiction is a thing of the past, but it soon becomes apparent that this is a lie. Only Mattie believes that her favorite son can do no wrong.

Joe decides to join the Navy, knowing that he must save himself and his brother Davey. Paul, who has no desire to help himself, just does not count anymore. Joe's plans for marriage are only slightly changed and he promises Ellie that one day they will live "in a magic place—where trouble never comes. In a teacup... full of roses" (p. 87). On the night of Joe's graduation, there is tragedy—Aunt Lou's predicted "trouble" comes.

The language in this novel is stark, the action is convincing; the shocking outcome is sad and yet a tribute to hope. Joe and his brothers represent all black children and teenagers who attempt to cope with the situations that face them daily.

Reading level: easy. Literary quality: very good.

Myers, Walter Dean. *Fast Sam, Cool Clyde, and Stuff*. Viking Pr, 1975.

This novel will have the reader both laughing and crying with "the 116th Street Good People," a group of young blacks and Puerto Ricans in a New York City community, as they live, learn, grow, and get it all together for each other, in a circle of friendship that provides protection, understanding, and love. With infectious humor, Stuff, one of the youngest, describes the year he falls in love, is unfaithful, almost wins a dance contest, goes to jail three times, and begins to change some preconceived notions about "being a man."

Readers will remember Fast Sam, who would rather run than fight; Cool Clyde, the coolest dude on the block; Gloria, who explains how and why sex is much more than simply "getting some"; Maria, who brings everything right down front, always saying what everyone else is only thinking; and Carnation Charley, who would "fall out in a cashmere suit, a silk shirt, a velvet vest, West Indian bracelets, an East African tiki, and Pro-Keds" (p. 46). There is poignant tenderness in Stuff's accounts of the grief-filled moments surrounding the death of Clyde's father, the leaving home of Gloria's father, and the death of Carnation Charley, ace dancer turned junkie.

The text of *Fast Sam, Cool Clyde, and Stuff* is easy to read, but some readers may have difficulty with the book's high level of cultural authenticity. Some slang expressions may not be understood, even in context. Some conclusions the characters reach, based on aspects of ghetto living and the nature of racism, may require more explanation than Myers provides. Nevertheless, young readers will have no problem identifying with Stuff's concerns and feelings, or understanding the bond among the 116th Street Good People as a vehicle for survival in a world that is sometimes insensitive to young needs.

Reading level: easy. Literary quality: excellent.

Richards, Nat. *Otis Dunn, Manhunter*. Edited by Billie Young. Ashley Bks, 1974.

Otis Dunn, Manhunter combines all of the elements essential to intrigue—suspense, mind-boggling twists and turns of circumstance, subtle clues, and compelling action. Otis Dunn, an ex-FBI agent, is a cool, calculating dude who always gets his man. He is a larger-than-life bounty hunter who hunts the men and women on the FBI's Ten Most Wanted list.

Otis is looking for Vernell Henderson, who with three other men had stolen the Super Bowl receipts two years before. By tricking some of Vernell's old gambling cronies, Otis is able to determine where Vernell is hiding out, and the chase to capture him is on. Otis works alone, relying only on his trusty .45 automatic (that rarely seems to need reloading in spite of all the gunplay) and his late-model, white Sedan de Ville (that never seems to require gas station visits despite an abundance of wheeling and dealing). Otis finds himself in some unbelievably difficult situations from time to time, but these are only momentary obstacles that he overcomes with incredible wit and instinct. As the drama builds, there is a raging hurricane, unmarked and crowded graves appear all over town, and a cast of characters provide Otis with clues that appear fertile one minute and unprofitable the next (or vice versa). But of course the novel's star is triumphant, capturing Vernell and solving a multitude of subplot mysteries that are skillfully woven into the primary action of a thrilling story.

The author's emphasis is on plot, so several characters seem to pop up out of nowhere; explanations for their appearance in the story tend to be superficial. But *Otis Dunn, Manhunter* is so well written that even though the protagonist is carried through a plethora of changes, the novel is never confusing. The exploits of Otis Dunn, super-hero, will excite and fascinate even the most reluctant reader.

Reading level: easy. Literary quality: good.

Steptoe, John. *Marcia*. Viking Pr, 1976.

Here is a book that "lets it all hang out" with the kind of humor, toughness, and candor that will touch the spirit of every young person growing up and the heart of every adult who remembers the confused feelings of those years.

Most of *Marcia* is devoted to fourteen-year-old Marcia Anne Williams' conversations with her best girlfriend, Millie, to shared experiences with Danny, her boyfriend, who is growing up with her, and to talks with her mother and the reader. Yet because everyone's growing up time is different and revelations come in different ways, Marcia is alone, trying to make some sense out of a tangled web of joy and pain, apprehension and frustration. Sex is an urgent and confusing issue, as Marcia admits to herself: "You know, it's funny how I'm feelin screwed up about all this and I ain't said nothin to my mother about it.... She must have gone through the same thing.... But now I'm not a little girl. She's still my mommy, but now I'm a woman too... that means a whole new way between us" (p. 66).

The "whole new way" leads Marcia to have a deeply serious "rap" with Moma, in which she expresses the pride and fear, the simultaneous blues and good feeling that accompany her growing up. She discusses love, babies, abortion, contraception, economics, self-respect, and Danny, and in the end, we know that Marcia is going to make it all right "in a world that don't make no sense."

Young readers will appreciate Marcia's frank simplicity as she explores the ins and outs of approaching adulthood and faces her problems with an attitude that says, "To thine own self be true." The novel could serve as an ideal supplement to the study of peer pressure or values clarification in the classroom.

Reading level: easy. Literary quality: very good.

Taylor, Mildred D. *Roll of Thunder, Hear My Cry.* Dial, 1976. Here is another memorable story of the Logans, first introduced in *Song of the Trees* (see the following annotation). Based on stories told by the author's father about his early life, it describes the profound physical and mental struggle for survival of a black family in rural Mississippi during the Depression. In her introduction, the author says of her father: "...I learned a history not then written in books but one passed from generation to generation... a history of great-grandparents and of slavery and of the days following slavery; of those who lived still not free, yet who would not let their spirits be enslaved. From my father the storyteller I learned to respect the past, to respect my own heritage and myself..."

This novel spans one chaotic year in which Cassie Logan's mother is fired from her teaching duties for inspiring black pride. Cassie's older brother, Stacey, reaches the threshold of adulthood, night riders terrorize blacks, and Cassie learns that there are white people who consider her inferior. In this year, the Logans experience suffering and joy, humiliation and pride, and deepen their desire for independence. Symbolically, their strength in their personal struggle is the strength generations of black people in this country have displayed in their struggle against overwhelming degradation.

In the concluding chapter, Mr. Morrison, a hired hand and friend, sings a song that tells the family's story:

> Roll of thunder
>   hear my cry
> Over the water
>   bye and bye.
> Old Man comin'
>   down the line
> Whip in hand to
>   beat me down
> But I ain't
>   gonna let him
> Turn me 'round.
>   (p. 242)

Reading level: average. Literary quality: excellent.

Taylor, Mildred D. *Song of the Trees*. Dial, 1975.

This book, based on the author's father's stories of his childhood, is listed as children's fiction, but would be both interesting and inspiring to some junior high students. The story is told from the point of view of eight-year-old Cassie Logan, who lives with her mother, grandmother ("Big Ma"), and three brothers, Little Man, Christopher-John, and Stacey, in rural Mississippi during the Depression. The father, David Logan, is working in Louisiana, trying to earn money for his family.

Cassie's love for the beautiful trees which grow on the Logans' land is evident throughout the story. She believes they speak and sing to her. Trouble comes when Mr. Andersen, a white man, sees the substantial profit he could make by leveling the trees for lumber. Desperately needing money for medicine, Big Ma accepts the paltry sum of sixty-five dollars for as much lumber as Mr. Andersen wants. Cassie's mother sends Stacey to Louisiana to bring his father home. In an intense confrontation between Logan and Andersen, black bravery is pitted against white power.

Many young readers will identify with the children who must deal with fear and adult responsibility in the same breath. Simply and convincingly, the author conveys their range of emotions as they see the trees marked with white X's, overhear Andersen's conversation with their mother and Big Ma, hear the trees begin to fall, and hear their father say, "a black man's always gotta be ready to die." In the end, most of the trees are gone, but the Logans' self-respect and pride have increased in the face of a severe test. *Song of the Trees* could be used in an effort to encourage young people to stand up for human rights and fight against oppression of all kinds.

Reading level: easy. Literary quality: excellent.

Young, Al. *Snakes*. [1970] Dell, pap., 1972.

To MC, music is everything—his world, the very essence of life itself: "I listen and look for it everywhere I go: in the street, in the country, in people's voices, in their movements, in the way they lead their lives. There are pictures that sing to me; the right words can set my head to vibrating with music; certain women arent melodies to me but lovable fields of musical energy" (p. 1). Al Young's musical background is evidenced in this novel. Through his writing, the author reveals his feeling that music can be a most powerful medium for expressing the varied rhythms and nuances of life.

MC lives in Detroit with his hard-working grandmother, Claude, a wise, loving woman, who plays numbers with a passion and has a penchant for paperback mysteries. Claude becomes ill when MC is ten, and he is sent to Mississippi to live with cousins whom he calls Uncle Donald and Aunt Didi. It is there that MC starts playing melodies by ear on an old, beat-up upright and begins noticing the subtle and yet strong connection between music and feeling. It is in Mississippi also that MC meets a musician, Tull, who moves in and out of his life very quickly, but introduces MC to blues.

Several years later, after settling back up North, MC, playing guitar, and his buddy, Shakes, a drummer with "a snapshot memory," organize a band. They are turned on to jazz and "Down Beat" magazine by another friend, Champ, a non-musician who "had his problems but, in many respects, was sharp and unique." Champ's influence adds a new dimension to their music and allows them to glimpse the world of entertainment that they hope to become a part of. The group's music matures with them, and they move from school dances, to a television talent show, to the cutting of a record that becomes a local hit, "Snakes," written by MC. Then the heat is on and MC's life becomes confused with the pressures of school, family, love, friendship, drugs and success. The novel ends with MC leaving Detroit, heading for New York, trying to sort it all out and find himself.

Here is a story that flows effortlessly. This book should appeal to young readers with an interest in music or show business. *Snakes* is realistic and offers no easy solutions to the problems of adolescence and fame.

Reading level: average. Literary quality: very good.

Short Story Collections by Black Writers

"Vibrant," "sensitive," "honest," and "compelling" are terms that have been used to describe the following short story collections. From the cultures of Africa through the agony of the Middle Passage, from the oppression of the slavery era to the trials and joys of today, the variety and universality of human experience and the uniqueness of the black experience are depicted by black writers who know how to capture the essence of blackness—the "soul" of a people.

Bambara, Toni Cade. *Gorilla, My Love*. Random, 1972.

This collection of fifteen stories is barely described by the adjective "superb." The author is able to reach in and touch the very core of black existence, as she deals excellently and accurately with the complexities of black lifestyles. She does this in such a way that the ineffable becomes something that we can see and feel.

Her use of black idiom is strong and sure as she speaks through the characters of black children ("Gorilla, My Love") and old people ("Blues Ain't No Mockin' Bird"), the street-wise ("My Man Bovanne") and the worldly sophisticate (Patsy's mother in "Basement").

Reading level: advanced. Literary quality: excellent.

Hunter, Kristin. *Guests in the Promised Land*. Scribner, 1973; pap., Avon, 1976.

Growth and survival are the focal points around which Kristin Hunter spins eleven tales of adolescent development and of existence (from a black frame of reference) in a black-white society. The difficulties of teenagers growing up are handled with understanding and compassion. In addition, the author probes perceptively into a world where racism is the name of the game.

Hunter expresses a sincere tenderness towards her young characters in a moving love story, "Two's Enough of a Crowd." She reveals her recognition of the contradictions inherent in adolescence, when one is no longer a child and not yet an adult, when self-discovery occupies nearly every waking moment. The title story is charged with emotional impact as it bitterly exposes the paternalistic kind of racial prejudice that hides beneath what is presumed to be charitable kindness. Hunter's handling of the black experience is like a caress—light but moving, tender and yet strong.

Reading level: average. Literary quality: very good.

Lester, Julius. *Black Folktales.* R W Baron, 1969; pap., Grove, 1970.

One speaks of "unlucky number thirteen," but lucky is the child or adult who encounters this collection of thirteen stories by Julius Lester. Some elicit laughter and others, tears, but all teach something about black Africa and/or black America. These tales are part of a heritage that is rich in storytelling, and the author brings them a new freshness by injecting the vernacular of "what's happenin' now." The centuries-old stories, retold for generations in both North and South, provide explanations of why the world exists as it does. Stories about Stagolee and High John the Conqueror, about black men who defy intimidation, offer not only entertainment but also inspiration to be successful and strong men and women, unwilling to compromise on innermost convictions.

Reading level: easy. Literary quality: good.

Lester, Julius. *Long Journey Home: Stories from Black History.* Dial, 1972; pap., Dell, 1975.

Here are expert reinterpretations of black history by Julius Lester. The author weaves the fabric of historical fiction out of the fiber of fact and legend. Black children today are interested in their past and need accurate information to counteract misconceptions that they have been exposed to through the established media. These six stories from black history are drawn from times in America's past when slaves and ex-slaves fought to survive, facing tremendous odds in an oppressive society. Although each story deals with the desire and the asserted will to be free, the author creates variety with an assortment of colorful characters and a range of storytelling devices. Although the situations and the people described in these stories may appear to be remote from today's experience, such is not the case. After reading the title story, for example, in which a group of slaves walks away from the master into the ocean, the reader cannot help but be impressed with the same courageous spirit of black people that exists today.

Reading level: easy to average. Literary quality: very good.

McPherson, James A. *Hue and Cry.* Fawcett World, 1969.
Anyone who has ever been hurt, confused, lonely, or just plain miserable, will see him- or herself somewhere between the covers of this book. These ten short stories of pain and need suggest that no one has cornered the market on misery. As McPherson embraces the human condition with his writing, he exposes fear, disgrace, and hunger. As he raises his "hue and cry" against them, readers know that courage, honor, and fulfillment are within reach, but the negatives must be dealt with first. McPherson is a writer of exceptional insight and sympathy. In each story he deals with hopelessness as a fact of life, but the reader is left with the distinct impression that the author views hope as a prevailing fact of living.

Reading level: advanced. Literary quality: excellent.

Mirer, Martin, ed. *Modern Black Stories.* Barron, pap., 1971.
Here is a short story anthology specifically designed for classroom use. Each story is followed by study aids which include "Questions for Discussion," "Building Vocabulary," suggestions for "Thinking and Writing," questions relating to techniques of plot development, characterization, setting, theme and mood, and a brief note about the author. The introduction includes a section on the essential elements of the short story and a note to students, which briefly explains the purpose and use of the study aids. This is therefore an excellent text for independent study.

This collection is wide-ranging and contains two short stories by black Africans: Adelaide Casely-Hayford of Sierra Leone ("Mista Courifer") and Richard Rive of the Union of South Africa ("The Bench"). Included also are well-known classics such as "A Summer Tragedy" by Arna Bontemps, "The Homecoming" by Frank Yerby, and "Miss Cynthie" by Rudolph Fisher. Excerpts from the following novels may also be found in this collection: *Go Tell It on the Mountain* (Baldwin), *Invisible Man* (Ellison), and *Native Son* (Wright). Short stories by black writers who are rarely anthologized, such as Lerone Bennett, Jr. (senior editor of *Ebony* magazine) and Ted Poston (feature writer for the *New York Post* since 1937), are an important part of this collection too.

This fourteen-story grouping is an exciting compilation of literature that portrays the condition of black life in varied settings from Kentucky to Africa. At the same time, it successfully encompasses the monumental range of the short story as a work of art.

Reading level: advanced. Literary quality: excellent.

The Black Experience in Junior Novels by White Writers

Seen from a black's perspective, most white writers, despite the best of intentions, frequently present a distorted (racist) portrayal of the black experience. Nevertheless, this writer believes there are a few books that deserve to be mentioned here, for some degree of honesty and insight and/or literary quality make them worthy of note. Evidence of the white perspective in these novels is apparent. This is inevitable. However, these white writers have recognized, in a positive manner, something about the richness and the limitless diversity of the black experience. With admiration they have looked at blackness, giving it more than the all-too-common patronizing glance.

Before discussing novels that have some merit, it seems useful for the sake of comparison to look at an example of a book that from the black point of view does everything wrong: *Linda's Raintree* by Dorothy Hamilton (Herald Pr, cloth & pap., 1975).

Like her raintree, Linda is growing up; and like her raintree, at the novel's end, she is blooming because "things are as they should be," whatever that means. Linda's mother, Mrs. Powell, speaks in a dialect so inauthentic as to make people who know richness of black idiom cringe. Never has this writer heard a black person say, "How be I different?" At the library, Linda meets Amory, a rich white girl whose father has deserted the family. She confides in Linda, who knows all about that problem (among blacks) because "This happens a lot around here." No explanation is provided for *why* it "happens a lot," but we are advised of Linda's surprise at discovering that it happens to white folks too. (Shades of elitism?) Paternalism (probably unintended) rears its ugly head when Linda thinks things like:

> "What could a girl my age say to help a senior, especially a white girl?" (p. 29).
>
> "Will [Mother] think it strange that [Amory]... felt free about talking to little old me?" (p. 39).
>
> "I'm just afraid Amory won't like me anymore if she sees where I live" (p. 92).

It is gratifying to find a novel that shows two black parents striving to make a good home for the children, but the characterizations of Mr. and Mrs. Powell leave a lot to be desired. Father is constantly being laid off and sometimes finds factory work which keeps him away from home for weeks at a time. To help pay the bills, Mother irons for white people. Neither ever expresses anger about their lot, and Father voices an unrealistically mild dissatisfaction when he talks about trying and hoping for betterment. Mother speaks of wanting her children to get a good education, but neither parent inspires the children to challenge the system. Nor do they seem to be interested in developing the instinct for survival that Linda and her brothers will need to deal with the realities of life in a society where there are problems because some people are black and others are white. This novel describes an impossibility: Linda "grows up" but her blackness appears to be of no consequence. The author's denial of blackness is racist and her denial of the existence of racism is misleading. When Mrs. Powell tells her daughter, "... problems don't come in colors. People do but not problems" (p. 47), she neglects to explain the nature of the society in which they live, where racism is dehumanizing to both the oppressor and the oppressed, but where problems stemming from racism are most often suffered by those who are non-white. The reading level of this book is easy; the literary quality, poor.

Bonham, Frank. *The Golden Bees of Tulami.* Dutton, 1974; pap., Dell, 1977.

Frank Bonham is well known for his many novels for young readers that often deal with West Coast ghetto life and gang activity. Having worked in the ghettos of Southern California with young people, the author has developed an acute awareness of and sincere concern for adolescent problems. His deep interest is reflected in his works.

The Golden Bees of Tulami combines Bonham's frequently used elements of ghetto life and gang activity with mystery and intrigue, to keep the reader fascinated from cover to cover. The novel's premise may appear to be just a little far-fetched but this is not an escapist book, for Walter ("Cool") Hankins, the central character, confronts reality at every turn. There is just enough fantasy to pique the imagination and enough reality to prevent this novel from slipping into the bizarre.

Cool Hankins is a high school senior and city boxing champion who lives in Dogtown with his Aunt Josie and the fourteen foster children she is raising. Cool has a problem: Turk Ransom, leader of nine Dogtown gangs, is leaning on him, pressuring him to join. Cool is opposed to joining, though he fears Turk's wrath and power. Just when it seems that all is lost and Cool may be forced to join Turk's ranks, a stranger appears, a handsome African with a mysterious mission and a hive of golden bees. His name is Joshua Smith Kinsman, and Cool becomes his trusted friend and right-hand man.

The African has been assigned to sell twenty-four queen bees to the United States for one million dollars each. The tiny golden bees from his country, Tulami, produce a honey that contains a substance which would lead to a miracle—world peace. Having read about the criminal exploits of Turk's gangs in the newspapers, Kinsman wants to feed the honey to them to prove the golden bees' worth and to interest someone, hopefully the U.S. Government, in buying them.

The action that follows includes hoodlums with an interest in brotherhood; selfish prospective buyers with more interest in profit than in peace; a cool Cool, whose interest is in aiding Kinsman; and a disappointed Prince of Peace, who discovers that yesterday's dream is still a dream. But those who have tasted the honey of peace now have a hope for tomorrow.

Reading level: average. Literary quality: very good.

The black experience is also dealt with in other recommended novels by Frank Bonham: *Durango Street* (1965), *The Nitty Gritty* (1968), *Cool Cat* (1971) and *Hey, Big Spender* (1972). Young people should also enjoy reading *Mystery of the Fat Cat* (1968), an intriguing novel in which Bonham introduces Cool and his friends (all Dutton; pap., Dell).

Lipsyte, Robert. *The Contender*. Har-Row, 1967; pap., Bantam, 1969.

The Contender is a novel that most students will appreciate for its entertainment value, information, and realism. Boys may identify with the main character's need to prove himself —to be a man—and all young readers will identify with his need to "be somebody special."

Alfred Brooks is a Harlem resident searching for meaning in his life. He has quit school and works at a "dead end" job in a grocery store. His father has abandoned him, his mother is dead, and Aunt Pearl's concern for his welfare, although appreciated, is stifling and at times disconcerting. Alfred's best friend, James, does not want to be bothered with him, after a ten-year friendship, and has joined a gang. Gang members, Sonny, Major, and Hollis, are pressuring Alfred to join them. Conflict and confusion become his day-to-day companions until Alfred gets involved in activities at Donatelli's gym, where his development of a positive attitude and self-respect begins.

In his eagerness to "be somebody special," Alfred turns to boxing, learning early that one must start by wanting to be a contender—"wanting to be a champion is not enough." He also learns from Mr. Donatelli that the failure is the guy who quits before ever really trying and that "nothing's ever promised you." Mr. Donatelli's words of inspiration and wisdom create a new attitude within Alfred, and with this new attitude, Alfred begins to change his world. The transformation does not happen overnight. Alfred experiences a great many reversals in what he wants and thinks. He must reinforce his closeness with Aunt Pearl. He must restore his friendship with James. He must gain the respect of his peers. And he must fulfill his need to "be somebody special." In this realistic portrayal, solutions do not come easily.

Realism in this novel is also evidenced in the author's descriptions of activities at the gym, actual boxing matches, and "behind-the-scenes" action in the boxing world. Most students will appreciate details of character, setting, and plot that are honest and accurate, and therefore believable.

The Contender tells the story of Alfred's struggle as he learns what it means to strive, to work hard, to concentrate, and persevere. At the novel's end, he has decided to return to school and work in a recreational center for children; having learned to think beyond his own problems, he is able to think about helping others.

Reading level: easy. Literary quality: very good.

Miklowitz, Gloria. *Turning Off*. Putnam, 1973.

Turning Off is about a black high school dropout's "turning off" drugs and "turning on" to a better understanding of human nature. As the novel begins, we meet the protagonist, eighteen-year-old Edison Cook, who has spent nearly a year at a rehabilitation camp for drug addicts. In a conversation with Rosie, his probation officer, we see that Edison is ready to leave the camp but fears that returning home may mean a return to old friends, old problems, and drugs. He asks that Rosie try to find him a job "somewhere" doing "anything" where drugs are not a part of the scene. Rosie honors his request and finds him a job working with animals at a place called Safari Land. From this point, the action mounts in a setting where Edison soon discovers that "so-called civilized people can sometimes be more difficult than so-called wild animals."

The novel is about Edison's proving, mostly to himself, that he is really through with drugs. It is also about Edison's not wanting to disappoint Rosie, who demonstrates a kind of faith and trust in him that no one else has. Edison's story is about doing a good job and about fighting for self-respect, against drugs and discrimination. When Edison proves his worth and is instrumental in saving several animals at Safari Land during a flash flood, he learns that kindness and gratitude, although warranted, do not always replace dislike and distrust. In an unusual setting, Edison achieves the insight that allows him to better understand and cope with himself and others.

Reading level: average. Literary quality: very good.

Neufeld, John. *Edgar Allan*. S G Phillips, 1968; pap., NAL, 1969.

Here is an honest and balanced picture of what happens to a white community and one of its families when the family decides to adopt a black child. There are problems, and the author neither denies nor overstates them. The realistic outcome is in total harmony with the balance of the novel and in keeping with some gut-level truths about the negative feelings that many whites have toward blacks in this country.

The Rev. Robert Fickett lives in a small, conservative, California town (which his son Michael describes as being "not really very real") with his wife and four children. The younger children, Stephen and Sally Ann, are ages three and four, Michael is nearly eleven, and Mary Nell, the eldest, is thirteen when Rev. Fickett and his wife adopt little Edgar Allan—cute, bright, and black. Sally Ann and Stephen are more than pleased to have a little brother; Michael is also delighted but with some reservations, for he senses future problems that the family may not be able to deal with. Mary Nell is adamantly opposed to the adoption and tells her parents: "Can you imagine the look on my friends' faces when I introduce him as my *brother*? Do you know what they're going to think to themselves, about *you*? . . . He *is* black! . . . He's visible, and he's different, and he is not *ours*!" (p. 25). Mary Nell's friends and most of the community share her attitude. The Ficketts face mounting pressures as neighbors express anger, disapproval and fear. After a year, Edgar Allan is returned to the orphanage, and the Ficketts must come to grips with a clearly recognizable conflict between personal ideals and the real world.

Michael, now twelve years old, describes the emotionally charged events of Edgar Allan's probationary year with the family. There is humor in his description and the captivating honesty of a child who can only tell it as it is. The author is especially adept at allowing us to view the events of this story through the eyes of a child. We witness and understand Michael's confusion, admire his candor, and celebrate his coming to the threshold of manhood as he is led to an examination of society's weaknesses.

John Neufeld is to be commended for having written a novel that neither slights nor exaggerates some hard, cold facts.

Reading level: average. Literary quality: very good.

Skulicz, Matthew. *Right On, Shane*. Putnam, 1972.

When it comes to knowing what respect is, how one can earn it, and who deserves it, sixteen-year-old Shane believes himself to be the "man" with all the answers. Living in Harlem, Shane, a gang member and good fighter, believes that a man must get respect, and the only way to get it is by protecting his own turf. Maintaining this belief, he encourages his gang to avenge an assault on one of their brothers. Although the result of this vengeful attack is not a satisfying end in itself, Shane holds true to the belief that respect may be attained in no other way.

Part Two of Shane's theory is that a man who wants respect cannot achieve it with women "hanging around." According to Shane, females are to be avoided and at best they represent "an easy way to spend the afternoon." After an "easy afternoon" with Luann, a girl who wants to be his, Shane says, "A man got to lead his own life. Can't waste no time hanging onto no girl" (p. 45). But whether he likes it or not, Shane's life *is* involved with the lives of his immediate family, two females, his mother and his fourteen-year-old sister, Lea.

When Shane discovers that Lea is pregnant, and that one of his gang brothers is responsible, respect takes on an entirely new dimension. When Shane persuades Lea to have an abortion, and when he steals the money to pay for it, his perception of the female takes on an entirely new meaning as well. When tragedy strikes and Lea's abortion results in her death, Shane is forced to take another look at "respect." In coming face to face with love, fear and grief, Shane comes to an understanding of goodness, selfishness, and freedom in life, and he learns that respect comes to the man who tries to know, understand and respect the people around him. "Respect isn't something you get so much as a thing you give."

In the final paragraph, which could have been omitted, the author stretches credibility just a bit too far; we see Shane heading for the office of the Black Community Organization, where he hopes to redeem himself.

This powerful and moving novel is an intense portrayal of a young boy trying to "get his head together." Shane's transformation is both honest and convincing.

Reading level: easy. Literary quality: good.

4 Biography and Autobiography

Barbara Dodds Stanford

Part history, part literature, biography and autobiography can serve many functions. Like novels, they can entertain, illustrate a philosophy, and illumine human nature. Or biography can be primarily an account of factual, historic events, exploring and expounding historical or sociological hypotheses. In addition, biography can serve as an effective way of rousing support for a cause.

Slave narratives were the earliest form of black biography and autobiography in the United States, and they served an important function in the abolitionist campaign. Usually written or dictated by former slaves who had escaped to the North, slave biographies provided vivid and convincing pictures of the evils of slavery, contradicting the popular portrait of happy, singing, childlike "darkies." Since a major argument of slaveowners was that black people were inferior, books like Frederick Douglass' autobiographies were needed to show the intelligence and even genius of black people. The simple fact of writing a slave narrative was evidence of superior intelligence and unusual courage, for slaves could be severely punished for learning to read, and after the passage of the Fugitive Slave Laws, an escaped slave who revealed his origins could be captured and returned to slavery. Frederick Douglass was forced to live in England for a time after he wrote his autobiography.

After the Civil War, black biography and autobiography continued to reveal the mistreatment of blacks and to demonstrate the achievements of black people. As histories of decade after decade were written omitting both the achievements of black people and the crimes against them, biography and autobiography became a means for the pursuit and preservation of the truth. The large number of children's and young people's biographies written in recent decades were inspired to a great extent by the omission of black people from history books. Writers like Shirley Graham Du

Bois and Dorothy Sterling hoped to increase the self-esteem of black youth by showing them the achievements of their ancestors, and to correct for all young people the stereotypes of blacks perpetuated in almost every other genre.

In addition to showing the achievements of blacks and the evils of segregation, a large number of writers used biography and autobiography to express philosophies or propose strategies for fighting for justice. Biographies and autobiographies of people like Booker T. Washington, Jacob Reddix, and Mary McLeod Bethune argue for the importance of education for blacks who hope to overcome poverty and discrimination, while showing the tremendous courage and effort required to achieve an education. W. E. B. Du Bois' last autobiography, *A Soliloquy on Viewing My Life . . .*, is a compelling argument for communism as the appropriate philosophy for black Americans, while biographies of Richard Wright and A. Philip Randolph devote much space to showing how communism failed black Americans. Biographies and autobiographies of modern political leaders such as Martin Luther King, Jr., Huey P. Newton, and Angela Davis describe in detail the development of their theories of the most appropriate way for blacks to fight for their rights, as well as the effects of their strategies. Several biographies such as Williams' *The King God Didn't Save* and Lomax's *To Kill a Black Man* are analyses of movements and ideas in the form of studies of individuals.

Assassination has prematurely ended the careers of many of the fighters for black rights, and biography has been a way of perpetuating a person's voice and influence. Stephen Butterfield in *Black Autobiography in America* (U of Mass Pr, pap., 1974), states that "The 'self' of black autobiography, on the whole, taking into account the effect of Western culture on the Afro-American, is not an individual with a private career, but a soldier in a long, historic march toward Canaan" (p. 3). A book like Mrs. Medgar Evers' *For Us, the Living* can stir contemporary "soldiers" and keep the old message alive.

Not all biographies have any kind of political purpose; some are written primarily for entertainment or even to make money. A large number of well-known sports or entertainment figures at some time in their careers either write an autobiography or are the subject of a biography. Most of these are simply extensions of their careers and appeal primarily to fans. Some of these books, however, because of the quality of the writing, the significance of the person, or the ideals and philosophy expressed, have wider appeal and more lasting value.

The books in this chapter vary more widely in quality and difficulty than those in the other chapters. Biographies of high literary quality, regardless of the subject, have been included. So as not to omit important historical figures, a few books of mediocre literary quality are discussed when no better biography is available.

A large number of the books are aimed at young readers. These biographies are usually highly fictionalized, emphasize the childhood and early life of the person, and stress the positive qualities of the subject, often ignoring flaws or departures from conventional morality. At the other extreme are academic biographies, filled with quotations and footnotes cataloguing facts with ponderous detail. The best books for high school students are usually in-between, presenting a balanced portrait and developing in detail several significant events.

Biographies of historical figures are arranged chronologically; biographies of moderns are arranged in alphabetical order. A few adult biographical novels are included in this chapter because they appear to be as closely based on fact as most of the fictionalized junior biographies. For a key to the reading levels listed, see the introduction to Chapter 3.

Biographies of Historical Figures

Estebanico (circa 1500–1539)

All that is definitely known of Estebanico is that he was one of four survivors of Cabeza de Vaca's expedition through the southern part of what is now the United States, beginning in 1528, and that he was described by Cabeza de Vaca as an Arabian Negro, a native of Azamur. Through detailed research on West Africa, Spanish genealogies, and early Spanish settlements in the Americas, Helen Rand Parish has reconstructed life in Africa and the Americas during that period and has recreated his story, partly from fact and partly from fancy, in *Estebanico* (Viking Pr, 1974).

It is a fascinating story, beginning in the Timbuctoo of Askia the Great and ending with the search for the Seven Cities of Cibola. The horrors of the slave trade in Africa and the murder and enslavement of the Indians in the New World are seen through the eyes of a victim of slavery. Told in the form of a report from Estebanico to the king, the story portrays Estebanico as a dreamer, but also a brave and resourceful explorer.

Although the length, type size, and cover art make *Estebanico* look like a book for junior high students, the device of telling the story in first person with archaic echoes in the language may not be appreciated by young readers. Readers of all ages, however, should be attracted by the adventure and by the vivid portrayal of little-known historical events.

Reading level: average. Literary quality: good.

Juan de Pareja (1606?–1670)

A fictionalized young adult biography, *I, Juan de Pareja* by Elizabeth Borton de Treviño (FS&G, 1965) is about a black slave who belonged to the seventeenth century Spanish painter Velazquez. Juan fell in love with the slave of the painter Rubens, but could not marry her because of his own slave status. Later, Juan found that his own artistic talents were beginning to develop, but he was fearful because it was illegal for a slave to paint. After painting in secret for a long time, he finally confesed and threw himself on the mercy of the king and Velazquez. Velazquez granted him freedom, and Juan was at last able to marry and become a painter himself.

Though slavery in Spain differed from slavery in America, it still destroyed the slave's self-respect. The author shows how Juan gains dignity from the kindness of Brother Isidro, a priest who befriends him, and from the development of his own talent. As she narrates Juan's life with Velazquez, the author develops important ideas about art, especially the concept of artistic integrity. The book is a Newbery Award winner.

Reading level: average. Literary quality: very good.

Tituba

Tituba of Salem Village by Ann Petry (T Y Crowell, 1964) explores the Salem witch trials of the 1690s from the point of view of Tituba, the Rev. Samuel Parris' Barbadian slave. Tituba, a simple folk character, contrasts with the social climbing Parris and his deceitful niece, Abigail. The story shows how Abigail and other girls began to play at witchcraft and, when they got into trouble, used Tituba as a scapegoat.

This fictionalized junior biography is well constructed; many minor incidents that seem unimportant at first are used later in Tituba's trial. The characters, however, are shallowly drawn, Tituba lacks depth of feeling, and most of the other people in the book are either villains or too good to be real. The style is simple, and at times talks down to the reader.

Reading level: easy. Literary quality: fair.

Amos Fortune (1710–1801)

Amos Fortune, an African slave, was purchased by a kindly Quaker, who taught him English, reading, and weaving. He was later sold to a tanner who taught him his skills and allowed him to buy his freedom. Fortune set up his trade and bought a wife. When she died, he acquired another wife and her daughter, freed them, and took them West with him. There he lived the rest of his life, a useful and respected man.

Amos Fortune, Free Man, by Elizabeth Yates ([1950] Dutton, 1967; pap., Dell, 1971) emphasizes the Quaker virtues of patience and forgiveness. Amos, by submission and acceptance of his fate, overcame slavery. His life is an illustration of nonviolence at work. However, some students might consider Amos Fortune an Uncle Tom and feel that he is too forgiving. The reading level and style are simple enough for elementary school children, but most of the material is mature enough for high school students.

Reading level: easy. Literary quality: good.

Benjamin Banneker (1731–1806)

Your Most Humble Servant: The Story of Benjamin Banneker, by Shirley Graham (Messner, 1949) describes one of those fascinating men of many talents of the Revolutionary era. The biography seems carefully researched, although it depends to a great extent on legend. A watch given him by a Jewish merchant first unlocked Benjamin's inventive ability. From the watch, he built one of the early clocks made in America. After the Revolutionary War, Banneker studied astronomy and made corrections in the calculations of some of the most noted astronomers of the day. When his neighbor, Major Ellicott, was asked to help plan the city of Washington, Banneker went with him. When planner Pierre L'Enfant, who was dismissed, took the plans for the city to France, Banneker reproduced them from memory. Banneker's fame also grew from a letter he sent to President Jefferson opposing slavery, and from his popular almanac.

Your Most Humble Servant emphasizes creativity, determination, and people's interdependence on each other. The book includes elements of patriotism, success, romance, suspense, and adventure, so it should appeal to adolescents.

Reading ability: average. Literary quality: very good.

Phillis Wheatley (1753?–1784)

The Story of Phillis Wheatley, by Shirley Graham (Messner, 1949; pap., Archway, n.d.), a biography of America's first important black poet, begins as Mr. Wheatley of Boston purchases Phillis, a small slave girl. The Wheatley family, amazed at the girl's intelligence, taught her reading, then literature, and finally Latin. Phillis gradually began writing poetry and soon became known in literary circles around Boston. Later she went to England, where her poetry was again applauded. During the Revolution, she wrote a poem to Washington. After the death of Mr. Wheatley, Phillis married John Peters, but in the postwar depression they were haunted by poverty, and she died young.

Phillis is portrayed in this young adult biography as a very sweet-natured, thoughtful girl. The story seems to be fairly accurate, though it glosses over some of the characters' faults. Interest factors include romance, family life, and the excitement of success. Students who are not advanced enough to read her poetry might enjoy reading about Phillis Wheatley's life.

Reading level: average. Literary quality: good.

James Forten (1766–1842)

James Forten was one of the black leaders in the abolitionist movement. During the Revolutionary War, Forten sailed on a privateer as a powder boy, and was captured by the British. Later he became quite wealthy from his sailmaking business and spent much of his life fighting for rights for black people. He helped to finance William Lloyd Garrison's newspaper and wrote several pamphlets and petitions of his own.

Forten the Sailmaker by Esther M. Douty (Rand, 1968) is an excellent biography combining the lively fictionalized narrative style of good junior biographies with the careful analysis of a historical period more common in adult biographies. In addition to telling the story of an outstanding leader, *Forten the Sailmaker* describes the gradually worsening conditions of free blacks in the period between the Revolution and the Civil War and the conflicts surrounding various proposals for their improvement, such as the colonization movement and abolition. *Forten the Sailmaker* is one of the best biographies of early black Americans. Excellent reproductions of daguerrotypes and paintings from the period illustrate the book.

Reading level: average. Literary quality: excellent.

Jim Beckwourth (1789–1867)

Jim Beckwourth was a mountain man and trapper in the early Northwest. His autobiography indicates that he was either one of the greatest fighters, hunters, runners, strategists, diplomats, administrators, and con men of his day or one of the best inventors of tall tales—perhaps some of both. Hired by the Rocky Mountain Fur Company in 1823, he immediately began a life of constant narrow escapes from hunger and hostile Indians. He was captured by Crow Indians, but because of his skin color and a joking remark by a companion, he was "identified" as the long lost child of a Crow family who had been kidnapped by whites. He was accepted by the Crows and, according to his account, eventually became the head chief of the Crows, a position he used to great benefit to increase his own profits in fur trading, though he claims to have also benefited the Crows by keeping them out of unnecessary wars and forbidding the sale of whiskey among them.

Not all of Beckwourth's qualities are likely to be admired by modern readers. His overwhelming loyalty to the white traders, who occasionally misused him, and his contempt for and trickery of the Crow Indians, who treated him so well, are often accompanied in his autobiography by apologies for not being even more pro-white. Except for descriptions of his skin color, he gives no hint of his African ancestry. And he seemed to feel that deserting his son and his nine or so Indian wives redeemed him for civilization. On the other hand, his contempt for the Indians was partly disgust at their constant, brutal warfare, and his race apparently had no effect on his relationships with other mountain men.

Several versions of Beckwourth's exciting life are available. *Mountain Man, Indian Chief: The Life and Adventures of Jim Beckwourth,* edited by Betty Shepard (HarBraceJ, 1968) is a condensed version of Beckwourth's autobiography as dictated to T. D. Bonner. It is not difficult to read and is full of excitement and adventure. Many parts are better written than the comparable passages in *Jim Beckwourth: Negro Mountain Man* by Harold W. Felton (Dodd, 1966; pap., Apollo Eds, 1970). The Felton version, a junior biography, is easier to read and contains more background information and more information about Beckwourth's later years than the autobiography, as well as a little less violence and gore. (See "Black Literature for a Unit on the World of the Imagination—Grade 8" in Chapter 8.) *Mountain Man: The Life of Jim Beckwourth* by Marian T. Place (Macmillan, 1970) is a still simpler biography aimed at fifth- to eighth-grade readers. Although very well written, it is much less realistic than the other two, omitting almost all of Beckwourth's life among the Crows and most events which show him violating conventional morality.

Jim Beckwourth: Negro Mountain Man: reading level—easy; literary quality—good. *Mountain Man, Indian Chief*: reading level—easy; literary quality—very good. *Mountain Man: The Life of Jim Beckwourth*: reading level—very easy; literary quality—very good.

Edward Rose

Edward Rose was a black mountain man, a talented hunter, guide and interpreter. Like Jim Beckwourth, he lived for many years among the Crows, but unlike Beckwourth, he did not leave an autobiography, so there are many gaps in his life story. An expert guide and a skilled interpreter, Rose several times saved the lives of the men who employed him, though he was often treated with unreasonable suspicion.

Edward Rose, Negro Trail Blazer by Harold W. Felton (Dodd, 1967) is an easy, fast-moving, exciting book that is most likely to appeal to upper elementary or junior high school students, but would not be unsuitable for high school students or even adults.

Reading level: easy. Literary quality: good.

Sojourner Truth (1797–1883)

Sojourner Truth was born a slave, but after her master reneged on his promise to free her, she ran away and then took the utterly remarkable step of going to court to demand that her son be freed because his master had sold him illegally. Amazingly, she won her case. This was the beginning of Sojourner Truth's fight for human rights, a fight that made her a central figure in both the abolitionist movement and the struggle for women's rights.

A deeply religious, mystical woman, Sojourner Truth often seemed to have almost supernatural powers. As she spoke or sang, audiences were deeply moved. In her travels around the country she was often attacked verbally and threatened physically—for neither a black nor a woman was supposed to speak in public, and she was both. But though she was attacked, she had a gift for responding in ways that either converted the attackers or humiliated them. During and before the Civil War, in addition to continuing the struggle for women's rights, Sojourner Truth went on speaking tours to raise support for the freedmen, taught newly freed women in Washington, and fought streetcar segregation.

Sojourner Truth: Narrative and Book of Life ([1875] Johnson Chi, 1970) is an interesting, if rather unusual biographical work. The first part consists of a biographical account written by a white friend, Olive Gilbert, from Sojourner Truth's memories. The simple, direct style lacks literary grace and does not capture her humor and imagination; however, the work is easy to read and often quite moving. The second part of the book contains excerpts from Sojourner's *Book of Life*, a combination diary, scrapbook, and autograph book. It tells the story of her speaking tours through newspaper clippings and letters. It is a fascinating record for a student of history, but becomes a little redundant for someone interested only in Sojourner's story.

Two very good biographies written for young people are unfortunately out of print at this writing. They are *Journey Toward Freedom: The Story of Sojourner Truth* by Jacqueline Bernard (Norton, 1967) and *Sojourner Truth: A Self-Made Woman* by Victoria Ortiz (Lippincott, 1974).

Journey Toward Freedom: reading level—average; literary quality—very good. *Sojourner Truth: A Self-Made Woman*: reading level—easy; literary quality—very good. *Sojourner Truth: Narrative and Book of Life*: reading level—average; literary quality—average.

Cinque (1811–1852)

Black Mutiny: The Revolt on the Schooner Amistad by William A. Owens ([1953] Pilgrim Press, 1968) should be received enthusiastically by high school students. The story of Cinque, the African who was captured as a slave but in turn captured the slave ship, is unusually exciting and appeals strongly to racial pride. Cinque's case is also of historical value in showing how extremely difficult it was for slaves to gain freedom through rebellion. Cinque, even after capturing the ship, was unable to steer it back to Africa and was finally captured off the northern coast of the United States. At the trial many of the conflicts and errors in the white men's thoughts about slavery and blacks were demonstrated.

The story, though historically accurate, is fictionalized so that it reads like a novel. Cinque is portrayed as a strong hero, sympathetic to children and friends; however, his occasional cruelty to his enemies and his desire for glory are not ignored. Perhaps the only drawback of this book for a high school audience is its length and difficulty; the trial is described in great detail. The book was originally published under the title *Slave Mutiny.*

Reading level: average to advanced. Literary quality: excellent.

Frederick Douglass (1817?-1895)

Frederick Douglass was born a slave on a Maryland plantation, but learned to read. Mistreated because he knew too much, he finally escaped from slavery and gained fame as an orator. After the publication of his autobiography, he traveled to England and preached abolition there until friends could buy his freedom and make it safe for him to return home. He became involved with John Brown's rebellion and was a major figure in the abolitionist movement. During the Civil War, Douglass recruited black soldiers for the Union Army and sent his own two sons. Later he served in important government posts such as ambassador to Haiti and marshal of the District of Columbia. Douglass is admirable for his courage in resisting oppression.

His autobiography, *The Life and Times of Frederick Douglass* (1881), a lengthy 674 pages, is full of excitement, particularly when it describes his attempts to escape from slavery. In the later parts, Douglass tends to ramble and editorialize. The first section pictures several different ways slavery was practiced: on a fairly typical plantation in the extremely brutal hands of a "slave breaker," and in the more flexible atmosphere of Baltimore. The second section deals with the rise and development of the abolitionist cause and Douglass' experiences in England. The last section emphasizes politics and Douglass' relationships with and opinions of Presidents Lincoln, Johnson, Hayes, Grant, Garfield, and Cleveland. Douglass presents a different view of the Reconstruction period from that given in most history books (Macmillan, pap., 1962; also Ritchie, Barbara, ed., T Y Crowell, 1966).

Also included are a number of Douglass' speeches, which could be studied for themselves, if shorter selections are desired. Several can also be found in Brawley's *Early Negro American Writers.*

An earlier autobiography, *Narrative of the Life of Frederick Douglass, an American Slave,* first published in 1845, only seven years after Douglass escaped from slavery, lacks the literary polish of his later work. It is a very short book and is simpler in style and vocabulary. Of course, it includes only the earlier part of Douglass' life. Even this account is less complete than the one in *The Life and Times,* because Douglass had to leave some information out to protect those who had helped him. More advanced students should be encouraged to read the later autobiography, but younger and less able readers would probably prefer the *Narrative* for its short, vivid descriptions. A modern edition was edited by Benjamin Quarles (Harvard U Pr, cloth & pap., 1960).

There Once Was a Slave: The Heroic Story of Frederick Douglass, by Shirley Graham (Messner, 1947), has more appeal for most high school students than either of the autobiographies. The author shows a certain amount of literary craftsmanship, with a clear and imaginative style, skill at switching point of view, and clever use of symbols. However, there is a slight tendency to stereotype the characters, and Douglass is portrayed as an almost superhuman hero. Although it emphasizes his positive qualities too much, this book makes him appear an exciting and interesting person.

The Life and Times of Frederick Douglass: reading level—advanced; literary quality—very good. *Narrative of the Life of Frederick Douglass*: reading level—average; literary quality—very good. *There Once Was a Slave*: reading level—average; literary quality—very good.

Harriet Tubman (1823–1913)

The heroic and exciting life of Harriet Tubman is interesting for high school students. As a young slave girl, Harriet had her skull fractured by her master, and consequently she was considered half-witted. Hearing that she was to be sold down-river, she fled to the North. After her own escape in 1849, she began to arrange for the flight of her friends and relatives. Eventually she became the most important conductor on the Underground Railroad and led a great number of slaves to freedom. When the Civil War came, she served the Union as a spy, and in her old age she founded an orphanage.

Harriet Tubman: Conductor on the Underground Railroad by Ann Petry (T Y Crowell, 1955) attempts to place the story in its historical context by discussing other events of the year at the end of each chapter. As a demonstration of the relationship of Harriet's life to our national history this junior biography would be very useful to history students. The style is fairly simple but shows a certain artistry.

Freedom Train: The Story of Harriet Tubman by Dorothy Sterling (Doubleday, 1954) tells the same story, but concentrates more on developing Harriet herself as an exciting personality and pays less attention to the historic significance of her life. As a result, *Freedom Train* is simpler, faster moving, and more exciting and, therefore, more appealing to reluctant readers.

A Woman Called Moses by Marcy Heidish (HM, 1976; pap., Bantam, 1977) is a mature, carefully researched biographical novel about Harriet Tubman. It begins as Harriet reviews her life after being kicked out of a whites-only railroad car and wonders if bringing a few hundred people to freedom a few years before Emancipation was really worth all of the suffering. She is not quite certain of the answer. Because this narrative shows the full bitterness of slavery, the pain and danger of escape, and the tragic disappointments of "the promised land," Harriet's strength and courage become even more significant. Frank in language and description, this strongly realistic book presents a quite different picture of Harriet from the junior biographies, but probably a much more accurate one. She is shown as a very human person who wanted love and freedom, whose courage was often spurred by desperation, and who suffered intensely on the long, hard journeys North.

Freedom Train: The Story of Harriet Tubman: reading level—easy; literary quality—very good. *Harriet Tubman: Conductor on the Underground Railroad*: reading level—easy to average; literary quality—very good. *A Woman Called Moses*: reading level—advanced; literary quality—excellent.

Robert Smalls (1839–1915)

In most history books, the contributions of blacks during the Civil War and Reconstruction are ignored. Robert Smalls was one of the rarely-mentioned heroes. He was a slave who stole a ship from the Confederates, served on it with the Union forces with distinction, and finally served in the U. S. Congress for several terms. All this was accomplished despite the handicaps first of slavery, then of the prejudice of the military, and finally of the Jim Crow laws, which eventually conquered him. Dorothy Sterling's biography, *Captain of the Planter: The Story of Robert Smalls* (Doubleday, 1958; pap., Archway, n.d.) is an exciting adventure story. Smalls' escape from slavery and his battle exploits make interesting reading, and the style is fast moving.

Reading level: average. Literary quality: excellent.

Booker T. Washington (1856–1915)

Booker T. Washington for many years was considered the major spokesman for his race. He and George Washington Carver were the two blacks occasionally mentioned in textbooks. The story of Washington's struggles, after Emancipation, to obtain an education and found Tuskegee Institute is fascinating. However, during his later years, Washington was used by segregationists to encourage black people to accept Jim Crow laws and to combat the influence of younger, more militant leaders.

His autobiography, *Up from Slavery* ([1900] Dodd, 1972; pap., Bantam, 1970), is written in the stilted, genteel style of the late nineteenth century. The early chapters, which tell of his efforts to get an education, have greater appeal for students than the detailed accounts of his fund-raising and school administration problems which follow.

Reading level: average. Literary quality: good.

Daniel Hale Williams (1858–1931)

Dr. Daniel Hale Williams was the first surgeon to operate on the human heart. He was also one of the founders of Chicago's Providence Hospital and leader in the improvement of medical training and facilities for blacks. Attending medical school in the 1880s, he received the best training available at that time and soon became a leading surgeon. A skillful and conscientious doctor, he was unfortunately hindered in his work by racial and political quarrels.

Daniel Hale Williams: Open Heart Doctor by Lewis H. Fenderson (McGraw, 1972) is a biography of Dr. Williams for young readers. It also provides interesting information on medical practices in the late nineteenth century.

Reading level: easy. Literary quality: good.

Ida B. Wells (1862–1931)

Ida B. Wells began her crusade for justice by biting a train conductor's hand when he grabbed her arm to force her to move to a Jim Crow car. She followed up her battle with a suit which she at first won, but later lost when the decision was appealed. This was the beginning of a lifelong struggle against injustice, a struggle by Wells that is not widely known. Her carefully researched articles and speeches on lynching provided evidence of the organized terror faced by blacks after the Civil War. Her struggle was a lonely one; she was often the only person who seemed concerned about the injustices that were occurring. She protested the hanging of twelve black soldiers during World War I in the face of threats by secret service officials that she could be accused of treason.

Among her other accomplishments was her work as one of the founders of the NAACP.

Crusade for Justice: The Autobiography of Ida B. Wells, edited by Alfreda M. Duster (U of Chicago Pr, cloth, 1970; pap., 1972) is a valuable historical document for advanced students interested in the struggles of blacks and women.

Reading level: advanced. Literary quality: good.

George Washington Carver (1864–1943)

George Washington Carver was a skillful scientist who devoted his life to research into the agricultural problems of his people during Reconstruction. He did remarkable work in finding uses for peanuts and sweet potatoes and in improving farming practices among the poor farmers of the South. His drive to obtain an education and his sacrifice of fame and wealth to help his people make him an inspirational figure.

For many years, George Washington Carver was one of the few blacks whose lives were studied in schools and included in texts. While he was undoubtedly a great man, one wonders whether his popularity owed as much to his quiet personality and to his refusal to fight segregation as it did to his achievements as a scientist. In contrast to many biographies that oversimplify Carver's character, Rackham Holt's *George Washington Carver: An American Biography* ([1942] Doubleday, 1963) presents Carver as a rounded human being. In Holt's portrait, Carver is still a gentle, kind scientist, but he is not perfect. The biography is thorough and shows careful research.

Reading level: average. Literary quality: good.

Matthew Henson (1867–1955)

Ahdoolo! Biography of Matthew A. Henson by Floyd Miller (Dutton, 1963) and *Dark Companion: The Story of Matthew Henson* by Bradley Robinson ([1947] Fawcett World, 1967) both tell the story of the black explorer who accompanied Admiral Robert E. Peary on his expeditions to the arctic and his final discovery of the North Pole in 1909. They are exciting accounts of men facing the dangers of nature. Henson is an excellent hero: his ability to make friends with the Eskimos shows his warm heart, and a number of incidents reveal his courage and endurance.

Dark Companion is an adult biography, but the writing style is lively enough to appeal to younger students. Henson's journeys through the dangerous arctic are described vividly.

Ahdoolo! is aimed more at the younger reader, but does not develop suspense so well as *Dark Companion.* The problems of exploration are explained in some detail, and sometimes minor, less interesting incidents are given exaggerated importance. However, like the word *Ahdoolo!* which Henson coined, the book effectively expresses hope and courage.

Both accounts are marred by a rather patronizing attitude toward the Eskimo explorers who worked with Peary. *Dark Companion* does describe their contributions, though it emphasizes their "childlike qualities." Neither book notes that the Eskimos Ootah and Seegloo received absolutely no recognition either for reaching the pole or for their essential roles in the expedition, though both devote extensive space to complaints that Henson was unjustly ignored.

Ahdoolo! reading level—average; literary quality—good. *Dark Companion*: reading level—average to advanced; literary quality—very good.

W. E. B. Du Bois (1868–1963)

For over half a century W. E. B. Du Bois was an important figure in literature, scholarship, political and reform movements, and peace work. For most of his life he was a center of controversy. In 1909, he was one of the founders of the Niagara Movement, which sought to resist the overwhelming influence of Booker T. Washington. Later, Du Bois helped found the NAACP. He served for many years on its Board of Directors and edited its magazine, *The Crisis*, which campaigned against lynching and the mistreatment of black troops in World War I. Although he opposed Marcus Garvey, he was chief organizer of the Pan African Movement beginning in 1919. More than forty years later, invited by President Nkrumah to head the *Encyclopaedia Africana* project, Du Bois became a citizen of Ghana.

Among the best of the biographies and autobiographies are *His Day Is Marching On: A Memoir of W. E. B. Du Bois* by Shirley Graham Du Bois (Lippincott, 1971) and *The Autobiography of W. E. B. Du Bois: A Soliloquy on Viewing My Life from the Last Decade of Its First Century* (Intl Pub Co, cloth & pap., 1968). *Soliloquy* begins with a glowing description of communism in eastern Europe, the Soviet Union and China and a declaration of faith in communism. Not until the age of 91 did Du Bois join the Communist Party, but during the 1950s he was arrested as a foreign agent because he belonged to several peace organizations, and even though he was acquitted of that charge, was denied a passport for seven years. Du Bois suffered for his race as well as his politics, losing his only son because hospitals refused to treat him. However, *Soliloquy* is far more than a recital of troubles. The ninety-year perspective, the outspoken honesty, and the thoughtful insights of this extraordinary man make this book well worth reading.

His Day Is Marching On is as much an autobiography of Shirley Graham Du Bois as it is a memoir of her more famous husband. But then, Shirley Graham, whose contribution to adolescent literature is evident to anyone reading Chapter 3, deserves a biography of her own. This biography focuses on the last years of Du Bois' life, a period dealt with only briefly in *Soliloquy.* Written with Shirley Graham's usual lively style, it is a loving and admiring—perhaps not completely objective—portrait.

The Autobiography of W. E. B. Du Bois: A Soliloquy . . . : reading level—advanced; literary quality—excellent. *His Day Is Marching On:* reading level—average; literary quality—very good.

James Weldon Johnson (1871–1938)

See Johnson, *Along This Way,* Chapter 2.

Paul Laurence Dunbar (1872-1906)

That Dunbar Boy by Jean Gould (Dodd, 1958) is obviously written for young readers. The book emphasizes Dunbar's childhood and school years and tends to gloss over unhappier periods in his life.

The style is simple but not outstanding. The plot development is good, but the characters are all idealized. Romance and overcoming prejudice are not handled effectively. The book describes Dunbar's problems in finding a job and publishing his poetry and his early death, but it ignores his marital difficulties and minimizes his problems with discrimination.

Reading level: easy. Literary quality: good.

Mary McLeod Bethune (1875–1955)

Education was the goal of all of Mary McLeod Bethune's life. First there was the struggle to obtain her own education during the hard times of the late nineteenth century. Then for many years she strove to build a school of her own, finally succeeding with Daytona Educational and Industrial Training School in Daytona Beach,

Florida, later a part of Bethune-Cookman College. She was nationally known for her educational work and for her work to improve conditions for women, was an advisor to Franklin Roosevelt, and, in 1935, founded the National Council of Negro Women.

Catherine Owens Peare's biography, *Mary McLeod Bethune* (Vanguard, 1951), is an interesting, readable account of her life. Somewhere between a junior and adult biography, Peare's book does not focus excessively on Ms. Bethune's childhood, but it presents incidents from throughout her life with enough fictionalized detail to make them exciting. Mary McLeod Bethune's courage, determination, strength, and imagination are well portrayed, but the picture seems a little unreal, as she is rarely shown with any negative emotions or weaknesses. However, a book that emphasizes the positive is probably quite appropriate for a woman who seemed to live so successfully by that philosophy.

Reading level: average. Literary quality: good.

Marcus Garvey (1887–1940)

During the 1920s, Marcus Garvey and his United Negro Improvement Association electrified Harlem with their brilliant pageantry and their revolutionary ideas. Among Garvey's many dreams were economic independence for blacks, pride in black achievements, international cooperation among blacks, and an independent homeland for blacks in Africa, which at that time was almost entirely under European colonial rule. While Garvey's ideas are commonplace today, they were so radical at the time that they were seen as a threat both by the United States Government and by most other black leaders, particularly members of the NAACP. Garvey was a charismatic speaker, a creative thinker and organizer, and a good journalist, but he was an abysmally poor businessman. To help make his dreams of international cooperation among blacks and economic independence a reality, Garvey poured his energies into the creation of a black-owned, black-run steamship line. Plagued by almost constant accidents with its ancient, decrepit ships, the Black Star Line lost the then incredible sum of $600,000 in two years of operation, and Garvey was arrested for using the mails to defraud. Garvey was sentenced to prison and later deported. Although he continued work with the UNIA in England and Jamaica until his death, the movement declined rapidly after Garvey was deported from the U.S., though it did have some impact on Jamaican politics.

A number of biographies of Garvey are available. The three listed here are somewhat similar. All present fairly objective, balanced portraits of Garvey and his movement. *Marcus Garvey* by Daniel S. Davis (Watts, 1972) is aimed at a high school audience. Moderately easy to read, it focuses on people and events more than philosophy and analysis, and is enlivened by a number of full-page photographs. *Garvey: The Story of a Pioneer Black Nationalist* by Elton C. Fax (Dodd, 1972) and *Black Moses: The Story of Marcus Garvey and the Universal Negro Improvement Association* by E. David Cronon (2d ed. U of Wis Pr, cloth & pap., 1969) are adult books which include extensive historical and sociological background that helps put Garvey and his movement in perspective. *Black Moses* seems to be somewhat more thoroughly researched, and ends with a less positive evaluation of Garvey. *Garvey* concludes with a chapter of quotations from more recent black leaders showing their use of Garvey's ideas.

Black Moses: reading level—advanced; literary quality—good. *Garvey*: reading level—advanced; literary quality—good. *Marcus Garvey*: reading level—average; literary quality—good.

Zora Neale Hurston (1901?–1960)

She was a flamboyant star of the Harlem Renaissance, the center of attention at parties full of celebrities. She was a serious folklorist, a graduate of Barnard College, and a student of anthropologist Franz Boas. She was a dedicated and talented writer of both fiction and academic works. She was a political conservative who supported Robert Taft and opposed school integration. She died a pauper in a county welfare home. A fascinating, contradictory personality, Zora Neale Hurston was a person whose life and experiences are very meaningful for anyone interested in black culture or in the struggle of black people and women for equality, or for anyone with hopes of becoming a serious artist or scholar.

Zora Neale Hurston: A Literary Biography by Robert E. Hemenway (U of Ill Pr, 1977) is not an entertaining book for the casual reader, though portions of it do contain fascinating stories; it is a book for the thoughtful, serious student. Hemenway carefully analyzes the many forces that influenced Hurston's writing and the ways that she reacted to them. He shows the conflicts between the patronizing whites, the older black critics, and the rebellious young blacks in Harlem in the 1920s, and Zora's success in impressing all three groups while remaining faithful to her own small-town Florida traditions. Her message was the beauty and strength of rural black culture, a message that was both radical and popular at the time; but this was a message that had previously been conveyed chiefly through oral literature. Zora struggled for years to find an appropriate medium to convey her folklore to a reading public. Hemenway shows her attempts to present folk ideas in the theater, in academic circles, and in short stories and novels, and her equally difficult struggle to support herself as a writer. During the 1930s Hurston's work was finally successful, and she published several good novels and an excellent folklore collection. However, her later projects were less successful. The final portion of the book shows her still writing, but coping with failure and poverty.

Reading level: advanced. Literary quality: very good.

Langston Hughes (1902–1967)

See Hughes, *The Big Sea,* Chapter 2.

Richard Wright (1908–1960)

Richard Wright's autobiography, *Black Boy* (see Wright in Chapter 2), is one of the most powerful indictments of Jim Crow society. John A. Williams' *The Most Native of Sons: A Biography of Richard Wright* (Doubleday, 1970), a short, interesting biography, also describes Wright's experiences growing up in the South, though not in such vivid detail, and then continues his life story after Wright moved to Chicago. While in Chicago, Wright was attracted to the Communist Party because of its interest in blacks and its willingness to encourage young writers. But later he left the communists because he was no longer convinced by their ideas. In 1940, Wright suddenly became famous with the publication of *Native Son,* which he followed with the equally successful *Black Boy.* In 1946, hoping to escape the racism that still plagued him after success and after moving North, Wright emigrated to France. Although he continued to write, none of his later works were as popular in the United States as *Native Son* and *Black Boy.*

Reading level: average. Literary quality: very good.

Biographies of Moderns

Muhammad Ali

Twice winner of the world heavyweight championship, Muhammad Ali is more than a sports superstar, and *The Greatest: My Own*

Story is more than a very good sports autobiography. Ali's conversion to the Black Muslim faith, his refusal to fight in the Vietnam War, and the persecution he faced as a result of those two decisions raise important political, moral, and religious issues.

More skillfully written than most sports biographies, *The Greatest* (written with Richard Durham. Random, 1975; pap., Ballantine, 1976) begins with Ali's reaction to his defeat by Ken Norton in 1973. From his return to Louisville after the fight, the book moves to a review of Ali's early years, when his name was Cassius Clay. Ali's early life, his training for his career, his winning an Olympic Gold Medal, and his subsequent disillusionment as he returned to a still-segregated Louisville are told in exciting detail. The remainder of the book is not written chronologically, but instead focuses on specific issues: two chapters describe the development of his decision to resist the draft, one explores the reasons for the failure of his first marriage, and other chapters give his impressions of Moslem world leaders he visited, such as Libya's Chairman, Col. Muammar el-Qaddafi, and a number of major boxing figures. The last part of the book, arranged more chronologically, tells how Ali gradually regained the right to box after being barred in all states, and culminates with the title fight against George Foreman in Zaire.

For the sports fan, *The Greatest* combines vivid descriptions of sports events with thoughtful analyses of boxing techniques and personalities. For the general reader, it provides insight into the reasons for the resentment of a contemporary black person, whose religion and politics annoyed and angered some Americans. Despite the title, the book contains little of the bragging and blustering for which Ali is famous; the tone, in fact, is rather serious and almost modest. This is a book which should appeal to most students, though slow readers may find the length (over 500 pages) discouraging and may be confused by the shifting chronology.

Reading level: average. Literary quality: excellent.

Marian Anderson

My Lord, What a Morning: An Autobiography (Viking Pr, 1956) tells of Marian Anderson's career from her childhood singing in churches through her successful tours abroad and finally her debut with the Metropolitan Opera. Among the incidents that might be particularly interesting to teenagers are her unsuccessful attempts to enter an all-white school and her failure in her first

Town Hall concert. National attention focused on her in 1939, when after she was refused permission to give a concert in Constitution Hall in Washington, D.C., by the Daughters of the American Revolution, she sang instead at the Lincoln Memorial on Easter Sunday to an audience of 75,000. Most of the incidents are interesting and sometimes humorous, but there are no great climaxes.

The style is simple and direct but not outstanding. The first part of the book, which pictures a teenager finding herself and her career, is of particular value to high school students, but the section on her concert tours tends to be repetitious.

Reading level: average. Literary quality: fair.

Maya Angelou

Angelou, a talented dancer, actress, journalist, and playwright, has written several autobiographical works that have literary merit.

In *I Know Why the Caged Bird Sings* (Random, 1970; pap., Bantam, 1971) she describes her childhood in a small Southern town and in a Northern city. In a series of vivid episodes, she chronicles the sometimes delightful but usually frightening experiences of a young black girl. In Stamps, Arkansas, a strong, loving grandmother cared for the two children who had been sent from California when their parents' marriage split up. Maya Angelou recaptures the child's perspective, in her recollections of pranks and images of church, social relationships and events. Later, living with her mother, life was more traumatic. Raped by her mother's boyfriend and forced to testify at the trial, young Ritie blamed herself when her relatives killed the rapist, and she remained mute for months until she was shipped back home to her grandmother. There she regained her spirits, and learned to cope with prejudiced white people.

The second volume, *Gather Together in My Name* (Random, 1974; pap., Bantam, 1975) continues her story through young adulthood. The first volume ends when she discovers she is pregnant. In the second book, a teenage girl tries to find work and love while caring for her infant son. As a dancer and a waitress, during a short stint in a whorehouse, and as manager of a restaurant, Maya Angelou has lived a hard life, but a proud, indomitable spirit pervades all.

Both volumes are books that most readers will find very hard to put down. Even in the most distressing circumstances, Angelou shows the capacity of the human being for resourcefulness and for love.

Reading level: average. Literary quality: excellent.

Arthur Ashe

Arthur Ashe: Tennis Champion by Louis Robinson, Jr. (Doubleday, 1970) is a junior biography of the famous tennis player, focusing on Ashe's childhood and the development of his interest and skill in tennis. It describes the hard work and sacrifices needed for success and the conflicts of operating in a previously segregated world.

Arthur Ashe: Portrait in Motion by Arthur Ashe with Frank Deford (HM, 1975; pap., Ballantine, 1976) is a diary of one year in Ashe's life, Wimbledon to Wimbledon, 1973–74. Ashe appears as a thoughtful, sensitive, intelligent person confronting the physically and psychologically demanding schedule of a pro tennis player. Among the other conflicts reported in the book are his decision to accept an invitation to South Africa, the fight against the banning of Nikki Pilic from Wimbledon, and his decision not to marry the woman he courts throughout the book. It is a frank and open discussion of Ashe's thoughts and feelings on a wide variety of subjects.

The two books will appeal to different audiences. *Tennis Champion* is a typical junior biography, an easy-to-read interesting story. *Portrait in Motion* is a book for more mature readers interested in deeper insights into a person and a sport.

Arthur Ashe: Portrait in Motion: reading level—easy; literary quality—average. *Arthur Ashe: Tennis Champion*: reading level—easy; literary quality—average.

Daisy Bates

In 1954, the Supreme Court declared segregation in public schools unconstitutional, a decision that has now been resisted by various school districts throughout the country for over twenty years. One of the most dramatic situations was in Little Rock, Arkansas, where it took the United States Army to get nine black students into Central High School. *The Long Shadow of Little Rock* by Daisy Bates (McKay, 1962) is the story of frightened but courageous high school students facing a dangerous mob, and of black parents who supported them. As president of the NAACP State Conference of Branches and a leader of the integration movement, Bates was arrested on the basis of a hastily passed ordinance, had two crosses burned on her lawn, and had rocks and shots fired into her house.

But the battle to get the students into the school was only the beginning. During the second half of the book, Ms. Bates bitterly describes the systematic destruction of the nine students by the mob that carried signs cheering "One down, eight to go." First, Minnijean was suspended when she finally fought back against constant attacks. Arrangements were made for her to continue schooling in New York. Jefferson Thomas suffered constant physical attacks, including one which knocked him unconscious. Gloria Ray was psychologically abused by constant threats. The families were also attacked. Three parents lost their jobs. Whites who supported them were also attacked. Two were finally hounded until they committed suicide; others left town.

Twenty years later, it is still disturbing to read this story, with its still unanswered closing question: "How long, how long?"

Reading level: average. Literary quality: very good.

E. R. Braithwaite

Though not about an American, E. R. Braithwaite's autobiographical account, *To Sir, with Love,* became popular in this country through a film version starring Sidney Poitier (P–H, 1960; pap., Pyramid Pubns, 1973). Braithwaite has written a beautiful book about the problems and joys of a black teacher from British Guiana, teaching in a school for difficult teenagers in a white slum in London. Parts of the book deal with effects of the race problem, among them Braithwaite's failure to secure employment in the fields for which he was trained and the obstacles he encountered when he decided to marry a white teacher. But the author focuses on his attempts to win the respect of his students and to develop their own self-respect.

Braithwaite's understanding of his students and his concern for them make him a person young people and adults can admire and like. Characters are portrayed with depth and feeling, and the pace of the narrative is sustained throughout.

Reading level: average. Literary quality: excellent.

Claude Brown

The autobiography *Manchild in the Promised Land* is controversial (Macmillan, 1965; pap., NAL, 1971). My students' reactions ranged from "It was one of the best books I have ever read," to "Books like that shouldn't be written."

Like *The Autobiography of Malcolm X, Manchild* pictures the squalor, crime, and terror of life in the ghetto. The descriptions of delinquent acts performed by three- to six-year-old boys are shocking. Although at times Brown seems to glory in the excitement of crime and delinquency, his primary attitude is relief and thankfulness for having escaped the horrors of the ghetto. What the author tells of his friends who were trapped by dope addiction or organized crime should be a warning to any prospective delinquent.

Manchild in the Promised Land provides a psychological and sociological study of the ghetto that would be significant for mature students. The conditions described in this book help explain the explosiveness of segregated slums in recent years. Brown's writing style is competent but not outstanding. The narrative jumps around, and too much of it is spent on reminiscence. But the overall impact is so powerful that weaknesses in style are scarcely noticed.

Reading level: advanced. Literary quality: good.

Roy Campanella

Although Roy Campanella's sports fame is now history, his autobiography has much to recommend it to high school students. It concerns one of the first blacks in major league baseball, a man who overcame many handicaps, even before an auto accident put him in a wheelchair. Campanella faced prejudice as a boy and later encountered opposition from his parents when he tried to enter baseball. For nine years he had to be content with the Negro and South American Leagues before getting a chance to play in the majors.

The great faith and courage reflected in Campanella's autobiography, *It's Good to Be Alive* (Little, 1959; pap., NAL, n.d.), make it a valuable and inspirational book. A good style adds to its attraction. Jackie Robinson, in his autobiography, *Wait till Next Year*, discusses Campanella's refusal to become involved in civil rights. An interesting assignment might be to compare the two ballplayers' personalities.

Reading level: average. Literary quality: good.

Wilt Chamberlain

Wilt Chamberlain is one of the all-time greats of pro basketball. Over seven feet tall, he created a well-deserved sensation when he played his first NBA game in 1959. In his more than ten years as a superstar he broke records for points scored and for money earned.

In *Wilt: Just Like Any Other 7-Foot Black Millionaire Who Lives Next Door* by Wilt Chamberlain and David Shaw (Macmillan, 1973; pap., Warner Bks, 1975) Chamberlain describes his childhood (which was not quite poverty-stricken) and the development of his skill, his competitive instinct, his determination, and his height. He then tells of his college career in Kansas, where he claims to have integrated every restaurant in the area, of his year with the Globetrotters, during which his exploits off the court chasing women rivaled his actions on the court, and finally of his lengthy career with the NBA. The book is filled with high-spirited bragging, humorous accounts of his pranks, and descriptions of team camaraderie and squabbles. A flaw in the book is the amount of space Chamberlain gives to refuting rumors and criticisms which have long since been forgotten. Overall, however, his is a lively, enjoyable book.

Reading level: average. Literary quality: good.

Angela Davis

Angela Davis: An Autobiography (Random, 1974; pap., Bantam, 1975) is a fascinating book by an interesting person. It reads more like a novel than most of the biographies of contemporary political figures. Davis begins with her attempts to elude the police during a suspenseful search, and then presents a detailed picture of her experiences in prison. The second part of the autobiography traces her early life and the beginnings of her involvement in Marxist movements and the black liberation struggle. Unfortunately, a few teachers report that parents object to students reading a book by an avowed communist.

Reading level: average. Literary quality: very good.

Sammy Davis, Jr.

For high school students, the chief drawback of singer-actor Sammy Davis, Jr.'s highly interesting autobiography is its length. But it includes so many engrossing episodes, told in such a lively, humorous style, that students read it despite its 650 pages. *Yes I Can: The Story of Sammy Davis, Jr.* written with Jane and Burt Boyar (FS&G, 1965; pap., PB, 1972) revolves around show business. It begins with three-year-old Sammy's first performances on the stage with his father, includes his adjustment to the loss of an eye during the height of his career, and ends with his celebrated appearances on Broadway and in films. A major theme is the constant struggle of a black entertainer against white prejudice, on as well as off the stage. Teenagers who dream of stage careers are bound to realize from this autobiography that having influential friends, as well as talent and luck, helps in show business. It was commendable of Frank Sinatra to fight the management so that Sammy could enter a nightclub, but, unfortunately, not every black is a friend of Frank Sinatra.

Reading level: average. Literary quality: good.

Katherine Dunham

Although *A Touch of Innocence* ([1959] HarBraceJ, 1969) is the autobiography of Katherine Dunham, a dancer whose troupe introduced black folk dances to Americans, it is not a career book. Instead it is a sensitive study of a girl growing up. The problems of attaining adulthood are compounded for Katherine by the death of her mother, and later, the estrangement of her father from the rest of the family. The quarrels among various branches of her family, which ranged from almost white to almost black, created another special problem. The story follows her life from birth through the various interesting places she lived to adulthood, when she moved away from home and got her first job.

A Touch of Innocence is a beautifully written book with poetic descriptions that only occasionally appear a bit overdone. Katherine's story of her struggles to find values is an exploration into the deeper levels of her personality as a child and adolescent. Although this is not a book with wide appeal, it is valuable for helping shy teenagers see that other people share the kinds of thoughts they have.

African Rhythm—American Dance: A Biography of Katherine Dunham by Terry Harnan (Knopf, 1974) is an easy-to-read but superficial biography of Katherine Dunham for younger readers. It outlines her story well, describing the development of her interest in dance, her research in the West Indies that provided the background for much of her work, and the success of her dance group, as well as the hard work and relentless pace which success requires. This book would be the best choice for someone interested in information about her career.

African Rhythm, American Dance: reading level—easy; literary quality—good. *A Touch of Innocence:* reading level—advanced; literary quality—very good.

Julius Erving

"He handles a basketball the way the average person handles a tennis ball," writes Marty Bell of Julius Erving, an exciting basketball star who began his pro career in 1971 with the Richmond, Virginia Squires. *The Legend of Dr. J.: The Story of Julius Erving* by Marty Bell (Coward, 1975; pap., NAL, 1976) is different from most sports biographies because it focuses more on Erving's impact on fans and on the sport than it does on his personal life and feelings. To some extent it lacks the human interest touches of an autobiography or authorized biography, but it provides some unique perspectives on the life of a basketball player. Vivid descriptions of Erving's style capture the excitement he generates in fans, and some of the most interesting parts of the book are interviews in which fans share their own excitement of watching Doctor J.

The Legend of Dr. J. is definitely for basketball fans; it does not have the more general appeal of books like *The Greatest* or *Foul.* It is short and full of lively descriptions of basketball action.

Reading level: average. Literary quality: good.

Medgar Evers

For Us, the Living, by Mrs. Medgar Evers with William Peters (Doubleday, 1967), is a moving and disturbing book. Medgar Evers worked for eight years in the 1950s and early 1960s as state field secretary for Mississippi for the NAACP, during a time when economic pressures, intimidation, and sometimes murder were used against blacks who tried to vote, petition for integration or join the NAACP. After years of threats Evers was assassinated in 1963.

The story is told vividly, simply, and frankly by his wife. After an exciting description of their childhoods and courtship, Mrs. Evers tells of Medgar's growing interest in and concern for the black sharecroppers who lived in hopeless poverty in the Mississippi Delta. She talks about her own opposition to his work at the beginning, when their own poverty seemed enough of a burden and when Evers' opposition to segregation threatened to destroy what little they had. She describes her growing pride in a man who could stand up against a system dedicated to the oppression of black people, and then the fears of knowing that he and perhaps the whole family would almost inevitably be killed. *For Us, the Living* is hard to put down. It is a beautiful portrait of courage and compassion as well as a chronicle of insane racism.

Reading level: average. Literary quality: excellent.

Althea Gibson

Althea Gibson became famous as a tennis star in the 1950s. Her autobiography, *I Always Wanted to Be Somebody* (Har-Row, 1958; pap., Noble, 1967), though not so thoroughly developed as many others, provides very interesting reading. She tells of her childhood as a Harlem tomboy, her life in a small town in the South, and her fight against the prejudice that barred her from playing in national tennis matches. After she achieves success, the story of her wins, her losses, and her various tours becomes somewhat routine, though accounts of her international tours add interest. Althea Gibson is an exciting personality whom teenagers can identify with.

Reading level: average. Literary quality: good.

Nikki Giovanni

Nikki Giovanni's *Gemini: An Extended Autobiographical Statement of My First Twenty-Five Years of Being a Black Poet* (Bobbs, 1971; pap., Penguin, 1976) is a confusing, contradictory book full of life and ideas. It is a collection of essays ranging from personal recollections of her grandmother and the birth of her son, to critical studies of black writers and music, to theories about race and revolution. In style, these range from straightforward, autobiographical narrative to experimental prose. In feeling and attitude, too, the essays show the full range of human emotions of a person who is both sensitive and hardened against anything that will detract from the revolution, who can call for the overthrow of white society, but who can also make practical suggestions for cleaning New York's subways.

There is something in *Gemini* for everyone. Universal experiences of family solidarity, childhood, and childbirth are described in a warm, friendly style in "400 Mulvaney St.," "For a Four-Year-Old," and "Don't Have a Baby till You Read This." Thought-provoking essays on oppression and the contrasts between black and white culture—"On Being Asked What It's Like to Be Black" and "The Weather as a Cultural Determiner"—show Giovanni as a master of the standard essay form. In "Convalescence—Compares to What?" and "Gemini—A Prolonged Autobiographical Statement on Why," the strident militant appears with a prose that combines myth, pun, and hyperbole for a powerful, almost poetic effect.

Reading level: advanced. Literary quality: excellent.

Ruby Berkley Goodwin

Life for a black girl in a small coal-mining town in southern Illinois was not easy. In her early years, described in *It's Good to Be Black* ([1953] pap., S Ill U Pr, 1976), there were mine disasters, there was sickness, there was poverty, and there was discrimination. But in addition, there was a true community that cared about its members; there were kind, friendly, and honest people of all races; and there were parents who could give their children love, strength, and models to imitate. In the introduction, Ruby Goodwin states,

> Until I once argued with a psychology teacher, I didn't know that all Negro children grow up with a sense of frustration and insecurity.... The philosophy behind this remark, however, I have since found implied in most books about Negroes. Whether the authors are black or white, they are equally guilty of representing us either as objects of pity or as objects of contempt...

While Goodwin is avowedly trying to counter the stereotypes of black childhood as deprived and sordid, her autobiography is honest rather than sentimental. The episodes range from descriptions of ordinary events such as a baptism and a carnival to character sketches to suspense-filled stories of murder. The style is not difficult, and the structure of the book lends itself to use of excerpts.

Reading level: easy. Literary quality: excellent.

Dick Gregory

Dick Gregory's *Nigger: An Autobiography,* written with Robert Lipsyte (Dutton, 1964; pap., PB, 1965), shows the effects of poverty on a boy's life and the hunger for both food and respect that accompanies poverty. The starkness of Gregory's early years is emphasized by his daydreams and his excessive pride in such a little thing as a clean Band-Aid. Gregory tells how he learned to bluff, to pretend, and to laugh—skills he would use later as an entertainer and campaigner for equality for blacks.

Nigger is written with considerable skill, at times using a modified stream-of-consciousness technique, and is always vivid and detailed. The ravaging effects of ghetto poverty are certainly not minimized, but neither are they exaggerated in this outstanding book.

Up from Nigger (Stein & Day, 1976; pap., Fawcett World, 1978) by Dick Gregory with James R. McGraw, continues Gregory's story after success as he climbs, not only financially but emotionally and spiritually, above the status of "nigger" and the "monster ... created within me by an oppressive and unjust social and political system." A self-confident book, occasionally bordering on good-humored egotism, *Up from Nigger* is full of Gregory's famous wit and unfailing spirit. But it is a serious book, too, devoting most of its space to Gregory's deep concern for justice, human rights, and most of all to his commitment to feeding the hungry. Gregory marched, ran, fasted, went to jail, sat-in, prayed-in, fished-in, and joked for the causes he believed in. He transported thousands of turkeys to Mississippi for Christmas, ran for President, and helped cool a riot in Watts.

Up from Nigger provides a model of a committed, dedicated individual whose personal courage contributed to a number of battles on many issues. In addition, it is an exciting, enjoyable book.

Nigger: reading level—average; literary quality—excellent. *Up from Nigger*: reading level—average; literary quality: excellent.

Connie Hawkins

Foul: The Connie Hawkins Story by David Wolf (HR&W, 1972; pap., Warner Bks, 1972) is the familiar ghetto-to-superstar story, but with problems and grief along the way. A poor, shy, lonely boy, Connie Hawkins had no abilities or advantages except for his extraordinary skill at basketball. Colleges from all over the country offered him all kinds of illegal inducements, but Connie was so poorly prepared for college that he did not last the first year. Another blow struck him his freshman year; he was accused of being involved in a point-fixing scandal. Although not himself convicted, he was cited in evidence against the major gamblers, and his reputation was ruined. For eight years, no National Basketball Association team would touch him, and he was forced to play for less prestigious and lower-paying teams. Finally he filed an antitrust suit against the NBA which allowed him the opportunity of clearing his name. The NBA settled for a contract and over a million dollars.

Most of *Foul* is interesting and well written. Although long (over 500 pages) it is a good mixture of personal interest, basketball activities, and insights into the obstacles to success faced by a ballplayer from the ghetto. Occasionally, however, the author's defense of the poor little deprived boy who couldn't be expected to learn to read or turn down bribes sounds somewhat patronizing.

Reading level: average. Literary quality: good.

Lena Horne

"They've never been given a chance to see a Negro woman as a woman. You've got to give them that chance," Count Basie once said to the singer-actress Lena Horne. Lena Horne was one of the first black performers to refuse to be stereotyped. A childhood that alternated between high society and lower class life gave her an independence of public opinion. Yet in escaping the stereotype, she was forced to look within herself for her identity as a woman, a performer, and a black.

Lena, by Lena Horne with Richard Schickel (Doubleday, 1965), is an interesting autobiography with information about the person as well as the performer. Lena's unusual background and childhood as well as her interracial marriage add interest. The style, though not unusual, is competent.

Reading level: average. Literary quality: very good.

George Jackson

George Jackson summarizes his life in this passage from *Soledad Brother: The Prison Letters of George Jackson* (Coward, 1970; pap., Bantam, 1970).

> When I was accused of robbing a gas station of seventy dollars, I accepted a deal—I agreed to confess and spare the county court costs in return for a light county jail sentence. I confessed but when time came for sentencing, they tossed me into the penitentiary with one to life. That was in 1960. I was 18 years old. I've been here ever since. I met Marx, Lenin, Trotsky, Engels, and Mao when I entered prison and they redeemed me . . . I met black guerillas, George "Big Jake" Lewis, and James Carr, W. L. Nolen, Bill Christmas, Torry B. Gibson and many, many others. We attempted to transform the black criminal mentality into a black revolutionary mentality.

> As a result, each of us has been subjected to years of the most vicious reactionary violence by the state. Our mortality rate is almost what you would expect to find in a history of Dachau (p. 26).

His story is told in a series of letters to the meaningful people in his life. The letters show clearly how a revolutionary mentality can develop out of the bitter experiences of prison and the systematic dehumanization of prisoners.

While fairly easy to read, this book is more appropriate for mature students. Immature students may either dismiss Jackson as paranoid or uncritically accept him as an expert on economics and foreign affairs. Mature students should be able to recognize and admire Jackson as a man struggling to maintain his integrity and to grow as a human being in a system that is as destructive of manhood as slavery. They should be able to empathize with the daily struggle to find meaning in a life from which all external forms of meaning have been removed. Both as the record of a strong and sensitive individual and as an exposition of black militant philosophy, *Soledad Brother* is well worth reading.

Reading level: average. Literary quality: very good.

Martin Luther King, Jr.

Dr. Martin Luther King, Jr., the leading spokesperson for the nonviolent civil rights struggle, has inspired a number of biographies, many of which were written either to attack or to support his nonviolent philosophy. As a young minister, King became the leader of the Montgomery, Alabama, bus boycott, one of the first successful mass movements in support of civil rights. During the next decade, his philosophy of nonviolent direct action and his dynamic personality inspired peaceful marches, sit-ins, freedom rides, and boycotts against an increasingly violent white opposition, and eventually culminated in his assassination. At the beginning of his struggle, King was supported by most blacks but attacked by many whites, who considered him a radical troublemaker. Toward the end of his career, many blacks began to reject his nonviolence and to insist on confronting violence with violence, but whites, after hearing Malcolm X, began to respect King.

Biographies of King range from almost worshipful to harshly critical. Lerone Bennett, Jr.'s *What Manner of Man: A Biography of Martin Luther King, Jr., 1929–1968* (Johnson Chi, 1968; pap., PB, n.d.) is one of the finest of the positive biographies. It is a thorough, adult work. Written with depth and insight, it traces the influences that helped King develop his commitment to nonviolent resistance: his family background, his education, and the events that led to the founding of the movement. This extensively illustrated book is excellent for advanced students who would like to investigate the philosophical background of King's movement.

King's own brief autobiographical book, *Why We Can't Wait* (Har-Row, 1964; pap., NAL, n.d.), is a more factual, less philosophical account of the early days of the Montgomery and Birmingham campaigns. A well written, readable account, the book provides an inside view of King's strategy and philosophy. Two of King's other books, *Where Do We Go From Here? Chaos or Community* (Har-Row, 1967; pap., Beacon Pr, n.d.) and *Stride Toward Freedom: The Montgomery Story* (Har-Row, 1958) contain both autobiographical information and King's theories.

My Life with Martin Luther King, Jr. ([1969] pap., Avon, 1970) is a pleasant, detailed autobiography of Coretta Scott King, which, of course, also tells her husband's story. The pride and honors, and the terrors of a bombed home and constant threats are described in detail.

A quite different version of the King story is told in *The King God Didn't Save: Reflections on the Life and Death of Martin Luther King* by John A. Williams (Coward, 1970). This book is an in-depth analysis of both the weaknesses and the strengths of King's philosophy and movement, rather than a life story. Williams believes that King underestimated the evil he faced and compromised too quickly during most of his life. He explores the hypothesis that King was largely a media-created phenomenon, speculates on the extent to which the threat of blackmail influenced King's behavior, and scathingly attacks the role of religious groups in King's campaign and their relationship to blacks in general. But he also points out the key role that King's campaign played in training young black leadership, in stimulating new movements, and in providing models for young blacks, of qualities to emulate and to avoid. "Martin King was no saint," Williams concludes, "But would a saint have fared better?"

The King God Didn't Save is a well written, carefully researched biography for the student who wants to read not just a life story but a careful analysis of the successes and failures of King's movement.

To Kill a Black Man by Louis E. Lomax (Holloway, pap., 1968) is a comparative biography of Martin Luther King and Malcolm X. In the similarities and differences between their lives, Lomax examines the issues that separated them and the personal as well as political reasons for their positions. The men and the political structure surrounding them are examined critically. Lomax finds King's eloquent expressions of love unrealistic, but considers Malcolm X's totally anti-white program equally unacceptable. He seems to feel that both were moving toward closer agreement when they were assassinated. His conjectures about the assassinations may interest students, especially in the light of recent reinvestigations into the assassinations of the 1960s.

All titles cited here: reading level—average; literary quality—very good.

Malcolm X

The Autobiography of Malcolm X, written with Alex Haley (Grove, pap., 1965), is a disturbing book about the spiritual growth of the militant advocate of black nationalism. The ideas of Malcolm X are so different from those of white middle class culture that they seemed bizarre to many readers when they first appeared in print, but they have influenced current thinking about racial issues in the United States. Those who can read critically, yet with an open mind, will finish this book with greater insight into history, world problems, and America's race problem.

Born in Omaha as Malcolm Little in 1925, Malcolm X grew up intimately acquainted with the problems of ghetto living and, like many boys, found that there was almost no legal way for a black man to make a good living. The description of his life of crime is so vivid that the first 150 pages of the book are almost a series of how-to-do-it lessons on burglary, gambling, pimping, and assorted other "hustles." While in prison, Malcolm X joined the Black Muslims, and soon became one of their leaders, but later founded a rival organization. Finally, on a pilgrimage to Mecca, he accepted the teachings of orthodox Islam and announced a new belief that there could be brotherhood between black and white. He was assassinated in 1965 by men who may have been Black Muslims.

The Autobiography of Malcolm X is an important book that Americans need to read, but students should be guided by a mature teacher who can keep them from being sidetracked by the descriptions of crime and the internal problems of the Black Muslims. (See the "Suggested Lesson Plan for Chapter One of *The Autobiography . . .* " in Chapter 7. For another study of Malcolm X, see *To Kill a Black Man*, under Martin Luther King, Jr., in this section.)

Reading level: average. Literary quality: very good.

Thurgood Marshall

Thurgood Marshall, Fighter for Justice by Lewis H. Fenderson (McGraw, 1969) tells for young readers the story of a man who won a number of victories for civil rights in American courts and became the first black man appointed to the United States Supreme Court. As the author describes incidents from Marshall's childhood, he develops the concept of rights and the conflicts blacks faced when their rights were violated. Obviously designed as an educational book, it mixes interesting incidents with explanations of the judicial system and legal terminology incorporated into the dialogue and narrative. The result is not a literary masterpiece, but is quite interesting, and an excellent introduction to and explanation of the legal aspects of the civil rights struggle. Several historic cases are described in detail, as are Marshall's financial problems and disappointments in working for the NAACP instead of in private practice.

Reading level: easy. Literary quality: good.

Willie Mays

Willie Mays, the home-run-hitting Giants outfielder, was a favorite of baseball fans for several years. The conversational, reminiscent style of *Willie Mays: My Life in and out of Baseball,* as told to Charles Einstein (Reprint of 1966 edition, Dutton, 1972), often captures the humor, innocence, and high spirits which created the Willie Mays legend. At times, the book rambles through seemingly unconnected events that never establish any point. Mays seems unconcerned about his image and relates in detail many of his problems and quarrels.

Reading level: average. Literary quality: good.

Anne Moody

Coming of Age in Mississippi: An Autobiography by Anne Moody ([1968] pap., Dell, 1970) is one of the finest books for understanding the civil rights movement of the 1960s. The biography describes the life of an ordinary black person in Mississippi before the civil rights struggle and the exhausting mental and physical strain young black activists experienced during the struggle for voting rights. However, in addition to being a valuable historical record, it is a very well written, engrossing life story. It describes the family, school, and church life of a young, poor black girl and her growing awareness of discrimination. As she grew older, Anne became interested in the struggle for civil rights for blacks, but had trouble finding someone who would even tell her what the NAACP was. When she herself became active, her mother warned her that the sheriff had told her that Anne had better not ever come home if she was going to be involved with that organization. But she persisted, participating in sit-ins, voter registration drives, and rallies. While she continued the struggle, the constant harassment, murders, and beatings left her feeling quite disillusioned.

Reading level: average. Literary quality: very good.

Pauli Murray

Proud Shoes: The Story of an American Family by Pauli Murray (Reprint of 1956 edition, Reprint, 1973), is a spirited book affirming the right of blacks to be proud of themselves, their race, and their ancestors. The author tells of four generations of her family. In her carefully researched story, there is a lot of information not generally known about blacks before and during the Civil War. Her grandmother was the black concubine of a white slaveowner. Her great-grandfather, a freedman, had married a white woman and had been a prosperous farmer, but they struggled to succeed in a world that did not accept them. It was her grandfather of whom she was the most proud, for despite ill health and bad eyesight, he had served with the Union Army during the Civil War and had taught in freedmen's schools after the war. Every aspect of these stories is portrayed with great sympathy and understanding.

Proud Shoes is well written; the characters, even the minor ones, are as alive as they were in the child's imagination. The book should be very valuable to both white and black students, who have too few opportunities to read about the accomplishments of ordinary blacks in Civil War times.

Reading level: average. Literary quality: good.

Huey P. Newton

Revolutionary Suicide by Huey P. Newton (HarBraceJ, 1973; pap., Ballantine, 1974) is a powerful and disturbing book. In it, Newton describes the events and thoughts that led him to revolutionary action and that made him consider revolution suicidal. Newton thoughtfully and carefully presents his story, using objective reporting and rational argument rather than propaganda and polemics. As a child, Newton began to recognize the experiences that stunt the growth of many black youths: the experiences that allowed him to reach his last year of high school as a functional illiterate and that made school a daily battle. As a college student, Newton tried to find a way of remaining loyal to his friends on the block while using his education and knowledge to work for black power.

The Black Panther Party grew out of these thoughts and experiences and study with Bobby Seale. Newton explains the goals and projects of the Black Panthers, and then he details the systematic attack on the party by white law-enforcement agencies. He describes how he was shot by a policeman and then accused of murder. He spent thirty-three brutal months in prison before the case was dismissed. The book ends with many of Newton's companions dead or imprisoned, but with Newton still hopeful: "We will touch God's heart; we will touch the people's heart, and together we will move the mountain."

Reading level: advanced. Literary quality: very good.

Gordon Parks

The world-famous photographer Gordon Parks explains the title of his autobiography, *A Choice of Weapons* (Har-Row, 1966; pap., Har-Row, 1973), in the prologue to this powerful, extraordinary book. As he watches the death of a man in a gas chamber, Parks recalls the period in his own life when he could easily have selected weapons that would have led him to that same chamber. The autobiography describes his choice of different weapons that kept him intact in a dangerous world.

His first choice of weapons was given him by his brother, who lay dying of an incurable disease. "I don't know why you're so mad at the world. You can't whip it the way you're going. It's too big. If you're going to fight it, use your brain. It's got a lot more power than your fists." After the death of his mother, Gordon moved from Kansas to live with his sister and brother-in-law in Minnesota, but he was soon kicked out of the house. In a second act of choice, he started to rob a trolley conductor with a knife, but at the last moment, offered the knife for sale and rejected that weapon. Playing the piano in a whorehouse, working in a diner, Parks tried to support himself well enough to stay in high school. Throughout months of cold, hunger, and poverty, Parks explored the use of violence and of brains to react to the frequent insults he received.

Later in Harlem, he stumbled into organized crime and found the anti-white speakers he heard were making a lot of sense. "White people were making it easy for me to hate white people."

Later, while working on a train, Parks discovered photography. He quickly learned photographic techniques, and then learned how to combat prejudice, discrimination, and suffering with film. His photographs in *Life* magazine helped educate the country to the cruelties of poverty.

Reading level: average. Literary quality: very good.

Adam Clayton Powell, Jr.

Adam by Adam (Dial, 1971) is the lively autobiography of the late Adam Clayton Powell, Jr., the controversial congressman. A man full of contrasts, Powell was a spiritual leader, pastor of one of the largest churches in the country, but was more widely known as a playboy who loved women and wealth. He organized protest marches, rent strikes, and bus boycotts in Harlem during the 1930s and '40s, fought almost alone for equality and fair employment practices in the House of Representatives during the 1950s, and was expelled from the House during the 1960s, when his civil rights causes were becoming fashionable.

Adam by Adam describes Powell's happy childhood, the development of his deep, if somewhat unorthodox, religious faith, his participation in early nonviolent action in Harlem, several significant issues and battles he was involved in with Congress, and the attacks he faced from both the IRS and the House during the 1960s. It closes with his ideas on black power. A generally well-written book, *Adam by Adam* conveys well the irrepressible congressman's wit and self-confidence. However, while the reading level is not difficult, the author assumes more knowledge of recent history than many readers who were not born during the 1950s and barely remember the 1960s will have.

Reading level: average. Literary quality: good.

A. Philip Randolph

A. Philip Randolph is best known as the organizer and leader of the Brotherhood of Sleeping Car Porters in their fight for recognition by the Pullman Company, but he championed black people's rights in a number of situations for many years. During the 1920s, he published a radical paper, *The Messenger*. After leading the Sleeping Car Porters to victory as a powerful, predominantly black union, Randolph fought within the AFL against discrimination. During World War II, Randolph threatened to lead a march of 100,000 people against Washington unless segregation in the armed forces was ended. Almost twenty years later, in 1963, Randolph was a major organizer of the civil rights movement's March on Washington.

A. Philip Randolph: A Biographical Portrait by Jervis P. Anderson and Peter Stone (HarBraceJ, 1973; pap., HarBraceJ, 1974) is a thorough, somewhat scholarly biography. It is a well-written book, but the detailed account of events and the many quotations make it suitable for the mature, serious reader. It provides a thorough description of Randolph's strategies for reaching his goal and their results and offers a useful historical perspective for contemporary civil rights struggles.

Reading level: advanced. Literary quality: good.

Jacob L. Reddix

A Voice Crying in the Wilderness: The Memoirs of Jacob L. Reddix (U Pr of Miss, 1974) is the success story of a family which, in three generations, rose from slavery to include a president of Jackson State College. Reddix devotes the first section of his book to his grandparents, who after Emancipation were fortunate and enterprising enough to homestead in a wilderness area of Mississippi and build a successful business. Both Reddix and his ancestors were blessed with ambition, determination and good fortune. Even as slaves, Reddix's ancestors were better treated than most, and their section of Mississippi, where the plantation system was never entrenched, was less repressive than others. The second half of the book, which focuses in detail on the development of curriculum and policy at Jackson State College, is of more interest to educators and to natives of Mississippi than to the general reader.

Reading level: average. Literary quality: good.

Jackie Robinson

As the first black to play in major league baseball, Jackie Robinson needed courage, determination, and the ability to remain calm under pressure, as well as superior skill as a ball-player. He endured prejudice from teammates and vicious verbal abuse from opposing teams and fans, and survived death threats and an attempt by one team to organize a strike against him. For two years, Robinson not only had to live with constant abuse and play outstanding baseball, but he was under strict orders to hold his tongue and absorb insults without retaliating. He was remarkably successful. He was named "Rookie of the Year" in 1948, and by the end of that year, other blacks were entering the major leagues with little comment. Robinson continued to grow as a ball-player and began to demand recognition of his rights. Soon he became known as much for his ability to unnerve the other team with his biting tongue and his daring attempts to steal bases as for his hitting and running ability.

Jackie Robinson of the Brooklyn Dodgers by Milton J. Shapiro ([1957] pap., Archway, n.d.) describes in detail the events that led to Jackie Robinson's historic breakthrough, the pressures from blacks and civil rights groups, and the support of key baseball leaders, as well as the many forces opposing blacks. Now, thirty years after Robinson's historic career, his story is still exciting, and a revealing study of a successful fight against prejudice. Shapiro's biography is short and easy, and should appeal to both young and older readers.

Reading level: easy to average. Literary quality: average.

Bill Russell

The six-foot-ten center for the Boston Celtics was one of the first of the giant basketball stars. As a boy, Russell was frustrated and unsuccessful in school and sports. Later, as a professional basketball player, he knew the excitement of success and the loneliness of fame. The opening lines of Bill Russell's autobiography, *Go Up for Glory* ([1966] Noble, pap., 1968), express his philosophy:

> There are no alibis in this book.
> There are no untruths.
> There is, within these pages, only a view of the world as I see it.

The candid, conversational style in which the book is written makes Russell's personality clear. Too much space is given to his personal complaints, but Russell discusses serious questions such as proper attitudes toward athletics and segregation. Highly fragmented, skipping from one event to another, the book is not a chronology but a series of memories of the important moments in Russell's life to that time.

Reading level: average. Literary quality: good.

Gale Sayers

I Am Third, by Gale Sayers with Al Silverman (Viking Pr, 1970; pap., Bantam, n.d.), is a reasonably good autobiography of a successful football star who joined the Chicago Bears in 1965.

Although this book is known for the chapter about Sayers' roommate, Brian Piccolo, whose death from cancer became the subject of a television drama, *Brian's Song, I Am Third* contains a number of other interesting chapters. The first section is devoted to Sayers' determined efforts to make a comeback after a serious knee injury in 1968. The second part describes his early life, and the third section is devoted to his experiences as a professional football player.

One important aspect of this book is Sayers' account of his positive relationships with other players and coaches, both black and white, as well as his model family life. The title comes from his motto, "The Lord is first, my friends are second, and I am third." While not a particularly religious book, it does have appeal to students who still have hope for brotherhood and who believe that success should reward hard work and persistence.

Reading level: easy. Literary quality: good.

Willie Stone (Pseudonym)

I Was a Black Panther by Chuck Moore (Doubleday, 1970) is an easy-to-read account of a high school student, real name not given, who was active in SNCC and then helped to form a New York chapter of the Black Panthers. Unfortunately, in his attempts to keep reading level easy, the author also keeps the intellectual level low. Events are summarized very briefly, and while many philosophical issues are raised, the author describes Stone's conversion from one viewpoint to another in one or two sentences. As a result, the Black Panthers appear to be little more than a teenage gang out for kicks. Any student who can read at higher than a fourth grade level should be steered to *Revolutionary Suicide* instead. This book might be useful, however, for very slow readers or for students who have a good enough understanding of black militant groups to appreciate seeing major events and personalities through the perspective of a high school student.

Reading level: easy. Literary quality: poor.

Ethel Waters

If ever a child was born in a hopeless environment, it was Ethel Waters. Her mother was a twelve-year-old rape victim, and the grandmother who raised her worked at jobs where she had to sleep in, leaving her children to care for themselves. Two cousins in the home died in early childhood. But intelligence, talent, a number of loving people, and a strong religious faith gave Ethel the strength to survive.

The title of her autobiography, *His Eye Is on the Sparrow,* is a line from a gospel song which emphasizes that God cares for all His creatures, an idea which permeates her book.

When Ethel Waters began her career as a singer in the Negro theater circuit in 1917, the toughness she had gained from her early life enabled her to cope with the almost unbelievable working conditions. The most harrowing experience was an automobile accident in which she almost lost her leg. Fortunately, Ethel's voice gained her quick recognition, and in less than ten years, her blues songs were among the most famous acts in theater. The last half of the book provides an inside look at the theater in the 1920s, Ethel's stormy love life, and her remarkable success. In one of the most touching sections, Ethel becomes deeply involved in her first dramatic role, that of a woman very much like her own mother, and then has to rush home to Philadelphia to rescue her mother from a mental hospital.

His Eye Is on the Sparrow, written with Charles Michel ([1951] pap., Pyramid Pubns, 1972), is an exciting, inspiring book. The style is frequently amusing and the events are certainly interesting.

Reading level: average. Literary quality: very good.

Biography Collections

David, Jay, and Catherine J. Green, eds. *Black Roots.* McDougal-Littell, pap., 1976.

This is an excellent anthology of autobiographical accounts written by twenty black Americans, some famous and some not nearly so renowned. Ideal for classroom use, it includes selections that high school students, both black and white, should find both interesting and inspiring. These descriptions of growing up black in white America come from Southern slave plantations and from America's black ghettos, from the early 1800s and from the turbulent 1960s. From widely scattered parts of the country, here is a collection of experiences of black men and women who sought pride and dignity in a society which oppressed them. The writers tell how they were able to attain full, rich, and rewarding lives in a society that denied their humanity.

Part I, "The South": Among the nine selections are excerpts from *Lay My Burden Down* by Joanna Draper, *Black*

Boy by Richard Wright, Anne Moody's *Coming of Age in Mississippi*, and Maya Angelou's *I Know Why the Caged Bird Sings*.

Part II, "The Cities": Included here are excerpts from the autobiographies of two outstanding sports personalities, Roy Campanella and Floyd Patterson. Brief portions of Baldwin's *Go Tell It on the Mountain* and Claude Brown's *Manchild in the Promised Land*, also in this section, may inspire students to read the full-length versions of these classics.

Part III, "Middle America": This grouping of five autobiographical sketches includes, among others, excerpts from *The Big Sea*, *The Autobiography of Malcolm X*, and *Nigger*, by Langston Hughes, Malcolm X, and Dick Gregory respectively.

This anthology could serve as an excellent introduction to the full-length works.

Lester, Julius. *To Be a Slave*. Dial, 1968; pap., Dell, 1970, 1975.

This short volume is a treasure for English and social studies teachers. A collection of writings by slaves and observers describing what life was like during slavery, almost every one is a moving account of the cruelties of the system and the strength of those who endured. Starting with descriptions of the voyage in slave ships, the narratives tell of life on the plantations (including those of Thomas Jefferson and George Washington), the experience of the auction block, resistance to slavery, and reactions to Emancipation. Skillfully selected and linked by well-written explanations, *To Be a Slave* preserves the experiences and feelings of ordinary black Americans.

Durham, Philip, and Everett L. Jones. *The Adventures of the Negro Cowboys*. Dodd, 1966; pap., Bantam, 1969.

An interesting collection of anecdotes about black men in the Wild West, *The Adventures of the Negro Cowboys* tells the stories of black cowboys, cooks, bronco busters, and outlaws. Easy to read, the book contains much interesting information about life in the Old West, as well as about some little-known black heroes and anti-heroes. It is a useful resource for filling in some of the gaps in American history, and a center section of photographs adds to the interest. Some more sophisticated students, however, might be offended by the tone of the book, which glosses over the discrimination against black cowboys almost to the point of implying that it was all right for a man to be a slave if he could be a cowboy.

Butterfield, Stephen. *Black Autobiography in America.* U of Mass Pr, pap., 1974.

A fascinating survey of black autobiographies from the slave narratives to modern polemics, this book explores the search of black people for an identity, and describes in detail some of the most significant autobiographies written by blacks. In his discussion of the autobiographies, Butterfield presents an analysis of American history and sociology: "Every writer must struggle to discover who and what he is; but if you are never able to take who you are for granted, and the social order around you seems deliberately designed to rub you out, stuff your head with little cartoon symbols of what it wants or fears you to be, and mock you with parodies of your highest hopes, then discovering who you really are takes on the dimensions of an epic battle with the social order. Autobiography then becomes both an arsenal and a battleground" (p. 284). Through a Marxist analysis of the autobiographies of such writers as Frederick Douglass, Richard Wright, James Baldwin, Ida Wells, Anne Moody, and George Jackson, the author chronicles the development of the revolutionary self.

Wilson, Ruth. *Our Blood and Tears: Black Freedom Fighters.* Putnam, 1972.

This easy-to-read group of short biographies, of Benjamin Banneker, Nat Turner, and Frederick Douglass, shows the roles that all three played in American history and the black struggle for freedom. Although written for elementary school readers, this book provides a good analysis of black people's choices and decisions in American history.

5 Supplementary Bibliographies of Black Literature

Whether a student is a skilled or a reluctant reader, the route to wider reading lies through existing interests. One engrossing book can lead to another. The supplementary bibliographies in this chapter can help teachers make the most of this fact. The reasons for including a list of books about blacks in sports, prepared by consultant Jack Busher, and the annotated bibliography of books on blacks on the western frontier, by Karima Amin, are evident. Curiosity about the life in blacks' original homelands in Africa may arise out of reading about black Americans, so Barbara Dodds Stanford has described some of the best of recent African literature in English. Because students who are able readers may want to read more black literature beyond course requirements, Karima Amin has supplied a list of especially interesting titles for this audience. Most novels and plays on this list are advanced in reading level, and some deal with adult subject matter. Discussions of a number of these books appear in Chapter 2 (see the Indexes).

A Booklist of Contemporary African Literature

Although a detailed survey of African literature is beyond the scope of this book, the following brief list is included because many American students are interested in learning more about Africa. Many aspects of black American literature are related to characteristics of African literature, and contemporary black Africa has produced a number of exciting writers with whom well-educated people today should be familiar.

Anthologies of Black Literature

Beier, Ulli, ed. *African Poetry.* Cambridge U Pr, cloth & pap., 1966.

This is a fascinating collection of traditional African poems and songs, one of the best sources of the literature before European influences.

Hughes, Langston, ed. *Poems from Black Africa*. Ind U Pr, cloth & pap., 1963.

This collection contains traditional poetry, African poetry in English, and translations of modern non-English poetry.

Marckward, Edris, and Leslie Lacy, eds. *Contemporary African Literature*. Random, pap., 1972.

A beautiful book, illustrated with lovely photographs, this is the best and most complete introduction to African literature of all genres for high school students.

Rutherford, Peggy, ed. *African Voices*. Vanguard, 1959.

Stories by modern writers from many parts of Africa. (See "Black Literature for a Unit on Myth and Legend: Grade 9" in Chapter 8.)

Wells, David, Marjorie Stevenson, and Nancy King, eds. *From Black Africa*. HarBraceJ, pap., 1970.

This is a shorter but well-selected anthology of poetry and short stories with pictures and brief notes about authors.

Major Authors Appropriate for High School Students

Peter Abrahams. A coloured South African who writes movingly of the suffering faced by blacks and coloureds (mulattos) under apartheid. *Tell Freedom* (Macmillan, pap., 1970) is the story of a boy growing to adulthood under that system.

Chinua Achebe. One of the most outstanding contemporary African novelists. His novel *Things Fall Apart* ([1959] Fawcett World, pap., 1976) describes traditional Ibo life and the effects on that life of the coming of Europeans. *No Longer at Ease* (Fawcett World, pap., 1975) describes the dilemmas facing a modern Nigerian government official. His short story collection, *Girls at War and Other Stories* (Fawcett World, pap., 1974) tells of contemporary Nigerian people and their problems, including the Biafran War. All three books would be valuable reading for high school students.

Ama Ata Aidoo. Writes about the problems of contemporary Ghanaian women. Her short story collection *No Sweetness Here* (Anch. Doubleday, pap., 1972), which pictures women emerging from tribal societies and confronting urban problems, contains a number of stories appropriate for high school classes. Aidoo uses many voices, in dialogues and monologues, to create dramatic situations.

Cyprian Ekwensi. Another Nigerian writer whose works include popular romances such as *Jagua Nana* ([1961] Fawcett World, pap., n.d.) as well as more traditional tales such as *Burning Grass* (Humanities, pap., 1966). Easy to read and full of romance and excitement, Ekwensi's works should be popular with high school students.

Bessie Head. In *When Rain Clouds Gather* (S&S, 1969), this writer tells of a South African refugee, an American, and a Botswanian woman who try to improve life in a very poor village. Although her later books, *Maru* and *A Question of Power*, are rather difficult and mystical, this one should appeal to high school students.

James Ngugi. A Kenyan whose writing about the Mau Mau wars is powerful and tragic. *Weep Not, Child* (Collier. Macmillan, pap., 1969) tells of the wars from the point of view of a young boy. *The River Between* (Humanities, pap., 1965) describes the conflicts of a person caught between the old and the new ways.

Amos Tutuola. A unique Nigerian writer, whose novels are based on folk tales and myths told in his own version of English. *The Palm-Wine Drinkard* (Grove, pap., 1954), *The Brave African Huntress* (Grove, pap., 1958), and *My Life in the Bush of Ghosts* (Grove, pap., 1962) are all exciting tales full of frightening spirits.

African Junior Novels

To meet the needs of schoolchildren in newly independent nations, African writers have produced a number of junior novels. Of generally lower quality than contemporary American adolescent fiction, African junior novels tend to be easy to read, full of adventure and romance, rather moralistic, and generally similar to American books from the 1950s. Because of their easy reading level, they might be quite useful for slow readers. The following books are all published by East African Publishing House, Koinage Street, P.O. Box 30571, Nairobi, Kenya:

Flying Doctor by William Radford

The Eighth Wife by Miriam K. Were

Daughter of Mumbi by Charity Waciuma

Loice: High School Student by students at Butere Girls High School

Truphena, City Nurse by Cynthia Hunter
(*Truphena, Student Nurse* is also available.)

Moses by Barbara Kimenye (There are seven books in the

Moses Series including *Moses and the Kidnappers*, *Moses and the Ghost*, and *Moses in Trouble*.)

Background Information on African Literature

A Reader's Guide to African Literature by Hans M. Zell and Helene Silver (Africana. Holmes & Meier, cloth & pap., 1971) is a thorough annotated bibliography with biographies of major writers and a very valuable list of addresses of sources of African literature.

African Writers Talking edited by Cosmo Pierterse and Dennis Duerden (Africana. Holmes & Meier, cloth & pap., 1972) contains interviews with sixteen writers.

A List of Novels and Plays by Black Writers for the Advanced Student's Supplementary Reading

Key to abbreviations: *N* designates novels, *D* designates dramas in this bibliography.

Baldwin, James. *Another Country*. Dial, 1962; pap., Dell, 1970 (N).

———. *Blues for Mister Charlie*. Dial, 1964; pap., Dell, 1964 (D).

———. *Giovanni's Room*. Dial, 1956 (N).

———. *Go Tell It on the Mountain*. Dial, 1953; pap., Dell, 1965 (N).

———. *If Beale Street Could Talk*. Dial, 1974; pap., NAL, 1975 (N).

———. *Tell Me How Long the Train's Been Gone*. Dial, 1968; pap., Dell, 1975 (N).

Baraka, Imamu Amiri (LeRoi Jones). *The Baptism and The Toilet*. Grove, pap., 1966 (D).

———. *The System of Dante's Hell*. [1965] pap., Grove, 1976 (N).

Bontemps, Arna. *Black Thunder*. [1936] pap., Beacon Pr, 1968 (N).

———. *Drums at Dusk*. Macmillan, 1939 (N).

———. *God Sends Sunday*. Harcourt Brace, 1931 (N).

Brooks, Gwendolyn. *Maud Martha*. Reprint of 1953 edition, AMS Pr, n.d. (N).

Brown, Frank L. *Trumbull Park*. Regnery, 1959 (N).

Bullins, Ed. *Clara's Ole Man* and *The Electronic Nigger*. In *Five Plays*. Bobbs, cloth & pap., 1969 (D).

Childress, Alice. *Like One of the Family*. Independence Pr, 1956 (short stories).

Cullen, Countee. *One Way to Heaven*. Reprint of 1932 edition, AMS Pr, n.d. (N).

Davis, Ossie. *Purlie Victorious*. In *Contemporary Black Drama*, edited by Stephanie Sills and Clinton F. Oliver. Scribner, pap., 1971 (D).

Dodson, Owen. *Boy at the Window*. Reprint of 1951 edition, Chatham Bkseller, 1972 (N).

Du Bois, W. E. B. *Dark Princess*. [1928] Kraus Repr, 1975 (N).

Dunbar, Paul Laurence. *The Fanatics*. [1901] pap., Mnemosyne, n.d. (N).

———. *The Love of Landry*. [1900] pap., Mnemosyne, n.d. (N).

Edwards, Junius. *If We Must Die*. Doubleday, 1963 (N).

Ellison, Ralph. *Invisible Man*. Random, 1951; pap., 1972 (N).

Fair, Ronald L. *Many Thousand Gone: An American Fable*. Reprint of 1965 edition, Chatham Bkseller, 1973 (N).

———. *We Can't Breathe*. Har-Row, 1972 (N).

Fisher, Rudolph. *The Conjure-Man Dies*. Reprint of 1932 edition, Arno, n.d. (N).

Gaines, Ernest J. *Catherine Carmier*. Reprint of 1964 edition, Chatham Bkseller, 1972 (N).

———. *Of Love and Dust*. Dial, 1967 (N).

Gordoné, Charles. *No Place to Be Somebody: A Black Comedy*. Bobbs, cloth & pap., 1969 (D).

Greenlee, Sam. *The Spook Who Sat by the Door*. [1969] pap., Bantam, 1970 (D).

Hansberry, Lorraine. *The Sign in Sidney Brustein's Window*. [1965] pap., NAL, n.d. (D).

Heard, Nathan C. *Howard Street*. [1968] pap., NAL, 1973 (N).

Hercules, Frank. *I Want a Black Doll*. S&S, 1967 (N).

Himes, Chester. *Cast the First Stone*. Reprint of 1952 edition, Chatham Bkseller, 1973; pap., NAL, 1972 (N).

———. *If He Hollers Let Him Go*. Reprint of 1945 edition, Chatham Bkseller, 1973; pap., NAL, 1971 (N).

———. *Pinktoes*. Reprint of 1965 edition, Chatham Bkseller, 1975 (N).

———. *The Third Generation*. Reprint of 1954 edition, Chatham Bkseller, 1973 (N).

Holder, Geoffrey. *Black Gods, Green Islands*. Reprint of 1959 edition, Negro U Pr, n.d. (N).

Hughes, Langston. *Not Without Laughter*. [1930] pap., Macmillan, 1969 (N).

———. *Tambourines to Glory*. [1958] Hill & Wang, 1970 (N).

Hunter, Kristin. *God Bless the Child*. Scribner, 1964 (N).

———. *The Landlord*. [1966] pap., Avon, 1970 (N).

Hurston, Zora Neale. *Their Eyes Were Watching God.* Reprint of 1937 edition, Negro U Pr, n.d.; pap., U of Ill Pr, 1978 (N).
Kelley, William Melvin. *dem.* Doubleday, 1967 (N).
———. *A Different Drummer.* [1962] pap., Doubleday, 1969 (N).
———. *A Drop of Patience.* Reprint of 1965 edition, Chatham Bkseller, 1973 (N).
Killens, John O. *And Then We Heard the Thunder.* Knopf, 1963 (N).
———. *'Sippi.* Trident, 1967 (N).
———. *Youngblood.* [1954] Trident, n.d. (N).
Lucas, Curtis. *Angel.* Lion, 1943 (N).
———. *Forbidden Fruit.* Universal, 1953 (N).
McKay, Claude. *Banana Bottom.* Reprint of 1933 edition, Chatham Bkseller, 1971; pap., HarBraceJ, 1974 (N).
———. *Home to Harlem.* Reprint of 1928 edition, Chatham Bkseller, 1973 (N).
Marshall, Paule. *Brown Girl, Brownstones.* Reprint of 1959 edition, Chatham Bkseller, 1972 (N).
Mayfield, Julian. *The Hit.* Vanguard, 1957 (N).
———. *The Long Night.* Vanguard, 1958 (N).
Moreau, Julian (J. Denis Jackson). *The Black Commandos.* Cultural Institute Pr, 1967 (N).
Parks, Gordon. *The Learning Tree.* Har-Row, 1963; pap., Fawcett World, 1975 (N).
Petry, Ann. *Country Place.* Reprint of 1947 edition, Chatham Bkseller, 1971 (N).
———. *The Narrows.* Reprint of 1953 edition, Chatham Bkseller, 1973 (N).
Redding, J. Saunders. *Stranger and Alone.* Harcourt Brace, 1950 (N).
Reed, Ishmael. *The Free-Lance Pallbearers.* Reprint of 1967 edition, Chatham Bkseller, 1975; pap., Avon, n.d. (N).
Wright, Richard. *Native Son.* Reprint of 1940 edition, Har-Row, 1969; pap., n.d. (N).
Yerby, Frank. *The Foxes of Harrow.* [1946] pap., Dell, 1976 (N).
———. *Goat Song.* Dial, 1967; pap., Dell, 1974 (N).
———. *The Golden Hawk.* [1948] pap., Dell, 1975 (N).
———. *The Vixens.* [1947] pap., Dell, 1976 (N).

The mature student may also consider reading some novels by black Africans. Especially recommended are:

Achebe, Chinua. *A Man of the People.* [1966] pap., Doubleday, n.d. (N).

———. *Things Fall Apart.* [1959] pap., Fawcett World, 1976 (N).

Ekwensi, Cyprian. *Jagua Nana.* [1961] pap., Fawcett World, n.d. (N).

The Black Presence on the American Frontier: An Annotated Bibliography

This bibliography brings light to an aspect of the black experience that has been singularly ignored by the American mass media and educational curricula. For the most part, movies, television, western fiction, and textbooks have been blatantly negligent in properly portraying the lives of blacks who were trappers, traders, soldiers, cowboys, and homesteaders on the American frontier. Covering the black frontier experience from the time of Columbus through the Spanish-American War in 1898, this bibliography includes fiction and nonfiction for the junior reader, pictorial accounts, adult fiction and nonfiction, and records.

Fiction for the Junior Reader

Essex, Harry. *Man and Boy.* Dell, pap., 1971.

A novel of the Old West about Caleb Revers, a proud black man with a fourteen-acre homestead, a loving wife, and a ten-year-old son who idolizes him. But there are white men who undermine Caleb's manhood, destroying the respect that his son has for him. Fighting for "life, pride and vengeance," with only sheer courage and an Army Colt, Caleb Revers struggles to regain his son's admiration and respect.

Lester, Julius. *Long Journey Home: Stories from Black History.* Dial, 1972; pap., Dell, 1975.

This is a collection of short stories from black history. The author has taken documented historical fact and enriched it with details of character and setting to amplify the human experience. Included in this collection is "The Man Who Was a Horse" (pp. 79–90), a story about Bob Lemmons, born a slave in 1847, freed in 1865, a cowboy who became well known for his ability to bring in a herd of mustangs single-handedly.

Walker, Drake. *Buck and the Preacher*. Popular Lib, pap., 1972.
This is a story of a little-known aspect of America's frontier days. The Civil War is over and black men, women, and children are now free—free to make their way West to new land and a new life. This is the story of Buck, a free black and scout who must guide a group of ex-slaves westward from Louisiana; of Ruth, Buck's beautiful and courageous woman; of Willis Oakes Rutherford, the colorful preacher; and of Deshay, ruthless white leader of a band of mercenary vigilantes, sworn to stop blacks, by any means necessary, from being free and independent.

Wormser, Richard. *The Black Mustanger*. Morrow, 1971.
An easy-to-read novel with illustrations by Don Bolognese. After the Civil War, the Rikers, a white family from Tennessee, move to the wide plains of Texas, seeking their fortune and a better life. They meet a mustanger, Will Mesteno, half black, half Apache, and with his help, their fresh start becomes a success.

Nonfiction for the Junior Reader

Booker, Simeon. *Susie King Taylor, Civil War Nurse*. McGraw, 1969.
According to the foreword, this illustrated narrative is based on a diary of Susie King Taylor's life during the Civil War, which included service on the western portions of the front. Her story covers important chapters in America's military history and the history of blacks in nursing. Booker's account is an exciting story of a proud black woman who served the black troops admirably as nurse and teacher in the face of tremendous difficulties.

Clark, Charlotte R. *Black Cowboy: The Story of Nat Love*. Hale, 1970.
A book for children with full-color illustrations by Leighton Fossum on every page. This is the story of one of America's first black cowboys, champion rider, roper, and sharpshooter Nat Love, better known as Deadwood Dick—a legend in his own time.

Cortesi, Lawrence. *Jim Beckwourth, Explorer-Patriot of the Rockies*. Criterion Bks, 1971.
Beckwourth went West from St. Louis in the early nineteenth

century to become a trapper, fur trader, and "mountain man." Captured by the Crow Indians, he rose to become an adopted chief of the tribe.

Downey, Fairfax. *The Buffalo Soldiers in the Indian Wars*. McGraw, 1969.

Illustrated by Harold James, this book is about the hardships and heroism of these gallant men.

Durham, Philip, and Everett L. Jones. *The Adventures of the Negro Cowboys*. Dodds, 1966; pap., Bantam, 1969.

The black cowboys rode the range through purple sage with white Texans, Mexicans, and Indians. They ate, slept, and faced the enemy together, but when history became legend, the black man was erased from the pages of western fiction, the scenes of western movies, and the pages of America's history textbooks. Durham and Jones fill in the gaps with this collection of true tales about the post-Civil War, pioneering blacks.

Felton, Harold W. *Edward Rose, Negro Trail Blazer*. Dodds, 1967.

An illustrated biography of a hero of the Old West, a skilled and courageous marksman, horseman, and hunter. Also known as Cut Nose for the deep cut across his face, Rose was an invaluable trail blazer, trapper, guide, and interpreter. Like Jim Beckwourth, he was a leader of the Crow Indians for several years. According to the author, Rose was "a figure in almost every major step taken in the early West."

Felton, Harold W. *Jim Beckwourth, Negro Mountain Man*. Dodd, 1966; pap., Apollo Eds, 1970.

Illustrated with photographs, prints, and maps. (See Cortesi, above.)

Felton, Harold W. *Nat Love, Negro Cowboy.* Dodd, 1969.

Another biography from the early cattle-raising days. Illustrated by David Hodges. (See Clark, above, and Love, below.)

Jackson, Florence. *The Black Man in America*, 1877–1905. Watts, 1973.

Illustrated with contemporary drawings and photographs, this volume is part of a historical series, with excellent chapters on "Settlers and Cowboys" and the "Black Soldiers."

Lee, Irvin H. *Negro Medal of Honor Men*. Rev. ed., Dodd, 1969.

Illustrated with photographs, the chapter "The Indian Fighters" is excellent, filling in a part of America's history where the black man is usually ignored. This book tells about black soldiers who proved their courage again and again. They were loyal fighters despite the brutality and humiliation of racial prejudice.

Love, Nat. *The Life and Adventures of Nat Love, Better Known in the Cattle Country as Deadwood Dick.* Reprint of 1907 edition, Arno, 1968.

Not specifically written for a junior reading audience, Love's autobiography is nevertheless very easy to read, though hard to believe.

Shepard, Betty, ed. *Mountain Man, Indian Chief: The Life and Adventures of Jim Beckwourth.* HarBraceJ, 1968.

Illustrated with reproductions of prints and a map. (See Cortesi, above.)

Wakin, Edward. *Black Fighting Men in U.S. History.* Lothrop, 1971.

Illustrated with photographs, this book covers blacks' role in major wars from the American Revolution through Vietnam.

Pictorial Accounts

All readers should enjoy the following collections of pictures. Only the Miller book has a text for the junior reader.

Carroll, John M. *Buffalo Soldiers West.* Old Army, 1971.

An exciting assemblage of pictures, including many by the art historian Frederic Remington, who is well known for his western art.

Franklin, John Hope. *An Illustrated History of Black Americans.* Time-Life, 1970.

Pages 46–54 of this survey volume deal with black troops in the Civil War; pages 130–33 give a brief description of the black soldier in the American Revolution, the War of 1812, the Civil War, and the Spanish-American War. Also mentioned are Henry O. Flipper, West Point's first black graduate, and Jim Beckwourth, the man who discovered a strategic pass through the Sierra Nevadas which bears his name.

Harris, Middleton A., et al. *The Black Book.* Random, cloth & pap., 1973.

A documented pictorial history of the Afro-American experience. For brief accounts of black pioneers, see: pp. 49–

54—Bill Pickett, Gobo Fango, the Bongas, Jim Beckwourth, Nat Love, and others; pp. 127–28—Edmonia Lewis, Prince Boston, Daniel Hale Williams, and black homesteaders; pp. 155–65—the black soldier in the Revolutionary War, the Civil War, and the Spanish-American War; also a brief section on Henry O. Flipper, West Point's first black graduate.

Katz, William Loren. *The Black West.* Rev. ed., Doubleday, cloth & pap., 1973.

A pictorial account with well-documented text and impressive bibliography. Beginning with Estevan, the first African known by name to have taken part in a government (Spanish) exploration of America's southwest region (1528), the text covers the black presence on the American frontier through the Spanish-American War of 1898. The young adult reader should be able to handle the text. Less capable readers will enjoy the many illustrations.

Miller, Major Donald L. *An Album of Black Americans in the Armed Forces.* Watts, 1969.

This account by a retired Army colonel is illustrated with photographs and reprints of paintings and sketches. For information about the pioneering black, see the following chapters: "Black Soldiers in the Far West," "Spanish-American War," "The Black Cadet," and "Pancho Villa Chase in Mexico."

Adult Fiction

Reed, Ishmael. *Yellow Back Radio Broke-Down.* Reprint of 1969 edition, Chatham Bkseller, 1975; pap., Avon, 1977.

This fantasy of a surrealistic Wild West features a black "hoodoo cowboy." (See the discussion under Ishmael Reed in the section on new black writers in Chapter 2.)

Williams, John A. *Captain Blackman.* Doubleday, 1972.

Captain Abraham Blackman is a black soldier, wounded in Vietnam. With the sounds of AK-47's, M-16, and M-60 fire bursting all around him, Blackman drifts in and out of consciousness, mentally reliving the black man's military history in the American Revolution, the Battle of New Orleans, the Civil War, the Indian Wars, the Spanish-American War, and World Wars I and II. Blackman's dreams describe the freedom and equality always promised to his people but never granted.

Adult Nonfiction

Beckwourth, James P. *The Life and Adventures of James P. Beckwourth.* Edited by Thomas D. Bonner. Reprint of 1856 edition, U of Nebr Pr, 1972.

This autobiography is exciting to read, and at times hard to believe. The author recounts childhood experiences, incidents of city life in St. Louis, Missouri, and tales of his life as a renowned mountain man and chief of the Crow Indians. (A condensed version is described under Jim Beckwourth in Chapter 4.)

Carroll, John M., ed. *The Black Military Experience in the American West.* Liveright, 1971; pap., 1974.

An illustrated text exploring the black soldiers' lives, both professional and social. The author delineates the soldiers' hardships and successes, the excitement and danger of frontier life, and the ugliness of unjustified prejudice. A good bibliography is included.

Cornish, Dudley Taylor. *The Sable Arm: Negro Troops in the Union Army, 1861–1865.* [1956] pap., Norton, 1966.

An amply documented account of the role of black soldiers fighting for the North in the Civil War.

Dobie, J. Frank. *The Mustangs.* [1934] pap., Little, 1952.

Basically this is a book about the mustang horse, but Chapter 13, "As the Mustangers Told It," describes the unique style of Bob Lemmons, black cowboy and mustanger.

Durham, Philip, and Everett L. Jones. *The Negro Cowboys.* Dodd, 1965.

This is the adult version of *The Adventures of the Negro Cowboys,* by Durham and Jones. (See young readers' list.)

Fowler, Arlen L. *The Black Infantry in the West, 1869–1891.* Negro U Pr, 1971.

Covers the important contributions made by the black infantry in the West, with emphasis on the Twenty-Fifth Infantry in the Dakotas and Montana and the Twenty-Fourth Infantry in the Southwest. An extensive bibliography is included.

Harris, Theodore D., ed. *Negro Frontiersman.* Tex Western, 1963.

One reviewer says, "This is the personal narrative of Henry O. Flipper, the first Black graduate of the U. S. Military

Academy at West Point. His account covers his civilian and military experiences along the untamed Mexican border from the years 1878 to 1916."

Leckie, William H. *The Buffalo Soldiers: A Narrative of the Negro Cavalry in the West.* U of Okla Pr, cloth & pap., 1970.
With photographs, drawings, and maps and a moving text, Leckie tells the story of the heroic fighting men of the Ninth and Tenth Regiments, who were able to overcome every obstacle in their path on the American frontier except "the twin foes of prejudice and discrimination."

McPherson, James M. *The Negro's Civil War.* Pantheon, 1965.
Subtitled "How American Negroes Felt and Acted during the War for the Union," this is an account of the black man's "contributions and achievements, his hopes and aspirations, his opinions and frustrations."

Porter, Kenneth Wiggins. *The Negro on the American Frontier.* Reprint of 1971 edition, Arno, n.d.
Two centuries of the black presence on the frontier are presented in this book, which also looks at blacks' relations with Native Americans.

Black Literature of Sports: A Recommended Bibliography

Ali, Muhammad. *The Greatest: My Own Story,* with Richard Durham. Random, 1975; pap., Ballantine, 1976.

Baker, Jim. *O. J. Simpson.* G&D, pap., 1974.

Bell, Marty. *The Legend of Dr. J.: The Story of Julius Erving.* Coward, 1975; pap., NAL, 1976.

Chamberlain, Wilt, and David Shaw. *Wilt: Just Like Any Other 7-Foot Black Millionaire Who Lives Next Door.* Macmillan, 1973; pap., Warner Bks, 1975.

Frazier, Walt, and Ira Berkow. *Rockin' Steady.* P-H, 1974; pap., Warner Bks, 1974.

Frazier, Walt, and Joe Jares. *Clyde: The Autobiography of Walt Frazier.* [1970] G&D, pap., n.d.

Gibson, Bob, and Phil Pepe. *From Ghetto to Glory: The Story of Bob Gibson.* P-H, 1968.

Gutman, Bill. *Hank Aaron.* G&D, pap., 1973.

Hano, Arnold. *Roberto Clemente: Batting King.* Rev. ed., Putnam, 1973; pap., Dell, 1973.

Jacobs, Linda. *Wilma Rudolph: Run for Glory.* EMC, cloth & pap., 1974.

Lardner, Rex. *Ali.* G&D, pap., n.d.

Pepe, Phil. *Kareem Abdul-Jabbar.* G&D, pap., n.d.

Robinson, Louis, Jr. *Arthur Ashe: Tennis Champion.* Doubleday, 1970.

Sayers, Gale, and Al Silverman. *I Am Third.* Viking Pr, 1970; pap., Bantam, n.d.

Wolf, David. *Foul: The Connie Hawkins Story.* HR&W, 1972; pap., Warner Bks, 1972.

Recordings of Black American Literature

Recordings may be used as a supplement to in-class reading and discussion of black literature, and as reference aids for the teacher. Literature comes alive on records by skillful performers, so teachers should if possible devote some class time to listening to records of black poetry, drama, folk tales, or stories. Such recordings can also serve as aids to independent study.

This list of recordings is by no means comprehensive—new discs are constantly appearing—but these are readily available in most public libraries. Addresses of recording companies are given at the end of the Directory of Publishers.

Anthology of Negro Poetry. Folkways Records, FL 9791.

Langston Hughes, Sterling Brown, Claude McKay, Countee Cullen, Margaret Walker, and Gwendolyn Brooks read their own poems. Arna Bontemps, editor.

Anthology of Negro Poets in the U. S. A.: 200 Years. Folkways Records, FL 9792.

Arna Bontemps reads the poetry of eighteen black writers. Some of those included are Lucy Terry, Phillis Wheatley, Paul Laurence Dunbar, Claude McKay, Langston Hughes, and Sterling Brown.

Black Pioneers in American History. Volume I: 19th Century. Caedmon Records, TC 1252.

Eartha Kitt and Moses Gunn read biographical sketches of Frederick Douglass, newspaper editor, publisher, and prominent black leader of the anti-slavery movement; Charlotte Forten, a young teacher who left her free and wealthy Philadelphia family to teach slaves recently freed in South

Carolina; Susie King Taylor, who taught, nursed, and cooked for black troops during the Civil War; and Nat Love, the black cowboy better known as Deadwood Dick. Suitable for younger listeners.

Buffalo Soldiers. Buddah Records, 2001.

Produced, directed, and narrated by Nathanial Montague, this recording chronicles the daring exploits of America's Buffalo Soldiers, organized in 1866 as the Tenth Cavalry Regiment. Also mentioned are black rangers, scouts, and hunters who aided them. The achievements of black cavalrymen and infantrymen are related in detail. For the adult listener. The musical accompaniment may be distracting to younger listeners.

Folk Tales of the Tribes of Africa as Told by Eartha Kitt. Caedmon Records, TC 1267.

Eartha Kitt reads folk tales of seven African tribes; each story is particularly relevant to American children.

God's Trombones. Folkways Records, FL 9788.

The poetry of James Weldon Johnson read by Bryce Bond with music by William Martin. Includes "The Creation," "Let My People Go," "Go Down Death," and others.

Gwendolyn Brooks Reading Her Poetry. Caedmon Records, TC 1244.

The author reads selections from *A Street in Bronzeville, Annie Allen, The Bean Eaters, Selected Poems, Black Expression* (Vol. I, No. 1), and *In the Mecca.* The record includes an introductory poem by Don L. Lee (Haki R. Madhubuti) entitled "Gwendolyn Brooks."

William Melvin Kelley. CMS Records, CMS 525.

The author reads "A Different Drummer," an excerpt from his novel *The African,* and "The Only Man on Liberty Street," from his collection of short stories, *Dancers on the Shore.*

The Last Poets. Douglas Records, 3.

Poems by Abiodun Oyewole, Alafia Pudim, and Omar Ben Hassen read by the poets with percussion accompaniment by Nilaja. For mature students.

The Last Poets: This Is Madness. Douglas Records, 7-Z 30583.

Poems by Alafia Pudim and Omar Ben Hassen with vocal and percussion accompaniment. For mature students.

Like a Ripple on a Pond. Nikton Records, NK 4200.
Nikki Giovanni reads poems from her collection, *My House*, with accompaniment by the New York Community Choir.

The Poetry of Langston Hughes. Caedmon Records, TC 1272.
"The Negro Speaks of Rivers," "Song for a Dark Girl," "I, Too," "Ballad of the Landlord," etc., read by Ruby Dee and Ossie Davis. Also selected poems from *The Panther and the Lash* and *One-Way Ticket.*

The Poetry of Margaret Walker. Folkways Records, FL 9795.
Margaret Walker reads several of her works, including ballads for two famous women, Phillis Wheatley and Harriet Tubman, and the ever-popular "We Have Been Believers" and "Let My People Go."

A Raisin in the Sun. Caedmon Records, TRS 355.
A drama by Lorraine Hansberry featuring the actor Ossie Davis as Walter Lee Younger and the actresses Ruby Dee as Ruth Younger, Claudia McNeil as Mama, and Diana Sands as Beneatha Younger.

Sidney Poitier Reads Poetry of the Black Man. United Artists, UAS 6693.
With Doris Belack, the Brooks Male Chorus, and instrumental accompaniment. Sixteen selections by seven black poets with a concentration on poetry by Langston Hughes, Paul Laurence Dunbar, and James Weldon Johnson.

Simple. Caedmon Records, TC 1222.
Seven stories from Langston Hughes' *The Best of Simple* and *Simple's Uncle Sam,* read by Ossie Davis.

16 Poems of Sterling A. Brown. Folkways Records, FL 9794.
Read by Sterling Brown himself and edited by Frederick Ramsey, Jr., these selections include "Old Lem," "Break of Day," "Remembering Nat Turner," and "Strong Men."

Sterling Brown and Langston Hughes. Folkways Records, FL 9790.
Sterling Brown reads his poems: "Break of Day," "Sharecropper," "Slim in Hell," "Old Lem," "Old King Cotton," and "Putting on Dog." Langston Hughes reads from *Simple Speaks His Mind*: "Feet Live Their Own Lives," "Simple Prays a Prayer," "Wooing the Muse," and "Landladies."

a sun lady for all seasons. Folkway Records, FL 9793.
Sonia Sanchez (Laila Mannan) reads her poetry about black people and love.

Truth Is on Its Way. Right-On Records/Farem Productions, RR 05001.

Nikki Giovanni reads poetry from two of her books, *Black Feeling Black Talk/Black Judgement* and *Re: Creation*, with accompaniment by the New York Community Choir.

Winter in America. Strata-East Records, SES 19742.

"New Renaissance" poetry about the "energy . . . beauty . . . and determination . . . " of black people by Gil Scott-Heron. Read by the author with vocal and piano accompaniment. For mature students.

II Classroom Uses of Black American Literature

This section is a potpourri of practical guides and activities to aid the teacher in creating and broadening black literature courses.

The first two outline guides grew out of my experience of being plunged into teaching black literature without benefit of adequate preparatory course work. I designed and used them with my senior high school students. At the time they were introduced, many looked upon black studies as a passing fancy, but the guides have been used successfully and have endured ignorant condescension.

The Cleveland and Pittsburgh guides are reprinted here to provide teachers with some knowledge of black literature curricula developed by school systems, and are typical of those used in most major cities. The Oneonta guide was designed by a teacher when an elective program was developed at her school.

Enrichment is the intent of the Supplementary Activities (Chapter 10). "Composition and Discussion Motivators," "Ideas for Role-Playing," and "A Word about Games" are all directed toward the affective objectives that characterize some black literature courses. They may be used by teachers who are interested in promoting positive behavioral change and/or an improved understanding of the black experience.

Karima Amin

6 Two Literature Units on the Black Experience

Karima Amin

Outline 1: From Africa to America

Introduction: This outline is based on one I devised in 1971, when I began teaching a course titled Literature by Black Writers in a senior high school. At that time, my knowledge of the subject was sadly lacking, and I barely managed to keep up a "one-page-ahead-of-my-students" pace in the first semester of my assignment. This course outline was designed for twenty weeks (one semester) of instruction for sixty twelfth graders in two classes. A few advanced eleventh graders were also permitted to take the course.

The past-present-future structure resulted from my need for a guiding framework as I simultaneously taught and studied, gleaning information from textbooks, magazines, recordings, and people with an interest in my plight. I also referred to the Buffalo, New York, Board of Education curriculum guide for Literature by Black Writers, which had been released in 1970. I reworked themes and concepts in it to accommodate my limited knowledge, piecemeal studies, and desire to make an exciting presentation. The outline as it appears here has the 1971 framework but incorporates many changes that grew out of trial-and-error learning along the way.

Facts of publication for the book-length works referred to in this outline can be found in the bibliography following Outline 2.

Unit I. The Past

A. Early black civilization. Before studying literature by black writers, students should first be helped to understand that black history did not begin in America. An excellent reference for the instructor to use at this point (and in connection with future studies) is John Hope Franklin's *Illustrated History of Black Americans* (1970). The following poems make reference to the African past.

1. "Heritage" by Gwendolyn Bennett (Adams, *Poetry,* 1970)
2. "Heritage" by Countee Cullen (Adams, *Poetry,* 1970)
3. "To Egypt" by Gloria Davis (Murray, *Journey,* 1971)
4. "Africa" by David Diop (Murray, *Journey,* 1971)
5. "The Negro Speaks of Rivers" by Langston Hughes (Adams, *Poetry,* 1970)

B. Slavery in America. It ought to be indicated here that Americans were not the first to practice slavery. In fact, blacks themselves enslaved other black people for centuries. However, in no other place and in no other era was the treatment of slaves crueller than in America. Another excellent reference for the teacher is *The Interesting Narrative of the Life of Olaudah Equiano, or Gustavus Vassa the African. Written by Himself* (Equiano, 1969; Equiano, 1970). Vassa was a slave to both black men and white. His book tells how the horrors of the latter far surpassed his prior state of servitude. The following poems illustrate the degradation slavery causes.

1. "The Slave Auction" by Frances E. W. Harper (Adams, *Poetry,* 1970)
2. "Middle Passage" by Robert Hayden (Adams, *Poetry,* 1970)

C. Black resistance to dehumanization. Some slaves fled persecution and several poems tell of their plight.

1. "Remembering Nat Turner" by Sterling A. Brown (Adams, *Poetry,* 1970)
2. "Runagate Runagate" by Robert Hayden (Adams, *Poetry,* 1970)
3. "Harriet Tubman" by Margaret Walker (Weisman, 1971)

Music is one aspect of African culture that the slave was able to salvage, and many slaves turned to song as a language of resistance. The teacher may refer to *Blues People: Negro Music in White America* (Jones, 1963) for more information about the role of music in early black American life. The mature student may be encouraged to read the first and final chapters of *The Souls of Black Folk*: Chapter 1: "Of Our Spiritual Strivings"; Chapter 14: "Of the Sorrow Songs" (Du Bois, 1965). *Three Negro Classics* combines this Du Bois work with other important early writing: *Up from Slavery* by Booker T. Washington and *The Autobiography of an Ex-Coloured Man* by James Weldon Johnson. Recordings of black religious music, work songs, field blues, and shouts should be utilized in this unit. The following poems tell of the solace and energizing spirit that black people have found in their music.

1. "Strong Men" by Sterling A. Brown (Murray, *Search*, 1971)
2. "On Listening to the Spirituals" by Lance Jeffers (Chapman, 1968)

Some folktales with African or Afro-American origins are also suitable for this section. The following deal with resistance to enslavement and may be found in *Black Folktales* (Lester, 1969).

1. "People Who Could Fly"
2. "Keep on Steppin'"
3. "High John the Conqueror"
4. "Stagolee"

D. Jim Crowism. To really understand what blacks were up against, the instructor may consider having the class read the following books by whites, which perpetuated the widely held belief that black people were somehow subhuman.

1. *The Negro a Beast* (Carroll, 1900)
2. *The Caucasian and the Negro in the United States* (Calhoun, [1902] 1977)
3. *The Negro, a Menace to Civilization* (Shufeldt, 1907)
4. *Folkways* (Sumner, 1906)

The mature student may be encouraged to read the preceding selections or may be provided with excerpts. The following poems discuss the inhumanity and brutality spawned by Jim Crow legislation.

1. "Old Lem" by Sterling A. Brown (Adoff, 1968)
2. "'So Quietly'" by Leslie Pinckney Hill (Adoff, 1968)
3. "Song for a Dark Girl" by Langston Hughes (Adoff, 1968)
4. "The Lynching" by Claude McKay (Adoff, 1968)
5. "Between the World and Me" by Richard Wright (Adoff, 1968)

Also appropriate for inclusion here are Richard Wright's autobiography, *Black Boy* (1945), and a short story by Lerone Bennett, Jr., "The Convert" (Mirer, 1971).

Unit II. The Present

The literature listed in this unit explores several facets of the contemporary scene from the viewpoint of blacks who find themselves on the outside looking in.

A. An appeal to the powers that be. Poetry
   1. "Merry-Go-Round" by Langston Hughes (Adams, *Poetry,* 1970)
   2. "America" by Claude McKay (Chapman, 1968)
   3. "The White House" by Claude McKay (Adams, *Poetry,* 1970)

B. The "Bootstrap Syndrome"
   1. Poetry. "We Have Been Believers" by Margaret Walker (Murray, *Black Perspectives,* 1971)
   2. Short story. "My Brother Went to College" by Frank Yerby (Murray, *Search,* 1971)
   3. Drama. *A Raisin in the Sun* by Lorraine Hansberry (Adams, *Drama,* 1970)

C. Individual worth
   1. Novels
      a. *Invisible Man (*Ellison, 1951)
      b. *Native Son* (Wright, 1940)
   2. Nonfiction
      a. *Nigger* (Gregory, 1964)
      b. *The Autobiography of Malcolm X* (Malcolm X & Haley, 1965)
   3. Short story. "A Summer Tragedy" by Arna Bontemps (Chapman, 1968)

D. A new person
   1. Poetry
      a. "Song of the Awakened Negro" by Ruby Berkeley Brown (Weisman, 1971)
      b. "The Emancipation of George-Hector (A Colored Turtle)" by Mari Evans (Murray, *Journey,* 1971)
      c. "The Rebel" by Mari Evans (Adoff, 1968)
      d. "—a poem for nina simone to put some music to and blow our nigguh/minds—" by Sonia Sanchez (Laila Mannan) (Murray, *Major Black Writers,* 1971)
   2. Short story. "The Homecoming" by Frank Yerby (Murray, *Search,* 1971)
   3. Nonfiction. *Look Out Whitey! Black Power's Gon' Get Your Mama* (Lester, 1969)

Unit III. The Future

A. "Where do we go from here?"
   1. Poetry
      a. "Dream Deferred" by Langston Hughes (Murray, *Search,* 1971)
      b. "Harlem" by Langston Hughes (Chapman, 1968)

2. Drama. *Dutchman* (Jones, 1964)

Students should be prompted to discuss or write about possible answers to the above question.

B. Make it better. Poetry that says, "Let's change the system!"
   1. "Democracy" by Langston Hughes (Murray, *Black Perspectives*, 1971)
   2. "Let America Be America Again" by Langston Hughes (Murray, *Search*, 1971)
   3. "If We Must Die" by Claude McKay (Murray, *Black Perspectives*, 1971)
   4. "Mad! Mad!" by Ernest White (Murray, *Search*, 1971)

C. Brighter days ahead. Nonfiction. The literature of optimism by Dr. Martin Luther King, Jr.
   1. "I Have a Dream" (Murray, *Black Perspectives*, 1971)
   2. *Stride Toward Freedom* (King, 1958)

Outline 2: Eye + Mind + Heart = Experience

Introduction: Unlike the preceding outline, with its historically based framework, this four-unit outline is structured upon attitudes and feelings resulting from and perpetuated by the black experience in America. Like "From Africa to America," this outline was also designed for twenty weeks of instruction. It, too, incorporates many changes made over the years to reflect my growing knowledge and my desire to challenge heterogeneous groups of students—some who entered the course with a sincere interest and others who entered out of simple curiosity. (For sources of the works cited, see the bibliography following this outline.)

Unit I. The Eye: Black Perspective

A. "The way I see it . . ." The black perspective is a kaleidoscope of opinion from a black point of view. The following selections reveal that the black perspective is influenced by: the "double-consciousness," i.e., being black in white America; black cultural values vs. white cultural values; slavery (past and present); racism (overt and covert); and that hard-to-define but easily recognizable quality called "soul."
   1. Essay collection. "Tales of Simple" by Langston Hughes (Chapman, 1968)
   2. Poetry. "Booker T. and W. E. B." by Dudley Randall (Chapman, 1968)

3. Drama. *Five on the Black Hand Side* by Charlie L. Russell (Murray, *Black Perspectives*, 1971)

B. Black vs. white
   1. Poetry
      a. "When in Rome" by Mari Evans (Emanuel, 1968)
      b. "Customs and Culture" by Ted Joans (Murray, *Search*, 1971)
      c. "Jungle Taste" by Edward S. Silvera (Adams, *Poetry*, 1970)
   2. Short story. "The Boy Who Painted Christ Black" by John Henrik Clarke (Murray, *Journey*, 1971)

C. The way it is. Poetry
   1. "Red" by Countee Cullen (Adams, *Poetry*, 1970)
   2. "I Am Not Lazy" by Mari Evans (Coombs, 1970)
   3. "Motto" by Langston Hughes (Murray, *Major Black Writers*, 1971)
   4. "Theme for English B" by Langston Hughes (Murray, *Major Black Writers*, 1971)
   5. "What We Know" by Raymond Patterson (Murray, *Search*, 1971)

Unit II. The Mind: Black People

In this country, blacks have had to deal with psychological oppression which has been intense and deeply penetrating, though often subtle. Blacks who give in to this abuse often allow their image of themselves to be governed by the white perspective. They frequently aim for white "acceptance," and at the same time, reject their blackness. Very often, they are people who applaud the material while neglecting the spiritual. Sometimes they labor in a world of illusions that does not allow them to function as a "necessary blackself" (see "A Poem to Complement Other Poems" by Don L. Lee [Haki R. Madhubuti]).

As an introduction to this unit, the class could discuss the extent of psychological damage that may occur when a child encounters racial prejudice, after reading the poem "Incident" by Countee Cullen. The teacher should read "The Black Psyche," the first chapter of John O. Killens' *Black Man's Burden* (1965).

A. The damage is done.
   1. Poetry
      a. "Incident" by Countee Cullen (Murray, *Journey*, 1971)
      b. "Black Bourgeoisie" by LeRoi Jones (Imamu A. Baraka) (Murray, *Black Perspectives*, 1971)

c. "But He Was Cool" by Don L. Lee (Haki R. Madhubuti) (Murray, *Scene*, 1971)
d. "A Poem to Complement Other Poems" by Don L. Lee (Haki R. Madhubuti) (Murray, *Black Perspectives*, 1971)

2. Short stories
   a. "Sonny's Blues" by James Baldwin (Emanuel, 1968)
   b. "Singing Dinah's Song" by Frank London Brown (Adams, *Fiction*, 1970)
   c. "In Darkness and Confusion" by Ann Petry (Chapman, 1968)

B. Constructive reaction. In an effort to cope with the abuse of a racist society, blacks have responded with four basic psychological attitudes: masking (hiding the black reality); adapting to alienation (accepting or adjusting to an inferior position); militancy (developing a new image and a sense of identity in a manner which may be either violent or nonviolent); and open hostility (an outspoken rejection of the status quo). The following poems are suitable examples of each stance.
   1. Masking: "We Wear the Mask" by Paul Laurence Dunbar (Weisman, 1971)
   2. Adapting to alienation: "I, Too, Sing America" by Langston Hughes (Weisman, 1971)
   3. Militancy: "Awareness" by Don L. Lee (Haki R. Madhubuti) (Lee, 1967). After reading this poem, students may be prompted to discuss the idea of "thinking black" as the first step in a move toward black militancy.
   4. Open hostility: "Mad! Mad!" by Ernest White (Murray, *Search*, 1971)

Unit III. The Heart: Black Struggle for Survival

Blacks have survived in spite of racial oppression and are still struggling, in the face of heavy odds, despite their numerous advances. In the following selections, black writers discuss some survival tactics that may be employed to insure and enhance the future of blacks.

A. Endurance
   1. Nonfiction
      a. *Manchild in the Promised Land* (Brown, 1965)
      b. *Up from Slavery* (Washington, 1965)
   2. Poetry

   a. "Mother to Son" by Langston Hughes (Murray, *Black Perspectives*, 1971)
   b. "The Negro Mother" by Langston Hughes (Emanuel, 1968)
   c. "Still Here" by Langston Hughes (Murray, *Black Hero*, 1971)
   d. "Lift Every Voice and Sing" by James Weldon Johnson (Weisman, 1971)

B. Brotherhood. Nonfiction. "Letter from Birmingham City Jail" (King, 1970)

C. Teach the children! Poem. "let us begin the real work" by Sonia Sanchez (Laila Mannan) (1970)

D. Black unity
   1. Short story. "A Love Song for Seven Little Boys Called Sam" by C. H. Fuller, Jr. (Murray, *Journey*, 1971)
   2. Poetry. "The New Integrationist" by Don L. Lee (Haki R. Madhubuti) (Murray, *Black Perspectives*, 1971)
   3. Nonfiction. "A Black Value System" by LeRoi Jones (Imamu A. Baraka) (Murray, *Black Perspectives*, 1971). This is an essay which explains the "Nguzo Saba" or "Seven Principles of Blackness," defined by Ron Maulana Karenga. Contact local black cultural centers for more information or write to: The East, 1310 Atlantic Avenue, Brooklyn, New York 11216.

Unit IV. The Product of Experience: Black Identity

A. Historical identification. In these selections, blacks celebrate their heritage and pay homage to their roots.
   1. Short stories
      a. "Mister Toussan" by Ralph Ellison (Murray, *Black Perspectives*, 1971)
      b. "Fishbelly's Discovery" by Richard Wright (Murray, *Journey*, 1971)
   2. Poetry
      a. "The Visitation" by Sun-Ra (Murray, *Journey*, 1971)
      b. "For My People" by Margaret Walker (Murray, *Major Black Writers*, 1971)

B. The badge of color
   1. Poetry
      a. "Mr. Z" by M. Carl Holman (Adams, *Poetry*, 1970)
      b. "Cross" by Langston Hughes (Weisman, 1971)
      c. "What Color is Black?" by Barbara D. Mahone (Murray, *Journey*, 1971)

2. Short story. "Revolt of the Evil Fairies" by Ted Poston (Murray, *Black Perspectives*, 1971)

C. Black pride. The following indicate the cultural identity, personal identity, and pride one attains upon achieving black awareness in a very personal sense.
   1. Drama. *Wine in the Wilderness* by Alice Childress (Murray, *Major Black Writers*, 1971)
   2. Short story. "Not Any More" by Eloise Greenfield (Murray, *Journey*, 1971)
   3. Poetry
      a. "In a Period of Growth" by Don L. Lee (Haki R. Madhubuti) (Lee, 1967)
      b. "Black Power" by Raymond Patterson (Murray, *Journey*, 1971)

Bibliography

Adams, William; Peter Conn; and Barry Slepian, eds. *Afro-American Literature: Drama*. HM, pap., 1970.

______. *Afro-American Literature: Fiction*. HM, pap., 1970.

______. *Afro-American Literature: Poetry*. HM, pap., 1970.

Adoff, Arnold, ed. *I Am the Darker Brother: An Anthology of Modern Poems by Negro Americans*. Macmillan, cloth & pap., 1968.

Brown, Claude. *Manchild in the Promised Land*. Macmillan, 1965; pap., NAL, 1971.

Calhoun, William P. *The Caucasian and the Negro in the United States*. Reprint of 1902 edition, Arno, 1977.

Carroll, Charles. *The Negro a Beast*. Arno, 1900.

Chapman, Abraham, ed. *Black Voices: An Anthology of Afro-American Literature*. NAL, pap., 1968.

Coombs, Orde, ed. *We Speak as Liberators: Young Black Poets, an Anthology*. Dodd, cloth & pap., 1970.

Du Bois, W. E. B. *The Souls of Black Folk*. In *Three Negro Classics*, edited by John H. Franklin. Avon, pap., 1965.

Ellison, Ralph. *Invisible Man*. Random, 1951; pap., 1972.

Emanuel, James A., and Theodore L. Gross, eds. *Dark Symphony: Negro Literature in America*. Free Pr, cloth & pap., 1968.

Equiano, Olaudah. *The Interesting Narrative of the Life of Olaudah Equiano, or Gustavus Vassa the African. Written by Himself*. 2 vols. Reprint of 1789 edition, Shoe String, 1969.

______. *The Slave Who Bought His Freedom: Equiano's Story*. Revised, abridged from the above, for young adults. Dutton, 1970.

Franklin, John Hope. *An Illustrated History of Black Americans*. Time-Life, 1970.

Gregory, Dick. *Nigger: An Autobiography,* with Robert Lipsyte. Dutton, 1964; pap., PB, 1965.

Jones, LeRoi (Imamu A. Baraka). *Blues People: Negro Music in White America.* Morrow, cloth & pap., 1963.

———. *Dutchman.* Morrow, pap., 1964.

Killens, John O. *Black Man's Burden.* [1965] Trident, n.d.; pap., S&S, 1970.

King, Martin Luther, Jr. "Letter from Birmingham City Jail." Excerpts in Chase and Collier, *Justice Denied: The Black Man in White America.* HarBraceJ, pap., 1970.

———. *Stride Toward Freedom: The Montgomery Story.* Har-Row, 1958.

Lee, Don L. (Haki R. Madhubuti). *Think Black.* 3d ed., Broadside, pap., 1967.

Lester, Julius. *Black Folktales.* R W Baron, 1969; pap., Grove, 1970.

———. *Look Out Whitey! Black Power's Gon' Get Your Mama!* [1968] pap., Grove, 1969.

Malcolm X, and Alex Haley. *The Autobiography of Malcolm X.* Grove, pap., 1965.

Mirer, Martin, ed. *Modern Black Stories.* Barron, pap., 1971.

Murray, Alma, and Robert Thomas, eds. *Scholastic Black Literature Series: The Black Hero.* Schol Bk Serv, pap., 1971.

———. *Scholastic Black Literature Series: Black Perspectives.* Schol Bk Serv, pap., 1971.

———. *Scholastic Black Literature Series: The Journey.* Schol Bk Serv, pap., 1971.

———. *Scholastic Black Literature Series: Major Black Writers.* Schol Bk Serv, pap., 1971.

———. *Scholastic Black Literature Series: The Search.* Schol Bk Serv, pap., 1971.

———. *Scholastic Black Literature Series: The Scene.* Schol Bk Serv, pap., 1971.

Sanchez, Sonia (Laila Mannan). *We a BaddDDD People.* Broadside, cloth & pap., 1970.

Shufeldt, Robert W. *The Negro, a Menace to Civilization.* Badger Press, 1907.

Sumner, William G. *Folkways.* [1906] NAL, pap., 1940.

Washington, Booker T. *Up from Slavery.* In *Three Negro Classics,* edited by John H. Franklin. Avon, pap., 1965.

Weisman, Leon, and Elfreda S. Wright, eds. *Black Poetry for All Americans.* Globe, pap., 1971.

Wright, Richard. *Black Boy: A Record of Childhood and Youth.* Reprint of 1945 edition, Har-Row, 1969; pap., n.d.

———. *Native Son.* Reprint of 1940 edition, Har-Row, 1969; pap., n.d.

7 Three Black Literature Units

Cleveland Public Schools

The following units, "Slave Narrative and Autobiography," "Introduction to Poetry," and "Introduction to the Short Story," were taken from a black American literature guide designed for teachers of grades 10–12 in the Cleveland Public Schools. The units were created by a special Curriculum Development Committee of the Department of English and Language Arts. The guide was published by the Board of Education in 1969, and Units 2, 3, and 4 are reprinted here with permission. The basal text for each of these units is the anthology *Black Voices*, edited by Abraham Chapman (NAL, pap., 1968). Facts of publication for works mentioned are listed in the bibliography at the end of this chapter.

Slave Narrative and Autobiography (5 weeks)

Introduction: In its early stages, nonfiction written by Negroes was largely autobiographical; it later included biographical works. Autobiographical prose by Negroes appeared as early as 1760. Frederick Douglass' *My Bondage and My Freedom* and *Life and Times of Frederick Douglass* are two of the mid-century prose works that complete the meaning of American culture. *Up from Slavery*, the autobiography of Booker T. Washington, tells of the illegitimate son of a white man and a Negro slave and his struggle for education for himself and his people.

In 1903 W. E. B. Du Bois published *The Souls of Black Folk*, a sociological document, which took issue with the ideas of Booker T. Washington.

Although James Weldon Johnson's *The Autobiography of an Ex-Coloured Man* is a document on the life of the American Negro, it gives his feeling toward the white man and toward his own race.

As John Hope Franklin points out in his introduction to *Three Negro Classics*, which includes the last three works above, "These three classic and crucial documents in the evolution of Negroes' consciousness of self—key documents, as well, in the development of white society's awareness of the Negro situation—have never been more timely."

This unit attempts to show pupils the progress black people have made in America. This unit begins with the slave narrative, the oldest form of Negro literature in America. The unit traces the Negro mood from slavery, through the Harlem Renaissance or Great Awakening to modern writers. This unit has five aims [for the student]:

1. To be able to identify by name eight black writers
2. To be able to identify and compare the writing styles of two authors
3. To be able to identify at least four conditions of slavery
4. To be able to identify with various authors through written and oral expressions
5. To be able to identify facts about the lives of various authors

General Discussion Guide

The following questions might be used with the biography unit as well as with the selected individual reading during this unit.

1. What specific contributions of the Negro to the American culture are represented by this author?
2. What view does the Negro have of himself? What events in the book contribute to this attitude?
3. What problems of the Negro, as discussed in the book, are common to all Americans?
4. What is each character's most outstanding personality trait? Cite evidence from the book to support your claims.
5. How does the main character achieve his goal?

Basal Text

Black Voices: An Anthology of Afro-American Literature, edited by Abraham Chapman [NAL, pap., 1968. Page numbers which follow refer to *Black Voices.*]

Objectives

1. To be able to identify by name the author of a slave narrative

2. To be able to identify an author's style of writing by citing examples
3. To be able to identify by name four adverse effects of slavery

Suggested Lesson Plan for Chapter I of *Narrative of the Life of Frederick Douglass, an American Slave*

Type of Reading: Autobiography (pp. 231–236)

Presentation

Play the recording "The Douglass Years" to class. (This is available at many high school libraries.) To give students the "feel" of the narrative, read several paragraphs aloud. Begin class discussion by asking the following questions:

1. What are the circumstances surrounding Douglass' birth?
2. Describe Douglass' parents. Be specific.
3. What does Frederick remember about his parents?
4. Which slaves, according to Douglass, suffered the greatest hardships? Why?
5. Who was Mr. Plummer?
6. Describe the whipping of Aunt Hester.
7. What effect does this experience have on Frederick?
8. Why hasn't he been exposed to this kind of brutality before?

Author's Style

To introduce students to Douglass' style of writing, point out sentence structure and vocabulary. (His sentences are short and vocabulary simple.) Let students read several of the more descriptive paragraphs aloud.

Paragraph Theme

What bad features would a modern psychologist find with Frederick Douglass' limited relationship with his parents, especially his mother?

Assignment

Assign Chapter VI (pp. 236–239) for next class. Teachers should have mimeographed questions from this chapter for students to use as a guide.

Additional Aids

Many students might be interested in other books about and by Douglass. *The Life and Times of Frederick Douglass* might be recommended. It deals particularly with his escape from slavery.

This approach can be used to some degree with other assignments.

Suggested Lesson Plan for Selected Episodes from James Weldon Johnson's *Along This Way* (pp. 269–287)

Objectives

1. To be able to identify by name three of the contributions James Weldon Johnson made to Negro American literature and culture
2. To be able to compare in several paragraphs the early childhood of Frederick Douglass with that of Johnson
3. To be able to identify Johnson's style of writing

Presentation

Have a student with a good reading voice read "The Creation" (p. 364 of *Black Voices*). Do not analyze poem, just discuss it purely for its beauty. Then introduce students to Johnson.

Short Quiz (True-False)

1. James Weldon Johnson was born on a plantation in Jacksonville, Florida, after the Civil War.
2. Johnson, instead of having a black mammy, had a white one.
3. This happened because his mother had to work in the fields with other slaves.
4. Johnson's mother visited a white church in Jacksonville and was invited to join its choir.
5. Johnson's father earned his first and second degrees from Atlanta University.
   [1 = F, 2 = T, 3 = F, 4 = F, 5 = F]

Discussion Topics

1. Describe Johnson's childhood home in Jacksonville.
2. What events led to his having a white mammy?
3. Why doesn't he boast of having had one?
4. Johnson says of his mother, "Racially she continued to be a nonconformist and a rebel." Cite several instances to substantiate that statement.

5. Describe Johnson's father. Be specific.
6. What quality in his father impressed him most?

Paragraph Theme

Compare the early years of James Weldon Johnson with those of Frederick Douglass. In what ways are they different? Similar? Find examples to support your statements.

Author's Style

Discuss sentence structure and vocabulary. Have students read aloud several passages where he is quite descriptive. Find other examples in the story that illustrate his style.

Suggested Lesson Plan for Richard Wright's "The Ethics of Living Jim Crow: An Autobiographical Sketch" (pp. 288–298)

Objectives

1. To gain an appreciation of Richard Wright's early life
2. To be able to write several paragraphs about the development of Wright's adjustment to life as a Negro
3. To be able to identify Wright's style of writing

Understanding the Facts

1. When does Wright receive his first lesson in how to live as a Negro?
2. How were cinders fine weapons, according to Wright?
3. What event made him fully realize the "appalling disadvantages of a cinder environment"?
4. What effect did the cinder incident have on Wright?

Discussion Topics

1. What is your reaction to Wright's mother after the cinder incident?
2. Put into your own words the meaning of Jim Crow.
3. What good fortune does Wright have by moving to Mississippi? Why?
4. Do you agree with the advice given Wright by his parents after the incident with Morrie and Pease? Why? What other advice might his parents have given?

Paragraph Themes

1. What does the title, "The Ethics of Living Jim Crow," say to you about the personality of Wright?
2. Do you think it is possible to keep one's manhood when one receives pressure from both sides? Why?

Author's Style

Wright's prose is quite descriptive. Sentence structure is short and simple. Note how he gives reality to his characters through the use of dialect.

Suggested Lesson Plan for Chapter One
of J. Saunders Redding's *No Day of Triumph* (pp. 300–315)

Objectives

1. To gain an appreciation of Redding's life
2. To develop an understanding of the style of J. Saunders Redding
3. To be able to draw conclusions
4. To be able to describe Redding's childhood
5. To be able to understand and use figurative language

Understanding the Facts

1. When does Redding become conscious of his environment?
2. What was the power that "turned the wheel" of his inner family life?
3. Where did Grandma Redding live?
4. Describe Grandma Redding.
5. How did Grandma Redding receive her limp?
6. Why is she so full of hate?

Discussion Topics

1. From the first paragraph, what kind of childhood did Redding have?
2. How does Redding let the reader know that his father is educated?

Author's Style

Point out to students how Redding uses figurative language ("Grandma Redding's telling was as bare and imageless as a lesson recited from the head and as coldly furious as the whine of a shot") etc. Notice his use of dialect to show some of the character of Grandma Redding.

Suggested Lesson Plan for James Baldwin's "Autobiographical Notes" (pp. 316–320)

Objectives

1. To gain an understanding and an appreciation of James Baldwin
2. To introduce students to Baldwin's style of writing
3. To be able to write a paragraph from a quotation by James Baldwin
4. To be able to write several paragraphs discussing students' interests

Understanding the Facts

1. Where was Baldwin born?
2. How old was he when this selection was written?
3. Describe some of the jobs held by Baldwin before his middle twenties.
4. What are some of the difficulties in being a Negro writer?
5. What are some of Baldwin's interests?

Discussion Topics

1. Do you agree with Baldwin about black people's heritage?
2. What has the American Negro been forced to hide according to Baldwin? Is this true of you?
3. What was the relationship between Baldwin and his brothers and sisters?

Composition Theme

1. In several paragraphs, discuss what Baldwin meant when he said, "If you don't know my name, you don't know your own."
2. In several paragraphs discuss your present interests.

Author's Style

Notice the elements of humor. Discuss understatement. How does Baldwin use it? Have students read the first paragraph and analyze the dry humor.

Suggested Lesson Plan for Arna Bontemps'
"Why I Returned" (pp. 321–332)

Objectives

1. To gain an appreciation of Bontemps' life
2. To gain an appreciation of Bontemps' style
3. To be able to write several paragraphs on the presentation of the Negro heritage

Understanding the Facts

1. Where was Bontemps born?
2. What significance did Bontemps attach to a nickname?
3. Describe Bontemps' father. Be specific.
4. Who was Buddy?
5. What were the two opposing attitudes toward the roots of the Negro as expressed by Bontemps' father and Buddy?
6. Where does Bontemps find himself during the Depression?
7. After leaving Alabama, where does Bontemps go?
8. Explain what Bontemps meant by the statement, "We had fled from the jungle of Alabama's Scottsboro era to the jungle of Chicago's crime ridden South Side, . . ."
9. Why does Bontemps go to Fisk University?
10. What reason does Bontemps give for staying in the South? Do you think this is a valid reason?

Discussion Topics

1. Why do you think Bontemps was surprised at the condition of the house where he was born?
2. From the first few paragraphs, what is his attitude toward the South?

Paragraph Theme

Explain in several paragraphs why you do or do not feel that "The Southern Negro's link with his past seems worth preserving."

Author's Style

Point out to students Bontemps' use of poetry and the way the autobiography is divided.

Suggested Lesson Plan for Chapter One of *The Autobiography of Malcolm X*, written with Alex Haley (pp. 332–347)

Objectives

1. To gain an appreciation for the early life of Malcolm X
2. To be able to identify the writing style of Alex Haley
3. To be able to identify what Malcolm feels are the horrors of welfare

Understanding the Facts

1. Who was Malcolm's father? Describe him.
2. What influenced Malcolm's father to become a follower of Marcus Garvey?
3. Who was Marcus Garvey? (This can be given as an oral assignment.)
4. What prophecy does Malcolm make early in the autobiography?
5. What vision does Malcolm's mother have?
6. What happens to Malcolm's father?
7. What had been Malcolm's father's attitude toward buying on credit? Do you agree? Why?
8. How does Malcolm get into trouble at an early age?
9. Describe the Halloween night incident.
10. What did Malcolm mean when he said that the state welfare "destroyed" their home?
11. What lesson did Malcolm learn from rabbit hunting with the old men?
12. What eventually happens to Malcolm's mother?
13. How long does she remain in the hospital?
14. What effect does this have on Malcolm X?
15. Why doesn't Malcolm talk freely about his mother?
16. What relationship does Malcolm have with his brothers and sisters after the separation?

Discussion Topics

1. What reason does Malcolm give for not visiting his mother after 1952? Is this, in your opinion, a valid reason?
2. Malcolm states that "a state social agency destroyed his family." Why do you agree or disagree with this? What could have been done to keep the family together?

Author's Style

How does Haley capture the attention of the reader? (Note title of Chapter One.) Have students read aloud the first paragraph and note how he intrigues the reader. Note use of sarcasm through Haley's quotations.

Suggested Lesson Plan for Stanley Sanders'
"I'll Never Escape the Ghetto" (pp. 347–353)

Objectives

1. To be able to write a paragraph explaining a given quotation
2. To be able to identify three facts about the early life of Stanley Sanders and to show the style of Sanders
3. To demonstrate to students that a meaningful career in a ghetto is possible
4. To give a picture of Watts in mid '60s
5. To be able to identify an autobiographical article

Discussion Topics

1. According to Sanders, how is the black ghetto a "transient status"?
2. Why was Sanders considered one of the lucky ones?
3. Why was a career in Watts a personal ambition for Sanders?
4. What does Sanders do to escape the stigma of Watts?
5. What changes occurred during Sanders' two years at Oxford?
6. In what sense was Sanders the archetype of the ghetto child?
7. Describe Watts in 1965.
8. What was Sanders' first reaction to the riot?
9. Explain why Sanders felt that riots were helpful. Do you agree with this thinking?
10. Explain Sanders' affectionate ties to Watts.
11. What were the logical ties for Sanders staying in Watts?
12. What was life like in England for black people?

Paragraph Theme

In several paragraphs, explain what Sanders meant by "The life of a black man in Watts is larger than a federal poverty program."

Author's Style

Discuss with students the difference between an autobiography and an autobiographical article. His sentences are short, simple. This article is easy to read.

Note: This article appeared in a special issue of *Ebony* (August 1967). This issue could be useful in class along with this lesson.

Introduction to Poetry (3 weeks)

Background: In Arna Bontemps' introduction to his *American Negro Poetry* (rev. ed., Hill & Wang, cloth & pap., 1974) he writes, "The poetry of the American Negro sometimes seems hard to pin down. Like his music, from spirituals and gospel songs to blues, jazz, and bebop, it is likely to be marked by a certain special riff, an extra glide, a kick where none is expected, and a beat for which there is no notation. It follows the literary traditions of the language it uses, but it does not hold them sacred. As a result, there has been a tendency for critics to put it in a category by itself, outside the main body of American poetry.

"But Negroes take to poetry as they do to music. In the Harlem Renaissance of the twenties poetry led the way for other arts. It touched off the awakening that brought novelists, painters, sculptors, dancers, dramatists, and scholars of many kinds to the notice of a nation that had nearly forgotten about the gifts of its people. And almost the first utterance of the revival struck an arresting new note: 'I've known rivers ancient as the world and older than the flow of human blood in human veins.'" ["The Negro Speaks of Rivers," Langston Hughes]

During the same era, Claude McKay's *Harlem Shadows* was published. One of his poems, "America," begins:

> Although she feeds me bread of bitterness,
> And sinks into my throat her tiger's tooth,
> Stealing my breath of life, I will confess
> I love this cultured hell that tests my youth!
>
> [*Black Voices*, p. 374]

It wasn't long before Jean Toomer began his literary experimentation:

> Come, brother, come. Lets lift it;
> Come now, hewit! roll away!
> Shackles fall upon the Judgment Day
> But lets not wait for it.
>
> ["Cotton Song," *Black Voices*, pp. 377–78]

Another central figure of the Harlem Renaissance was Countee Cullen. Keats is acknowledged as an influence on the style of Cullen's writings. One of his famous epitaphs, "For Paul Laurence Dunbar," follows:

Born of the sorrowful of heart
Mirth was a crown upon his head;
Pride kept his twisted lips apart
In jest, to hide a heart that bled.

[*Black Voices*, p. 386]

Although Phillis Wheatley and Jupiter Hammon stand out in the history of Negro poetry, Paul Laurence Dunbar was the first Negro poet to win any national recognition in America. Dunbar gained recognition with several volumes of lyrics, including such poems as "Dawn," "The Party," and "We Wear the Mask."

The literary explosion of the twentieth century brought into American literature the early works of such writers as James Weldon Johnson, W. E. B. Du Bois, Claude McKay, Arna Bontemps, Langston Hughes, Mari Evans, LeRoi Jones, and many others listed in *Black Voices*.

Basal Text: *Black Voices*, edited by Abraham Chapman

Objectives

1. To be able to identify by name four black poets
2. To be able to write several paragraphs comparing two poems with similar themes
3. To be able to identify figurative language through use in a paragraph
4. To be able to identify and compare the two techniques of writing used by Dunbar (dialect or "plantation tradition" and literary English)

Type of Reading: Poetry

Suggested Lesson Plan I

Vocabulary

Review literary terms which are applicable to a unit on poetry, beginning with *imagery*.

Presentation

Spend several minutes giving students some historical background on poetry written by blacks. This can be done in the form of oral reports by students on such poets as Lucy Terry, Jupiter Hammon, and Phillis Wheatley. Introduce students to Dunbar by giving them the following facts:

1. Dunbar was born and educated in Dayton, Ohio.
2. Dunbar was the first black poet to win national recognition and full acceptance in America.
3. He began writing verse as a youth.
4. He held several positions as a high school student—editor in chief of his school newspaper, president of the literary society, and class poet.
5. His first book of poems, *Oak and Ivy* (1893), was distributed and sold by the poet.
6. His book *Lyrics of Lowly Life* (1896), with an introduction by William Dean Howells, made him a celebrity.

Have several students read "We Wear the Mask" aloud to the class. You may have three different students read each stanza. As students read, discuss any vocabulary problems that might arise. Ask students to explain in their own words what Dunbar is saying.

Class Discussion

Begin class discussion by asking the following questions:

1. Who are the "We" in the poem?
2. What is meant by "mask"?
3. Explain what Dunbar means by "This debt we pay to human guile."
4. What is happening to the Negro as he smiles?
5. What is meant by lines 12 and 13 of the poem?
6. What stereotype of the Negro is represented here?

Extending Language Skills

1. In several paragraphs, compare "We Wear the Mask" with Claude McKay's "Harlem Dancer." In what ways are the two poems similar, different? Cite examples. What general theme is present in both poems?
2. Have a student who is good in reading dialect read "The Party" by Dunbar. Show how Dunbar uses the "plantation tradition" on which much of the fame of his poetry rested.

Suggested Lesson Plan II

Another possible way of teaching the unit on poetry is to arrange the poems into thematic units. Use themes that appeal to your pupils. One possible theme, together with poems selected [from *Black Voices*], is listed below.

Materials

"Aunt Jane Allen" by Fenton Johnson (p. 371)
"Booker T. and W. E. B." by Dudley Randall (p. 470)
"The Ballad of Joe Meek" by Sterling Brown (p. 414)
"Robert Whitmore" by Frank Davis (p. 435)
"Theme for English B" by Langston Hughes (p. 429)
"Her Story" by Naomi Madgett (p. 476)
"We Real Cool" by Gwendolyn Brooks (p. 465)
"The Scarlet Woman" by Fenton Johnson (p. 370)

Theme 1: People

First read "The Ballad of Joe Meek" and then read "Aunt Jane Allen." Compare the techniques and effects of the two poems.

Next read a group of poems that suggest a story in a character sketch: Davis's "Robert Whitmore," Naomi Madgett's "Her Story." Have students write a paragraph describing one of the above characters.

Have several pupils who read well read Brooks' "We Real Cool," and Johnson's "The Scarlet Woman." Discuss how Brooks and Johnson paint a picture of a group of people.

Other themes. Some examples of other themes that could be especially interesting to a particular class are *Courage*, *Death*, *Love*, and *Friendship*.

Introduction to the Short Story (3 weeks)

Background: Slaves were the first makers of Afro-American legend and myth. They retold and adapted the many tales their people had brought from Africa. These stories were about heroes, animal and human, whose character traits were well known to the listeners. They revealed the dreams and aspirations of the black people of America. Since many of these were imaginative and different from the Anglo-Saxon traditions, they were added to the American culture.

During this era, folktales were circulated orally. The development of short stories written by Negroes proceeded very slowly for many reasons. The most obvious reason was that only a few Negroes knew how to write, and many southern states did not allow education of black Americans.

It was more than twenty years after the Emancipation Proclamation that the first short story by a black author appeared in *The Atlantic Monthly.* This story was written by Charles Waddell Chesnutt, who was a native Clevelander. Chesnutt passed the Ohio bar examination and worked for years as a legal stenographer in Cleveland. Even though *The Atlantic Monthly* continued to publish Chesnutt's work, the editor avoided identifying the writer as a Negro.

By the late forties and fifties, the list of significant short story writers grew tremendously. The most prominent are probably the ones listed in *Black Voices*—Jean Toomer, Rudolph Fisher, Arna Bontemps, Ralph Ellison, Langston Hughes, Richard Wright, James Baldwin, and others.

Basal Text: *Black Voices*, edited by Abraham Chapman

Objectives

1. To be able to identify by name the first black author to perfect the short story form
2. To be able to write several paragraphs accepting or rejecting a given philosophy
3. To be able to identify the term *allusion* and discuss how the author uses allusion in this story

Type of Reading: Short Stories

Skills and Concepts

Responding to the story:
- Interpreting title
- Determining theme
- Grasping implications

Recognizing the writer's skill:
- Characterization
- Language and word choice
- Logical endings

Suggested Lesson plan for Charles W. Chesnutt's "Baxter's Procrustes" (pp. 52–62)

Terms

Review the terms that are necessary in understanding the short story. These terms may be given in vocabulary exercises before the teacher begins this unit or as he or she progresses in the unit.

Presenting the Story

Have several students read the first few paragraphs aloud. The teacher will possibly have to stop to explain who several of the authors mentioned are. No definite date or place is given for setting. We can assume that the story takes place in the later 1800s or early 1900s. (The club had entertained Mark Twain.) Note that the story is told in the first person and Baxter is the main character.

Vocabulary

1. rubricated, p. 56
2. consternation, p. 54
3. coterie, p. 55
4. hypothesis, p. 54
5. remuneration, p. 56
6. enigmatical, p. 58

Introducing the Author

1. Stress the fact that Chesnutt was born in Cleveland.
2. He is considered the first Negro writer to master the short story form and the craft of fiction.
3. He established a national literary reputation as a novelist and short story writer before his death.
4. His race was kept a secret for nearly a decade by the editor of *The Atlantic Monthly.*
5. Chesnutt studied law and passed the Ohio bar examination, but he never practiced law; he became a legal stenographer instead.
6. "Baxter's Procrustes" was written for *The Atlantic Monthly* in June, 1904.

Understanding the Story

1. What was the main interest of the members of the Bodleian Club?
2. Where did the club gets its name?
3. Name several literary figures that the club had entertained.
4. Relate what happened at the club on the anniversary of Sir Walter Raleigh's death.
5. What happens at the club once or twice a year?
6. Describe Baxter.

7. How did the members of the Bodleian Club first get the notion of publishing "Baxter's Procrustes"?
8. What was Baxter's philosophy of life?
9. Why did the club members refrain from reading the poem?
10. Describe the paper and the cover of the Procrustes.
11. How did the members of the club discover that they had been duped?
12. What explanation does Baxter give for deceiving the members? Is it a logical one?
13. What finally happens to Baxter?
14. What does the president of the club finally conclude about Baxter?
15. What does the title mean?

Developing Language Skills

1. Define the term *allusion*. Discuss in several paragraphs how Chesnutt uses allusion in this story.
2. Baxter's philosophy was, "Society was the Procrustes which, like the Greek bandit of old, caught every man born into the world, and endeavored to fit him to some preconceived standard, generally to the one for which he was least adapted." In several paragraphs, tell why you agree or disagree with that philosophy.

Suggested Reading

Students who enjoyed this story might like to read "The Goophered Grapevine," a tale of Negro folk psychology, and "The Sheriff's Children" by Charles Chesnutt.

Bibliography

Bontemps, Arna, ed. *American Negro Poetry*. Rev. ed., Hill & Wang, cloth & pap., 1974.

Chapman, Abraham, ed. *Black Voices: An Anthology of Afro-American Literature*. NAL, pap., 1968.

Douglass, Frederick. *The Life and Times of Frederick Douglass: The Complete Autobiography*. Macmillan, pap., 1962.

______. *My Bondage and My Freedom*. In *Black Rediscovery Series*. Dover, pap., 1969.

Dunbar, Paul Laurence. *Lyrics of Lowly Life*. Reprint of 1896 edition, Irvington, pap., 1977.

______. *Oak and Ivy*. [1893].

Du Bois, W. E. B. *The Souls of Black Folk.* In *Three Negro Classics*, edited by John H. Franklin. Avon, pap., 1965.

Franklin, John H., ed. *Three Negro Classics: Up from Slavery; The Souls of Black Folk; and The Autobiography of an Ex-Coloured Man.* Avon, pap., 1965.

Johnson, James Weldon. *The Autobiography of an Ex-Coloured Man.* In *Three Negro Classics*, edited by John H. Franklin. Avon, pap., 1965.

Washington, Booker T. *Up from Slavery.* In *Three Negro Classics*, edited by John H. Franklin. Avon, pap., 1965.

Acknowledgments

Division of English and Language Arts, Cleveland Board of Education, Cleveland, Ohio, 1969.

Curriculum Development Committee. Evelyn Gunn, Editor, Glenville High School; Mary Grinage, English Department Chair, Addison Junior High School; and Betty Bonner, Advisory English Teacher

Organization. Verda Evans, Directing Supervisor of English and Language Arts; Raymond W. Clifford, Supervisor of English; James D. Mills, Supervisor of English; William P. Hoffman, Director of Secondary Schools; James R. Tanner, Assistant Superintendent, Curriculum; Darian H. Smith, Assistant Superintendent, Personnel; and George E. Theobald, Deputy Superintendent

8 Afro-American Literature: An Addendum to the Course of Study in Literature

Pittsburgh Public Schools

In November of 1969, the Board of Public Education, Pittsburgh, Pennsylvania, published "Afro-American Literature: An Addendum to the Course of Study in Literature, Grades 7–12." That part of the addendum which covers Grades 7 through 9 is reprinted here with permission.

Basic texts used for the units were as follows: For Grade 7, *The Long Black Schooner* by Emma Gelders Sterne; for Grade 8, *Jim Beckwourth: Negro Mountain Man* by Harold W. Felton; for Grade 9, *African Voices: An Anthology of Native African Writings*, edited by Peggy Rutherford; and *The Life and Times of Frederick Douglass* by Frederick Douglass, edited by Barbara Ritchie.

Facts of publication for the books referred to in these units can be found in the bibliography at the end of this chapter.

Black Literature for a Unit on Human Relationships: Grade 7

During the nineteenth century slave trading was abolished on the high seas. Nevertheless, slave trading persisted. Its very illegality made the practice more lucrative than it had been previously. It was during this period, in 1839, that a slave mutiny occurred aboard the *Amistad* off the coast of Cuba. This mutiny, in fictionalized form, is the subject matter of *The Long Black Schooner*, by Emma Gelders Sterne [reissued under the title *Slave Ship*].

It should be kept in mind that although the story has been fictionalized, it is based upon historical fact. The mutiny did occur, and John Quincy Adams in 1841 did represent the mutinous slaves as free men in the Supreme Court of the United States.

The historical relevance of this book, however, should not be the teacher's emphasis. These facts are mentioned to assist in and not to indicate the direction of the study. This narrative is of value because it is a good beginning for seventh graders in the study of human relationships. Both black and white students will learn that many different kinds of people inhabit the earth and that the color of a person's skin has nothing to do with his or her honor, pride, and personal integrity.

Questions for Discussion and Composition. (Asterisks mark items appropriate for composition activities.)

1. What was the basic contradiction in Thomas Jefferson's attitude about slavery? (See the Introduction, page 8.)*
2. Discuss Whitman's comments on equality, "Of Equality—As if it harm'd me, giving others the same chances and rights as myself—As if it were not indispensable to my own rights that others possess the same."
3. Compare the attitudes of Montez, Ruiz, Captain Stone, and the governor toward slavery. Were they for or against the institution? How are these attitudes indicated by their conversation?
4. Describe the capture of the slaves as seen through Ka-le's eyes.*
5. Discuss Cinque's character. Why does he stand out? Remember his remarks to Ka-le and to his people.*
6. Why does Ramon Ferrer consent to transport the slaves around the island?
7. As a result of tribal custom, Cinque is beaten because he will not touch the body of Goona. What significance does his reaction—snapping his fingers after the beating—have on the coming action of the narrative?
8. What kind of person is Antonio? Note his behavior prior to and during the mutiny.
9. During the mutiny why does the captain say, "Throw them bread, Antonio"? (This is, in a sense, another underestimation of the slaves.)
10. Discuss African culture as seen through the behavior of Cinque, Tua, and Fulway during and after the mutiny.*
11. How do the people of New York react to the black schooner before and after Ruiz' and Montez' landings?
12. Graham Ellis, Gil Johnson, and Green are different kinds of people. Discuss their varying viewpoints about slavery.
13. Describe the conditions of the slaves' imprisonment during the period in which they were being tried for mutiny and murder.

14. Discuss James Covey's role in the legal fight to free the slaves.
15. Why do some of the slaves decide to stay in America?
16. What factors control the ability of people to view others with respect and understanding? For example, what characteristics do Ellis and Adams possess that others in the story do not?
17. In what way is this narrative a study in human relationships?*

Vocabulary

1. contradiction
2. abolition
3. palaver
4. shrewd
5. engulf
6. tumultuous
7. confidence
8. cassava
9. pendulum
10. constellation
11. compass
12. mutiny
13. salvage
14. alien

Related Activities

1. Using knowledge acquired from the book and outside readings, have students prepare panel discussions dealing with slavery. General but relevant observations can be made about topics such as "The Legacy of Slavery," or "Slavery's Effect on Human Relationships in the United States during the 1800s."
2. Have students do dramatizations of scenes from the book. For example, the mutiny is a scene which lends itself to presentation. Other students might prefer to do monologues. Cinque's statement to his people or John Quincy Adams' comments on slavery are suggestions.
3. Have students do graphs for bulletin board display which depict the differences between African and American culture during the 1800s. For this, they can simply use information from the text or outside readings.
4. Encourage students to do additional reading about the history of this period in the United States. Such topics would include the abolitionist movement, the *Amistad,* slavery legislation, and John Quincy Adams.
5. Have students write compositions which contrast Cinque as a slave leader with Travis as the head of his household during his father's absence in *Old Yeller*.

6. Suggest that students contrast the attitudes which influence human relationships in *Romeo and Juliet* and *The Long Black Schooner*. This may be done orally or in written form. An example of such a comparison would be Ka-le's response to adult supervision as compared with Romeo's response to Friar Laurence's advice.
7. Have students compare the relationships of blacks and whites during the 1800s with those of blacks and whites today.

Independent Reading

Nonfiction

Angell, Pauline K. *To the Top of the World: The Story of Peary and Henson*. Rand, 1964.

Bennett, Lerone, Jr. *What Manner of Man: A Biography of Martin Luther King, Jr., 1929–1968*. Johnson Chi, 1968; pap., PB, n.d.

Buckmaster, Henrietta. *Women Who Shaped History*. Macmillan, 1968; pap., 1974.

Douty, Esther M. *Under the New Roof: Five Patriots of the New Republic*. Rand, 1965.

Graham, Shirley. *Your Most Humble Servant: The Story of Benjamin Banneker*. Messner, 1949.

Owens, William A. *Black Mutiny: The Revolt on the Schooner Amistad*. [1953] Pilgrim Press, 1968.

Scherman, Katharine. *The Slave Who Freed Haiti: The Story of Touissant Louverture*. Random, 1964.

Sterne, Emma Gelders. *Mary McLeod Bethune*. Knopf, 1957.

Yates, Elizabeth. *Amos Fortune: Free Man*. [1950] Dutton, 1967; pap., Dell, 1971.

Fiction

Hamilton, Virginia. *The House of Dies Drear*. Macmillan, 1968; pap., 1970.

Poetry

Hughes, Langston. *The Dream Keeper and Other Poems*. Knopf, 1932.

Black Literature for a Unit on the World of the Imagination: Grade 8

The purpose of including *Jim Beckwourth: Negro Mountain Man* in a unit on American folklore is to give students an awareness of the contributions of both black and white mountain men to the development of their country.

As a trapper, fur trader, Crow Indian chief, and dispatcher, Jim Beckwourth broadened the western frontier of this nation. His experiences are vividly depicted and largely involve conflicts between man and nature.

Beckwourth appears larger than life because of his unhesitating nature in the face of danger and his fierceness in battle. However, the teacher should always emphasize that here was an American, a black American, who did much to further the development of his country.

Another emphasis should be that of Jim Beckwourth's background. Blacksmithing prepared him for his isolated wanderings, and his associations with the Rocky Mountain Fur Company prepared him to become an independent trapper. These preparations were essential in making him the man of greatness that he was.

Questions for Discussion and Composition. (Asterisks mark items appropriate for composition activities.)

1. What was the influence of Jim Beckwourth's background on his future life?
2. Discuss General Ashley's Rocky Mountain Fur Company and Beckwourth's association with it.
3. Considering Jim Beckwourth and other trappers mentioned in the story, such as Moses Harris and Caleb Greenwood, discuss the characteristics of the mountain man.*
4. Contrast the cultures of the trappers and Indians.
5. Discuss the social implications of the following statement:* "The broad valley that held the Green River would become famous as a place where mountain men would hold their rendezvous in the years to come; where they would meet in the late summer and trade peltries for the goods of the East . . . where Indians would meet the white men and the Negroes, among them Jim Beckwourth . . . where men of

all races and colors would meet and mix; where there was no distinction between men, except the superior and the inferior, the lucky and the unlucky, and where death came to those who failed."

6. Why does Jim Beckwourth decide to become a free trapper?
7. What enables Beckwourth to become accepted by the Crow Indians? Remember Greenwood's story.
8. Describe Beckwourth's life with the Crow Indians.
9. Discuss possible exaggerations in the biography, especially the saving of Ashley's life on two occasions by Beckwourth and the 95-mile chase by the Blackfeet. What is the relationship between these possible exaggerations and the popularity of legendary heroes?
10. Discuss the trapping process.
11. Discuss Beckwourth's later years as a trader, soldier, and dispatch carrier.
12. What made the Crows poison their chief? Was it an excess or lack of love? Explain.*
13. Which aspects of Beckwourth's life did you find most interesting?
14. What kind of man was Jim Beckwourth? Would the world be a better place if more people were like him? Why or why not would it be a better place?

Vocabulary

1. ague
2. primitive
3. frigid
4. militia
5. expedition
6. desolate
7. tributary
8. sustain
9. fatigue
10. exaggeration
11. mammoth
12. draught
13. gauntlet
14. barter
15. boisterous
16. rendezvous
17. tumultuous
18. avalanche
19. ferocious
20. environment
21. culture
22. pursuit
23. babel
24. civilization
25. legitimate
26. coup
27. degradation
28. profane
29. majestic
30. inaugural

Related Activities

1. Have students develop a map during the reading of the biography which will indicate the places where Beckwourth lived and trapped during the development of the western portion of this country.
2. Have students do group reports on other mountain men mentioned in the text such as:
   a. William H. Ashley
   b. Thomas Fitzpatrick
   c. Robert Campbell
   d. Caleb Greenwood
   e. Edward Rose
   f. William Sublette
   g. Jim Bridger
   h. John Colter
   i. John Jacob Astor
   j. Kit Carson
   k. Stephen Kearny
   l. John Frémont
3. Have students do group or individual reports on the various Indian cultures. Some of those mentioned in the text are:
   a. Pawnees
   b. Sioux
   c. Iroquois
   d. Blackfeet
   e. Navajos
   f. Snakes
   g. Cheyennes
   h. Arapahos
   i. Shoshones
   j. Dakotas
4. Have students do research work on famous contemporary black Americans. Have them contrast Beckwourth's preparation, attitude, and accomplishment of goal with similar characteristics of a contemporary black American.
5. Have students do individual research on other black Americans who assisted in the development of this country such as Crispus Attucks, Frederick Douglass, Sojourner Truth, Estebanico, and Benjamin Banneker.
6. Have students contrast life in the West during the early 1800s with life today. Have them discuss occupations, family relationships, and the role of men. Have students present their findings through small group discussions.
7. Students may dramatize the sections of the text which concern Jim's trapping expeditions for the Rocky Mountain Fur Company and his life with the Crow Indians.
8. Have students compare Beckwourth and other legendary characters mentioned in the unit such as Paul Bunyan and Pecos Bill.

Independent Reading

Nonfiction

Bontemps, Arna. *The Story of the Negro*. Knopf, 1958.
Bradford, Sarah. *Harriet Tubman: The Moses of Her People*. Peter Smith, n.d.
de Treviño, Elizabeth Borton. *I, Juan de Pareja*. FS&G, 1965.
Durham, Philip, and Everett L. Jones. *The Adventures of the Negro Cowboys*. Dodd, 1966; pap., Bantam, 1969.
Felton, Harold W. *Edward Rose, Negro Trail Blazer*. Dodd, 1967.
Graham, Shirley. *Jean Baptiste Pointe de Sable: Founder of Chicago*. Messner, 1953.
Petry, Ann. *Tituba of Salem Village*. T Y Crowell, 1964.
Rollins, Charlemae. *They Showed the Way: Forty American Negro Leaders*. T Y Crowell, 1964.
Sterling, Dorothy. *Captain of the Planter: The Story of Robert Smalls*. Doubleday, 1958; pap., Archway, n.d.
Zagoren, Ruby. *Venture for Freedom*. Dell, pap., 1971.

Fiction

Clarke, Mary. *Petticoat Rebel*. Viking Pr, 1964.
Cluff, Tom. *Minutemen of the Sea*. Follett, 1955.
Rodman, Bella. *Lions in the Way*. Follett, 1966.

Anthology

Brooks, Charlotte. *The Outnumbered: Stories, Essays and Poems about Minority Groups by America's Leading Writers*. Dell, pap., 1967.

Black Literature for a Unit on Myth and Legend: Grade 9

The selections from this book are to be read as a part of the ninth-grade unit "Myth and Legend" in the *Course of Study in Literature, Grades 7–12*. It is important that both the teacher and the student have some geographical and historical knowledge of Africa before reading these stories. The universal themes of star-crossed lovers, rejected wives, faith in God, and lack of trust are developed in the suggested selections.

The "Foreword" and "Introduction" to Rutherford's *African Voices: An Anthology of Native African Writings* will be helpful to the teacher in preparation and presentation of the material. In addition to these aids, the "Preliminary Activities" contain three comprehensive initial activities which should prepare the students for this study.

Preliminary Activities

1. Have students do group work on the geography and cultures of Southern Africa, East Africa, Ethiopia, and West Africa. Mention that visual aids such as maps and charts are expected as a part of their oral presentations. These aids can also be used throughout the discussion of the selections from the text.
2. After the students have studied African life, pair students and have them write and present dialogues which contrast the attitudes about the Africa of the European colonist and the African native. This is important because some students may not understand the sometimes uncomplimentary references to the colonists.
3. Have students investigate African history as far as Southern Africa, East Africa, Ethiopia, and West Africa are concerned. Have selected students debate the effects of colonization. A suggested topic would be: Resolved: That colonization has had a positive effect on the peoples of Africa.

Questions for Discussion and Composition. (Asterisks mark items appropriate for composition activities.)

1. Southern Africa
   a. "Under the Blue Gum Trees" by Dyke Sentso
      (1) What is the relationship between Japie Genade and Moiloa?
      (2) Discuss Moiloa's reaction to the death of his son and to his displacement after Genade's farm is sold.
      (3) What is the difference between the way of life of Japie's family and Moiloa's family?*
   b. "Mob Passion" by D. C. Themba
      (1) Why is the relationship between Linga and Mapula destined to be tragic?
      (2) What is the cultural significance of the ritual which precedes the violence?
      (3) Name other stories of "star-crossed" lovers. Compare them.
      (4) Contrast the reactions of the men and women after the violence.

c. "The Dignity of Begging" by William Modisane
   (1) What does the reader learn about the narrator's character throughout the story?
   (2) Compare the narrator's conception of himself with his conception of Blushing Groom. Are they as different as the narrator seems to feel they are?*
   (3) Why are Richard and Nathaniel beggars?
   (4) What is it in this society which permits begging to become a profession? How does the satire in this selection make this point?

2. East Africa
   "The Story of Liongo" by Hamisi Wa Kayi
   (1) Why is Liongo imprisoned?
   (2) This selection is an exercise in cleverness. Give some examples of the cunning of the villagers and of Liongo as well.*
   (3) Why does Liongo accept his fate at the hands of his nephew?

   Note: The reference to Liongo as "father" and to his murderer as "nephew" is probably not in the same sense as would be inferred in the Western cultures.

3. Ethiopia
   "How the Ethiopian Woman Tamed Her Husband" retold by Professor Murad Kamel
   What is the universal truth in this story?

4. West Africa
   a. "The Stolen Jacket" by Camara Laye
      (1) Contrast the attitudes toward their court experiences of Clarence in this story and of Nathaniel in "The Dignity of Begging."*
      (2) How is Clarence a victim of the innkeeper, the judge, the landlord, the beggar, and the two boys?
      (3) What is the irony of Clarence's situation?
   b. "Truth and Falsehood" by Birago Diop
      (1) Explain the personification in the story.
      (2) Fene-Falsehood bears no resemblance to the "good Lord." Prove or disprove this statement by using evidence from the text.
      (3) Discuss what Fene-Falsehood means when he states, "I am begining to think that even if the good Lord loves you [Deug-Truth], man doesn't appreciate you overmuch."*

(4) Compare the reactions of the husband and village chief to Deug-Truth's advice with the reaction of the king to Fene-Falsehood's advice. Evaluate the advice of the two men.

c. "Shadow of Darkness" by Gladys Casely-Hayford
(1) Compare the loyalty between Shadow of Darkness and Jalona with the loyalty shown in other stories of boys and their pets such as Travis and Old Yeller.*
(2) Why is Shadow of Darkness such a prize bull?
(3) Jalona says of Shadow of Darkness, "He was with me in my darkest hours. . . ." Explain.
(4) What will become of Sori?

d. "There's Always a Way Out" by Gbemi
(1) What problems does Fasasi face automatically if he accepts the position as chieftain?
(2) What are his wife's reasons for assisting him in finding a solution?
(3) What makes his daughters attractive to the suitors?
(4) What does the story tell us about marriage customs in West Africa?

e. "The Parable of the Eagle" by James Aggrey
What is the significance of the statement, "Thou art an eagle . . . stretch forth thy wings and fly"? Discuss this as it relates to the narrator's people.*

Related Activities

1. Have selected students write and present satirical dramatizations with themes similar to that of "The Dignity of Begging."
2. Have students construct a list of distinctively African aspects of life as seen in the selections. An example is the sense of tribal honor in "Mob Passion."
3. Have students select passages from other works they have read and contrast the style of these African myths with these other works. For example, selections from Carl Sandburg's *Abe Lincoln Grows Up* and Charles Dickens' *Great Expectations* could be used. The students should contrast sentence structure, diction, and the use of figurative language.
4. Have students contrast family relationships in Africa and in the United States.

5. Have students write original fables using Africa as the setting.
6. Have students write original compositions in which they personify inanimate things such as peace, hope, despair, and love. An alternative assignment would be the use of the same topics for a connotative theme.
7. Have a group of students investigate marriage customs from different countries. Have them contrast these with the custom seen in "There's Always a Way Out." In addition, students can indicate different customs their American families observe.
8. Have students contrast legendary heroes. Such a contrast would integrate this unit and the course of study. An example of such a contrast would be of Liongo and his nephew with Odysseus and Telemachus of Greek mythology.
9. Have students write a contemporary original story, poem, or play that has the same theme as "The Parable of the Eagle."
10. Have students discuss the universal themes found in the selections. Of what importance is this universality?

Independent Reading

Moore, Gerald, and Ulli Beier, eds. *Modern Poetry from Africa.* Penguin, pap., 1963.

Mphahlele, Ezekiel, ed. *African Writing Today.* Penguin, pap., 1967.

Black Literature for a Unit on Prose Nonfiction: Grade 9

Without some mention of Frederick Douglass, this curriculum would be incomplete. He was one of the most outstanding black orators of the pre-Civil War period and was well known through his antislavery-oriented *The North Star,* a newspaper which he published himself.

Douglass' autobiography, *The Life and Times of Frederick Douglass,* is an excellent reading selection for the ninth-grade unit of prose nonfiction. However, because of its length, sentence structure, and vocabulary, a compromise must be made. The compromise is an adaptation by Barbara Ritchie. It is well written, and students will enjoy reading of the life of Douglass, the slave, who lived to escape to freedom and to dedicate the rest of his life to the elimination of slavery in this country. The fact that some of his thoughts are written in his own words will give the students insight into the pre-Civil War period. The book also presents commentary on the institution of slavery.

The life of Frederick Douglass will be an inspiration to many students. They will identify easily with his desire for freedom, security, and peace among people.

Questions for Discussion and Composition. (Asterisks mark items appropriate for composition activities.)

1. Discuss Douglass' birth, childhood, and early relationships on the Anthony plantation.
2. What were the physical characteristics of the plantation? Describe the slave quarters, the Great House, and the other surroundings.
3. Describe the living conditions of the slaves.
4. Discuss Douglass' remarks about the attitude of blacks to slavery:* "The remark in the olden time was not unfrequently made that slaves were the most contented and happy laborers in the world, and their dancing and singing were referred to in proof of this alleged fact; but it was a great mistake to suppose them happy because they sometimes made those joyful noises. The songs of the slaves represented their sorrows, rather than their joys. Like tears, they were a relief to aching hearts."
5. What are the implications of the relationship between slave and overseer found in this passage: "The doctrine that submission to violence is the best cure for violence did not hold good between slaves and overseers. He [the slave] was whipped oftener who was whipped easiest."?
6. Describe the various classes found on the plantation and their relationships to each other. Mention the slaveholder, the slaves, and the overseer.
7. When did Frederick first think of escaping to the North? What event precipitated this desire?
8. Discuss the means used by slaveholders to control the lives of their slaves. For example, why does Auld say, "Learning will spoil the best nigger in the world. . . . He should know nothing but the will of his master and learn to obey it"?*

9. What significant part does Father Lawson play in Frederick's early intellectual development?
10. How does Douglass rationalize stealing from Thomas Auld?
11. Discuss the paragraph that begins, "The morality of free society could have no application to slave society. . . ." (The passage is found on page 59.)*
12. What was ironic about Thomas Auld's conversion to a religious life?
13. Discuss Douglass' relationship with Covey. Consider the required labor, his flight, and his eventual confrontation with Covey.
14. Describe Douglass' first escape attempt. Why was it unsuccessful?
15. What trade does he learn in Baltimore? What were the complications?
16. How does Douglass eventually escape?
17. How does Frederick's name happen to change?
18. Describe Douglass' association with the abolitionists in the 1840s.*
19. Describe some of the racial conflicts that Douglass meets in the North. Note his reception in some cities and the treatment of his children in school.
20. Characterize John Brown. What were some of the flaws in his thinking according to Douglass?
21. What was Douglass' evaluation of Abraham Lincoln? Agree or disagree with his thinking.
22. Why did Douglass encourage blacks to fight in the war? Were they treated equally?
23. After the Civil War, Douglass made the right of blacks to vote one of his most important causes. Why was this right so important?
24. What was Douglass' contribution to society? In other words, what did he do for himself and others as far as black people in this country are concerned?*

Vocabulary

1. indigent
2. incur
3. ineffaceably
4. sedate
5. impose

31. disconsolate
32. censure
33. cordial
34. contemplation
35. abhorred

6. ponderous
7. countenance
8. indignation
9. disparage
10. indolent
11. baronial
12. intersperse
13. diminution
14. destitute
15. redress
16. capricious
17. debase
18. emanate
19. perpetrate
20. atrocity
21. grapple
22. balsam
23. compensation
24. termagant
25. malediction
26. benevolent
27. stringent
28. denunciation
29. vindication
30. advocate
36. conversion
37. laudable
38. goad
39. allegation
40. benignant
41. defensive
42. aggressive
43. enervate
44. congenial
45. feasible
46. agitate
47. formidable
48. mortify
49. emancipate
50. nigger (connotation)
51. assailant
52. solicit
53. tarpaulin
54. peremptory
55. fugitive
56. proscription
57. mobocrat
58. discretion
59. assail
60. sagacious

Related Activities

1. Have students do connotative paragraphs about slavery as an introductory assignment. At the conclusion of the reading, these compositions should be discussed again in the light of acquired knowledge.
2. Have students compare the lives of Frederick Douglass and other people mentioned in the unit on prose nonfiction.
3. Have students present group discussions which emphasize life in the United States during the 1800s. For example, one group might discuss dedication to country when one's country does not recognize every member as a full citizen.
4. Guide students to read and to present oral reports of related books which discuss the struggles of other well-known blacks in the United States.

5. Have students present group skits which dramatize some aspect of Douglass' life. Students will in this activity have a chance to identify with Douglass and react in their own way to Douglass' experiences.
6. Have students increase their knowledge of other black people in history, such as Harriet Tubman, Sojourner Truth, and Robert Smalls. Individual or group work in these areas should be shared with the class through oral discussions.
7. Encourage students in the making of slavery collages, illustrations of passages from the text, and pictorial interpretations of portions of *The Life and Times of Frederick Douglass.*

Independent Reading

Nonfiction

Davis, Sammy, Jr. *Yes I Can: The Story of Sammy Davis, Jr.*, with Jane and Burt Boyar. FS&G, 1965; pap., PB, 1972.

Douglass, Frederick. *The Mind and Heart of Frederick Douglass: Excerpts from Speeches of the Great Negro Orator*, edited by Barbara Ritchie. T Y Crowell, 1968.

Gregory, Dick. *From the Back of the Bus*. Dutton, 1963.

______. *Nigger: An Autobiography*, with Robert Lipsyte. Dutton, 1964; pap., PB, 1965.

______. *The Shadow That Scares Me*. PB, pap., n.d.

Griffin, John H. *Black Like Me*. [1961] 2d ed., HM, 1977; pap., NAL, n.d.

Murray, Pauli. *Proud Shoes: The Story of an American Family.* Reprint of 1956 edition, Reprint, 1973.

Fiction

Bonham, Frank. *Durango Street*. Dutton, 1965; pap., Dell, 1972.

Bontemps, Arna. *Black Thunder*. [1936] pap., Beacon Pr, 1968.

Booth, Esma. *Kalena*. McKay, 1958.

Graham, Lorenz. *North Town*. T Y Crowell, 1965; pap., NAL, 1977.

______. *South Town*. NAL, pap., 1966.

Hentoff, Nat. *Jazz Country*. Har-Row, 1965; pap., Dell, 1967.

Hunter, Kristin. *The Soul Brothers and Sister Lou*. Scribner, 1968; pap., Avon, 1976.

Marshall, Catherine. *Julie's Heritage*. McKay, 1957.

Means, Florence C. *Tolliver*. HM, 1963.

Sterling, Dorothy. *Mary Jane*. [1959] Schol Bk Serv, pap., 1972.

Poetry

Adoff, Arnold, ed. *I Am the Darker Brother: An Anthology of Modern Poems by Negro Americans*. Macmillan, cloth & pap., 1968.

Bibliography

Adoff, Arnold, ed. *I Am the Darker Brother: An Anthology of Modern Poems by Negro Americans*. Macmillan, cloth & pap., 1968.

Angell, Pauline K. *To the Top of the World: The Story of Peary and Henson*. Rand, 1964.

Bennett, Lerone, Jr. *What Manner of Man: A Biography of Martin Luther King, Jr., 1929–1968*. Johnson Chi, 1968; pap., PB, n.d.

Bonham, Frank. *Durango Street*. Dutton, 1965; pap., Dell, 1972.

Bontemps, Arna. *Black Thunder*. [1936] pap., Beacon Pr, 1968.

______. *The Story of the Negro*. Knopf, 1958.

Bradford, Sarah. *Harriet Tubman: The Moses of Her People*. Peter Smith, n.d.

Brooks, Charlotte. *The Outnumbered: Stories, Essays and Poems about Minority Groups by America's Leading Writers*. Dell, pap., 1967.

Buckmaster, Henrietta. *Women Who Shaped History*. Macmillan, 1968; pap., 1974.

Clarke, Mary. *Petticoat Rebel*. Viking Pr, 1964.

Cluff, Tom. *Minutemen of the Sea*. Follett, 1955.

Davis, Sammy, Jr. *Yes I Can: The Story of Sammy Davis, Jr.*, with Jane and Burt Boyar. FS&G, 1965; pap., PB, 1972.

de Treviño, Elizabeth Borton. *I, Juan de Pareja*. FS&G, 1965.

Douglass, Frederick. *The Life and Times of Frederick Douglass*, edited by Barbara Ritchie. T Y Crowell, 1966.

______. *The Mind and Heart of Frederick Douglass: Excerpts from Speeches of the Great Negro Orator*, edited by Barbara Ritchie. T Y Crowell, 1968.

Douty, Esther M. *Under the New Roof: Five Patriots of the New Republic*. Rand, 1965.

Durham, Philip, and Everett L. Jones. *The Adventures of the Negro Cowboys*. Dodd, 1966; pap., Bantam, 1969.

Felton, Harold W. *Edward Rose, Negro Trail Blazer*. Dodd, 1967.

______. *Jim Beckwourth: Negro Mountain Man*. Dodd, 1966; pap., Apollo Eds, 1970.

Graham, Lorenz. *North Town*. T Y Crowell, 1965; pap., NAL, 1977.

______. *South Town*. NAL, pap., 1966.

Graham, Shirley. *Jean Baptiste Pointe de Sable: Founder of Chicago*. Messner, 1953.

______. *Your Most Humble Servant: The Story of Benjamin Banneker*. Messner, 1949.

Gregory, Dick. *From the Back of the Bus*. Dutton, 1963.

———. *Nigger: An Autobiography,* with Robert Lipsyte. Dutton, 1964; pap., PB, 1965.

———. *The Shadow That Scares Me.* PB, pap., n.d.

Griffin, John H. *Black Like Me.* [1961] 2d ed., HM, 1977; pap., NAL, n.d.

Hamilton, Virginia. *The House of Dies Drear.* Macmillan, 1968; pap., 1970.

Hentoff, Nat. *Jazz Country.* Har-Row, 1965; pap., Dell, 1967.

Hughes, Langston. *The Dream Keeper and Other Poems.* Knopf, 1932.

Hunter, Kristin. *The Soul Brothers and Sister Lou.* Scribner, 1968; pap., Avon, 1976.

James, Charles L., ed. *From the Roots: Short Stories by Black Americans.* Har-Row, pap., 1970.

Marshall, Catherine. *Julie's Heritage.* McKay, 1957.

Means, Florence C. *Tolliver.* HM, 1963.

Moore, Gerald, and Ulli Beier, eds. *Modern Poetry from Africa.* Penguin, pap., 1963.

Mphahlele, Ezekiel, ed. *African Writing Today.* Penguin, pap., 1967.

Murray, Pauli. *Proud Shoes: The Story of an American Family.* Reprint of 1956 edition, Reprint, 1973.

Owens, William A. *Black Mutiny: The Revolt on the Schooner Amistad.* [1953] Pilgrim Press, 1968.

Petry, Ann. *Tituba of Salem Village.* T Y Crowell, 1964.

Rodman, Bella. *Lions in the Way.* Follett, 1966.

Rollins, Charlemae. *They Showed the Way: Forty American Negro Leaders.* T Y Crowell, 1964.

Rutherford, Peggy, ed. *African Voices: An Anthology of Native African Writings.* Vanguard, 1959.

Scherman, Katharine. *The Slave Who Freed Haiti: The Story of Touissant Louverture.* Random, 1964.

Sterling, Dorothy. *Captain of the Planter: The Story of Robert Smalls.* Doubleday, 1958; pap., Archway, n.d.

———. *Mary Jane.* [1959] Schol Bk Serv, pap., 1972.

Sterne, Emma Gelders. *Mary McLeod Bethune.* Knopf, 1957.

———. *The Long Black Schooner.* Follett, 1953. Reissued as *The Slave Ship.* Schol Bk Serv, pap., 1973.

Yates, Elizabeth. *Amos Fortune: Free Man.* [1950] Dutton, 1967; pap., Dell, 1971.

Zagoren, Ruby. *Venture for Freedom.* Dell, pap., 1971.

Acknowledgments

Department of Curriculum and Instruction of the Board of Public Education, Pittsburgh, Pennsylvania

Committee: Juanita S. Alston, Elizabeth Claytor, Vickie Hamlin, Herman McClain, Dee Jay Oshry, Helen B. Gorman, retired, Supervisor, English; Lois M. Grose, retired, Associate Director for English; Margaret Band, Supervisor, English; Jane C. Tygard, Associate Director for English; Francine Gross, Senior Curriculum Editor; Francis J. Rifugiato, Director of Curriculum; Mary L. Molyneaux, Assistant Superintendent for Curriculum and Instruction

9 Black Literature: A Senior Elective

The following course outline describes a program that has been successful for several years. Its author, Grace Larkin, a teacher at Oneonta Senior High School, New York, says that initially some people looked upon the course as a fad. Having little or no knowledge of black literature, these individuals "had no idea of the hidden treasures of the past or of the wonderful things coming from the exciting writers of today." She began developing the course with two ideas in mind: (1) "to expose students to good literature not included in the existing program," and (2) "to expose them to new ideas and the basis for those ideas that are part of the world in which they live." Her students, many of whom may have decided out of curiosity to take the course, have found it to be exciting, informative, enjoyable, and a real eye-opener.

Oneonta is in an isolated location in upstate New York but receives stimulus from two colleges, Hartwick College and a campus of the State University of New York. Student population at the high school, therefore, is diverse, including rural residents as well as children of professors. The course runs ten weeks and forms part of a senior elective program. It is usually taught three times a year, reaching about ninety students.

Grace Larkin developed this senior elective after taking courses from Charles L. James, short story writer and editor of *From the Roots: Short Stories by Black Americans*, a text used in the program at Oneonta Senior High (Har-Row, pap., 1970). The "three basic traditions present in black literature" referred to in the course objectives exist in black literature from pre-Civil War times, and continue to influence black writers today. They are (1) folktale, (2) the plantation tradition, a romanticized view of slavery and plantation life which is evident in some of the fiction of Dunbar and others, and (3) the abolitionist tradition, which ranges from slave autobiographies to the rejection of white culture by the new black writers of the 1970s.

Facts of publication for the other works mentioned are given in the bibliography at the end of this chapter.

Course of Study

I. Major objectives
   A. Develop an appreciation of the existence and worth of a distinctive body of literature written by black Americans
   B. Recognize the cultural differences responsible for a separate and distinct black literature
   C. Understand the three basic traditions present in black literature
   D. Develop an understanding of the myths and themes functioning within black literature
   E. Recognize major black authors and their contributions to the literary world
   F. Develop an understanding of the black author's point of view

II. Course description

This course will use the short story and poetry forms to cover the five basic periods of black literature. Texts will be *From the Roots*, edited by Charles L. James, and *American Negro Poetry*, edited by Arna Bontemps. Students will be required to do independent reading in one particular period or in one particular author as a course project.

III. Course outline
   A. The roots (1890–1920)
      1. The folktale tradition
      2. The plantation tradition
      3. The abolitionist tradition
   B. A new writer (1920–1930)
      1. From the folk
      2. Expatriates
   C. Dark naturalism (1930–1940)
      1. Figures in transition
      2. Young protestors
   D. Toward literary assimilation (1940–1950)
      1. The war years
      2. Postwar dissent
      3. From the "Talented Tenth"
      4. A woman's voice
   E. Toward a black art (1950–present)
      1. Tales of the black sixties
      2. Modern voices

IV. Texts

A. The basic texts used in the course are *From the Roots* and *American Negro Poetry.*

B. A number of selections of independent reading and required projects are available in the classroom. Examples:

Baldwin, James. *Another Country*; *The Fire Next Time*; *Nobody Knows My Name*

Chapman, Abraham. *New Black Voices*

Du Bois, W. E. B. *The Souls of Black Folk*

Ellison, Ralph. *Invisible Man*

Frazier, E. Franklin. *Black Bourgeoisie*

Gaines, Ernest J. *The Autobiography of Miss Jane Pittman*

Gregory, Dick. *Nigger*; *The Shadow That Scares Me*

Hansberry, Lorraine. *To Be Young, Gifted and Black*; *A Raisin in the Sun*

Hentoff, Nat. *The New Equality*

Lomax, Louis E. *The Negro Revolt*

Parks, Gordon. *The Learning Tree*

Teague, Bob. *Letters to a Black Boy*

Washington, Booker T. *Up from Slavery*

Wright, Richard. *Native Son*

C. Non-textual materials [can] include records, films, and videotapes.

1. A selection of records including major black poets
2. On tape: *Black History: Lost, Stolen or Strayed* (a book by Otto Lindenmeyer)
3. Other selections depend on availability.

V. Course requirements

A. Assigned short stories and poetry for each unit

B. An independent reading project of longer works

VI. Evaluation

Evaluation of each student is based on three unit tests, a paper resulting from the independent reading, and class participation.

Bibliography

Baldwin, James. *Another Country.* Dial, 1962; pap., Dell, 1970.

______. *The Fire Next Time.* Dial, 1963; pap., Dell, 1970.

______. *Nobody Knows My Name.* Dial, 1961; pap., Dell, n.d.

Bontemps, Arna, ed. *American Negro Poetry.* Rev. ed., Hill & Wang, cloth & pap., 1974.

Chapman, Abraham, ed. *New Black Voices*. NAL, pap., n.d.

Du Bois, W. E. B. *The Souls of Black Folk: Essays and Sketches*. [1903] pap., WSP, 1970.

Ellison, Ralph. *Invisible Man*. Random, 1951; pap., 1972.

Frazier, E. Franklin. *Black Bourgeoisie: The Rise of a New Middle Class in the United States*. Macmillan, pap., 1962.

Gaines, Ernest J. *The Autobiography of Miss Jane Pittman*. Dial, 1971; pap., Bantam, 1972.

Gregory, Dick. *Nigger: An Autobiography*, with Robert Lipsyte. Dutton, 1964, pap., PB, 1965.

______. *The Shadow That Scares Me*. PB, pap., n.d.

Hansberry, Lorraine. *A Raisin in the Sun*. Random, 1969; pap., NAL, 1961.

______. *To Be Young, Gifted and Black: Lorraine Hansberry in Her Own Words*, edited by Robert Nemiroff. P-H, 1969; pap., NAL, 1970.

Hentoff, Nat. *The New Equality*. Viking Pr, cloth & pap., 1965.

James, Charles L., ed. *From the Roots: Short Stories by Black Americans*. Har-Row, pap., 1970.

Lindenmeyer, Otto. *Black History: Lost, Stolen or Strayed*. Avon, pap., 1970.

Lomax, Louis E. *The Negro Revolt*. Har-Row, 1962.

Parks, Gordon. *The Learning Tree*. Har-Row, 1963; pap., Fawcett World, 1975.

Teague, Bob. *Letters to a Black Boy*. Walker & Co, 1968.

Washington, Booker T. *Up from Slavery*. [1900] Dodd, 1972; pap., Bantam, 1970.

Wright, Richard. *Native Son*. Reprint of 1940 edition, Har-Row, 1969; pap., n.d.

10 Supplementary Activities

Karima Amin

Concepts of what a teacher can do in class to involve students actively in the subject they are studying have expanded greatly in recent years. This chapter offers suggestions for several kinds of classroom activities that can encourage students to shed self-consciousness and express ideas and feelings triggered by their reading. Included are ideas for both formal and informal classrooms that encourage students to examine many facets of black literature on several levels.

The "Composition and Discussion Motivators" are designed to help students (and teachers) reach a depth of understanding that is essential to the study of literature by black writers. In addition, these motivators should enrich vocabularies through speech and writing, and should encourage students to form and express opinions based on some degree of logical reasoning and critical thinking.

The "Ideas for Role-Playing" are flexible and provide vehicles for freely and creatively expressing feelings and attitudes. Through these improvised scenes and the discussions which may follow the acting, students can also be led to understand and appreciate the feelings of others.

Games in the classroom can be entertaining and enlightening for both students and teachers. The games mentioned in this section provide a break in the routine that allows students to have some fun while discovering more about the black experience. Increased knowledge of "the experience" will undoubtedly lead to a better understanding of black literature itself.

Composition and Discussion Motivators

The following provocative quotations provide topics which may be used for composition assignments, for discussions by an entire class, by small groups, by panels, or for debate.

1. "If young whites can change, then there is hope for America" (Eldridge Cleaver, *Soul on Ice*, Dell, 1970, p. 84).
2. "The negro race here and now is inferior to the white race. The negro is a beast" (Charles Carroll, *The Negro, a Beast*, Arno, 1900).
3. "Blues belongs to the black man. No white man can sing the blues and really know what he's talking about" (Ray Charles, narrator of the film "Soul," Part II of "Body and Soul," produced by BEA Educational Media, a division of CBS, in 1970).
4. "Black is beautiful" (a slogan popularized during the 1960s).
5. "Black Woman" by Don L. Lee (Haki R. Madhubuti), in Don L. Lee, *Don't Cry, Scream*, Broadside, 1969, p. 55.

   blackwoman:
   is an
   in and out
   rightsideup
   action-image
   of her man...
   in other
   (blacker) words,
   she's together,
   if
   he
   bes

6. "Each Negro is a little bit white, and every white is a little bit Negro.... Both are caught in a common human predicament. Each needs the other ..." (Kenneth B. Clark, *Dark Ghetto*, Har-Row, 1965, p. 223).
7. "...the white man said we were free ... but, he never let us practice freedom" (from the poem "Mad! Mad!" by Ernest White. In Alma Murray and Robert Thomas, eds., *The Search*, Schol Bk Serv, 1971, p. 27).
8. "The strong men keep coming" (from the poem "Strong Men" by Sterling Brown. In Alma Murray and Robert Thomas, eds., *The Search*, Schol Bk Serv, 1971, p. 36).
9. Comments on the television production of Alex Haley's *Roots* ("Why 'Roots' Hit Home," *Time*, Feb. 14, 1977, pp. 68–71):

a. "We now know our roots are inextricably bound with the roots of blacks and cannot be separated" (John Callahan, professor of American literature, Lewis and Clark College, Portland, Oregon, p. 70).
b. "It sounded like us, it looked like us, it was us. We've always wanted whites to understand how our backgrounds are different from theirs. Now they should understand a little better where we are coming from" (Allen Counter, biologist, Harvard University, p. 71).
c. "It helps people identify and gets conversations started, but I can't see any lasting effect" (Charles Rangel, U.S. Congressman from New York, p. 71).
d. "Everything converged—the right time, the right story and the right form. The country, I feel, was ready for it . . . in the 60's . . . it might have spawned resentments and apprehensions the country couldn't have taken" (Barbara Jordan, U. S. Congresswoman from Texas, p. 71).

10. "And now we're ready to change a system, a system where a white man can destroy a black man with a single word. Nigger" (Dick Gregory, *Nigger*, Dutton, 1964, p. 209).
11. ". . . I think there's a way to deal with this society's racial madness, peacefully and effectively, if Mister Charlie (the white man) is man enough to face it. But, as you realize by now, facing things squarely is not how Mister Charlie made his reputation" (Bob Teague, *Letters to a Black Boy*, Walker & Co, 1968, p. 194).
12. "Axiom: White folks do nothing that is not to their advantage.

    Correction: White folks do nothing that they *think* is not to their advantage.

    Conclusion: White folks do nothing that is not to the disadvantage of blacks"

    (Julius Lester, *Look Out Whitey! Black Power's Gon' Get Your Mama!*, Grove, 1969, p. 57).
13. Quotations from *Wine in the Wilderness*, a play by Alice Childress (In Alma Murray and Robert Thomas, eds., *Major Black Writers*, Schol Bk Serv, 1971). Tommy speaks:

    a. "Niggers, niggers, niggers, I'm sick-a-niggers ain't you? A nigger will mess up every time . . ." (p. 146).
    b. "Just you wait, one hundred years from now all the

honkys gonna claim our poets just like they stole our blues" (p. 173).

   c. "Straightened hair, naturals, wigs are accessories like shoes, hats, and bags. The real thing is taking place on the inside" (p. 184).

14. Quotations from *Five on the Black Hand Side*, a play by Charlie L. Russell (In Murray and Thomas, eds., *Black Perspectives*, Schol Bk Serv, 1971):
    a. Gideon: "The family is the basic unit in a society" (p. 62).
    b. Booker T.: "Different strokes for different folks" (p. 63).
    c. Stormy Monday: "... when you ... get into a black thing, more is expected of you. It's not only about how you look, it's also about how you live. Being black means being involved in the struggle" (p. 138).
    d. Sim: "... blackie's already got enough religion. It's whitey who needs to be turned on to God" (p. 92).
    e. Gideon: "As long as we think only of ourselves (individually) we'll always be a weak people" (p. 63).
    f. Sweetmeat: "Can't nobody tell me about black women, man. They're evil!" (p. 92).

Ideas for Role-Playing

1. An incident showing master-slave relationship
2. A slave being sold on the block
3. A slave learning to read and write in secret
4. "All black folks got rhythm!"
5. "Some of my best friends are colored!"
6. Brief re-enactment of a scene from a short story or play read in class
7. Invite someone to your home for their first "soul food" dinner.
8. "Jim Crowism":
   a. Blacks are refused restaurant service.
   b. A black person is expected to give his seat to a white person on a bus.
9. A person who is white awakens to discover that he has turned black overnight, or vice versa.
10. An incident involving the "Klan"
11. Encourage a friend to recognize the importance of studying black literature.

12. A scene based on the idea expressed in the poem "We Wear the Mask" by Paul Laurence Dunbar.
13. "The Black Experience":
    a. Black student, white teacher (or vice versa)
    b. Black customer, white salesperson
    c. Black welfare recipient, white caseworker
    d. Black employee, white employer (or vice versa)
    e. Black student, white student
    f. Black doctor, white patient
    g. Black child, white child (both age 5)
    h. Black youth, white policeman
    i. Black housekeeper, white employer
    j. Black celebrity, white interviewer

Students may give impromptu presentations or may be given time for advance planning. The time limit for delivery is best kept at three to five minutes, and groups should include two to four people. If time is provided for advance planning, the instructor should encourage *group effort*. Each member of a group should understand that he or she is to be an active contributor in the preparatory stage before delivery. Better results will be achieved also if students prepare without writing out and memorizing complete scripts; preparation should instead provide a degree of structure and control for some ad libbing. The instructor should also encourage imaginative approaches. The situations suggested above may be modified in an unlimited number of ways. A decision should also be made regarding whether a presentation is to be serious or humorous; in either case, it should exhibit logical development with a clear premise and a reasonable conclusion. Also consider the use of props and partial costuming.

For the purpose of evaluation, the following may be appraised:

1. Organization
2. Voice
3. Gestures
4. Audience contact
5. Choice of language
6. Imagination

A Word about Games

Many teachers who have experimented with games in the classroom have found that they help motivate students to take an active part in learning. This is especially true for students who react with anxiety to more formal reading and writing assignments. Besides adding an element of fun to the classroom atmosphere, a well designed game undoubtedly helps develop students' thinking, decision-making, and problem-solving abilities. When selecting games, teachers should consider the ages and personalities of the students who will be involved. Teachers should also recognize that game-playing requires that they shift their role from authority figure to facilitator and resource person.

Simulation games are especially useful, because they provide an approach to learning which is primarily affective, dealing with the emotions that surround ideas. A few simulation games are briefly described in this section. When studying literature, students certainly need to learn something of the artistic techniques involved in creating a work of fiction, for example. But to appreciate that work fully, they also need to know some of the personal experiences which shape and color such a work. This becomes more necessary if the reader's and the writer's experiences differ widely. Simulation games may encourage such probing into the black experience, if the teacher is careful to select games which minimize competitiveness and emphasize cooperation and reflection. Through such games, students can gain greater awareness of their own personal feelings.

Two books deal in general with the use of simulation games in the classroom:

Inventing and Playing Games in the English Classroom: A Handbook for Teachers, edited by Kenneth Davis and John Hollowell (NCTE, pap., 1977), discusses the value of simulation games as a teaching method, the best ways to integrate them into the framework of a course, and guidelines for designing your own classroom game. The book deals frankly with the challenges to the teacher posed by classroom activities in which students are not asked for cut-and-dried, right-or-wrong answers. It discusses ways for teachers to prepare themselves and their students for playing games. While the original games described in detail do not include one on black literature, several of the game designs could be adapted to it.

Simulation Games: An Approach to Learning by Dennis M. Adams (C A Jones, 1973) is another useful guide for educators who are interested in using games in the classroom. It also comments on the usefulness of simulation games and potential problems with gaming, and offers guidelines for teachers who want to design their own games. The book cites several games that are potentially useful for classes on black literature.

"The Ghetto Game," developed at Johns Hopkins University, is described as "a fairly advanced board game simulating what it is like to live in an urban ghetto" (p. 39). Eight to ten players using the game board must role-play inner-city characters according to game rules. The game has a playing time of one to three hours. (Source: School and Library Department, Western Publishing Co., Inc.)

"Blacks and Whites," designed by Communications Research Machines, Inc., also simulates ghetto life. Four to eight players are "black people" and "white people" who "play on the same board while living in different worlds . . . " (p. 41). The players invent new strategies and make changes, redistributing power and money. (Source: Psychology Today Games.)

"Simulating Events Found in Literature," described in Chapter 4 of *Simulation Games*, is a teacher-made, non-competitive game. After reading a selection, students role-play new scenes in which they may alter events which occur later in the plot, insert an event that fits the plot but is not depicted in the work, simply change a scene, or, after discussion, add a scene which makes the author's work more understandable. The text also suggests follow-up discussions relating the fictional story line to similar real-life behavior and its motivations.

Teachers might also check in their communities for commercially distributed games relating to the black experience, although games not produced by the mass manufacturers are often not widely available. One of these, "The Black Community Game," invented by Malik Ali, a former chemical engineer and teacher, simulates the lifestyle of black people in the ghetto. A classroom module requiring two to three class periods has been developed from it. The game puts up to seven players, ages eight through adult, in situations common to ghetto life. For example: "Your car breaks down. Get one brother or sister to help you." Or: "Your slumlord refuses to fix your heater." The game develops problem-solving and communications skills as it teaches the political, social, and economic forces at work in the black community. The players try to survive the rigors of the ghetto through interaction and cooperation. The game enables both teachers and students to better understand some of the ideas expressed by black writers. (Source: Motherland, Inc.)

Directory of Publishers

Book and Game Publishers

Africana. Holmes & Meier Africana Pub. Imprint of Holmes & Meier Pubs., Inc.

AMS Pr AMS Press, Inc., 56 E. 13th St., New York, NY 10003

Anch. Doubleday Anchor Books. Imprint of Doubleday & Co., Inc.

Apollo Eds Apollo Editions. Orders to: Harper & Row Pubs., Inc., Scranton, PA 18512

Appleton-Century-Crofts Appleton-Century-Crofts, 292 Madison Ave., New York, NY 10017

Archway Archway Paperbacks, 630 Fifth Ave., New York, NY 10020

Arno Arno Press, 3 Park Ave., New York, NY 10017

Ashley Bks Ashley Books, Inc., 223 Main St., Port Washington, NY 11050

Avon Avon Books, 959 Eighth Ave., New York, NY 10019

Badger Press No business address available.

Ballantine Ballantine Books, Inc., Div. of Random House, Inc. Orders to Westminster, MD 21157

Bantam Bantam Books, Inc. Orders to: 414 E. Golf Rd., Des Plaines, IL 60016

Barron Barron's Educational Series, Inc., 113 Crossways Park Dr., Woodbury, NY 11797

Beacon Pr Beacon Press, Inc., 25 Beacon St., Boston, MA 02108; Keystone Industrial Park, Scranton, PA 18512

Bobbs Bobbs-Merrill Co., Inc., A Thomas Audel Co., 4300 W. 62nd St., Indianapolis, IN 46206

Breman No business address available.

Broadside Broadside Crummell Press, 74 Glendale Ave., Highland Park, MI 48203

C A Jones No business address available.

Cambridge U Pr Cambridge Univ. Press. Orders to: 510 North Ave., New Rochelle, NY 10801

Chatham Bkseller Chatham Bookseller, 38 Maple St., Chatham, NJ 07928

Collier. Macmillan Collier Books. Imprint of Macmillan Publishing Co., Inc.

Columbia U Pr Columbia Univ. Press. Orders to: 136 S. Broadway, Irvington-on-Hudson, NY 10533

Corinth Bks Corinth Books. Dist. by: Book Organization, Elm St., Millerton, NY 12546

Coward Coward, McCann & Geoghegan, Inc. Orders to: 390 Murray Hill Pkwy., East Rutherford, NJ 07073

Criterion Bks Criterion Books, Inc., 666 Fifth Ave., New York, NY 10019

Crown Crown Pubs., Inc., 419 Park Ave., S., New York, NY 10016

Cultural Institute Press No business address available.

Da Capo Da Capo Press, Inc., 227 W. 17th St., New York, NY 10011

Dell Dell Publishing Co., Inc., 1 Dag Hammarskjold Plaza, 245 E. 47th St., New York, NY 10017

Dial Dial Press, 1 Dag Hammarskjold Plaza, 245 E. 47th St., New York, NY 10017

Dodd Dodd, Mead & Co., 79 Madison Ave., New York, NY 10016

Doubleday Doubleday & Co., Inc. Orders to: 501 Franklin Ave., Garden City, NY 11530

Dover Dover Pubns., Inc., 180 Varick St., New York, NY 10014

Dutton E. P. Dutton & Co., Inc., 201 Park Ave., S., New York, NY 10003

East African Publishing House East African Publishing House, Koinage Street, P. O. Box 30571, Nairobi, Kenya

EMC EMC Corp., 180 E. Sixth St., St. Paul, MN 55101

Falcon Pr No business address available.

Fawcett World Fawcett World Library, 1515 Broadway, New York, NY 10036

Follett Follett Publishing Co., Div. of Follett Corp., 1010 W. Washington Blvd., Chicago, IL 60607

Free Pr Free Press. Dist. by: Macmillan Co., Riverside, NJ 08075

FS&G Farrar, Straus & Giroux, Inc., 19 Union Square, W., New York, NY 10003

G&D Grosset & Dunlap, Inc., 51 Madison Ave., New York, NY 10010

Ginn Ginn & Co., A Xerox Publishing Co., 191 Spring St., Lexington, MA 02173

Globe Globe Book Co., Inc., 175 Fifth Ave., New York, NY 10010

Greenwood Greenwood Press, Inc., 51 Riverside Ave., Westport, CT 06880

Grove Grove Press, Inc., 196 W. Houston St., New York, NY 10014

Hale E. M. Hale & Co., 128 W. River St., Chippewa Falls, WI 54729

Har-Row Harper & Row Pubs., Inc. Orders to: Scranton, PA 18512

HarBraceJ Harcourt Brace Jovanovich, Inc., 757 Third Ave., New York, NY 10017

Harcourt Brace. Harcourt, Brace & World Predecessors of Harcourt Brace Jovanovich (HarBraceJ)

Harper Harper & Brothers. Predecessor of Harper & Row (Har-Row)

Harvard U Pr Harvard Univ. Press, 79 Garden St., Cambridge, MA 02138

Hayden Hayden Book Co., Inc., 50 Essex St., Rochelle Park, NJ 07662

Hemphill Hemphill Publishing Co., 1400 Wathen Ave., Austin, TX 78703

Henry Holt Predecessor of Holt, Rinehart & Winston (HR&W)

Herald Pr Herald Press, 616 Walnut Ave., Scottdale, PA 15683

Hill & Wang Hill & Wang, Inc., Div. of Farrar, Straus & Giroux, Inc., 19 Union Square, New York, NY 10003

HM Houghton Mifflin Co., 2 Park St., Boston, MA 02107; 551 Fifth Ave., New York, NY 10017

Holloway Holloway House Publishing Co., 8060 Melrose Ave., Los Angeles, CA 90046

Howard U Pr Howard Univ. Press, 2935 Upton St. N. W., Washington, DC 20008

HR&W Holt, Rinehart & Winston, Inc., 383 Madison Ave., New York, NY 10017

Humanities Humanities Press, Inc., Atlantic Highlands, NJ 07716

Ind U Pr Indiana Univ. Press, Tenth & Morton Sts., Bloomington, IN 47401

Independence Pr Independence Press, Div. of Herald House, Drawer HH, Independence, MO 64055

Intl Pub Co International Pubs. Co., 381 Park Ave., S., Suite 1301, New York, NY 10036

Irvington Irvington Pubs., 551 Fifth Ave., New York, NY 10017

Jihad No business address available.

Johnson Chi Johnson Publishing Co., Inc., 820 S. Michigan Ave., Chicago, IL 60605

Knopf Alfred A. Knopf, Inc., Subs. of Random House, Inc. Orders to: 400 Hahn Rd., Westminster, MD 21157

Kraus Repr Kraus Reprint Co., Div. of Kraus-Thompson Organization, Ltd., Rte. 100, Millwood, NY 10546

Lion Lion Press. Dist. by: Sayre Publishing, Inc., 111 E. 39th St., New York, NY 10016

Lippincott J. B. Lippincott Co., East Washington Sq., Philadelphia, PA 19105

Little Little, Brown & Co. Orders to: 200 West St., Waltham, MA 02154

Littlefield Littlefield, Adams & Co., 81 Adams Dr., Totowa, NJ 07511

Liveright Liveright Publishing Corp., Subs. of W. W. Norton Co., Inc., 500 Fifth Ave., New York, NY 10036

Lothrop Lothrop, Lee & Shepard Co., Div. of William Morrow & Co., Inc. Orders to: William Morrow & Co., Inc., Wilmor Warehouse, 6 Henderson Dr., West Caldwell, NJ 07006

Lotus Lotus Press, P. O. Box 601, College Sta., Detroit, MI 48221

McDougal-Littell McDougal, Littell & Co., P. O. Box 1667, Evanston, IL 60204

McGraw McGraw-Hill Book Co., 1221 Ave. of the Americas, New York, NY 10036

McKay David McKay Co., Inc., 750 Third Ave., New York, NY 10017

Macmillan Macmillan Publishing Co., Inc. Orders to: Riverside, NJ 08075

Merrill Charles E. Merrill Publishing Co., Div. of Bell & Howell Co., 1300 Alum Creek Dr., Columbus, OH 43216

Messner Julian Messner, Inc., A Simon & Schuster Div. of Gulf & Western Corp., 1230 Ave. of the Americas, New York, NY 10020

Mnemosyne Mnemosyne Publishing Co., Inc., 410 Alcazar Ave., Coral Gables, FL 33134

Morrow William Morrow & Co., Inc. Orders to: Wilmor Warehouse, 6 Henderson Dr., West Caldwell, NJ 07006

Motherland Motherland, Inc., 45 Wellington Hill St., Boston, MA 02126

NAL New American Library, 1301 Ave. of the Americas, New York, NY 10019

NCTE National Council of Teachers of English, 1111 Kenyon Road, Urbana, IL 61801

Negro U Pr Negro Universities Press, Affiliate of Greenwood Press, Inc., 51 Riverside Ave., Westport, CT 06880

Nelson-Hall Nelson-Hall, Inc., 325 W. Jackson Blvd., Chicago, IL 60606

Noble Noble & Noble Pubs., Inc., 1 Dag Hammarskjold Plaza, 245 E. 47th St., New York, NY 10017

Norton W. W. Norton & Co., Inc., 500 Fifth Ave., New York, NY 10036

October October House, Inc., P. O. Box 454, Stonington, CT 06378

Old Army Old Army Press, 1513 Welch, Fort Collins, CO 80521

P-H Prentice-Hall, Inc., Englewood Cliffs, NJ 07632

Pantheon Pantheon Books, Div. of Random House, Inc. Orders to: Random House, Inc., 457 Hahn Rd., Westminster, MD 21157

PB Pocket Books, Inc., Div. of Simon & Schuster, Inc., 1230 Ave. of the Americas, New York, NY 10020

Penguin Penguin Books, Inc., 625 Madison Ave., New York, NY 10022

Peter Smith Peter Smith Publisher Inc., 6 Lexington Ave., Magnolia, MA 01930

Pilgrim Press Pilgrim Press, 287 Park Ave., S., New York, NY 10010

Popular Lib Popular Library, Inc., Unit of CBS Pubns., 600 Third Ave., New York, NY 10011

Psychology Today Games Psychology Today Games, P. O. Box 4758, Clinton, IA 52732

Putnam G. P. Putnam's Sons. Orders to: 390 Murray Hill Pkwy., East Rutherford, NJ 07073

Pyramid Pubns Pyramid Pubns., Inc., 9 Garden St., Moonachie, NJ 07074

R W Baron Richard W. Baron Publishing Co. Orders to: E. P. Dutton & Co., Inc., 210 Park Ave., S., New York, NY 10003

Rand Rand McNally & Co., P. O. Box 7600, Chicago, IL 60680

Random Random House, Inc. Orders to: 457 Hahn Rd., Westminster, MD 21157

Regnery Henry Regnery Co. Now Contemporary Books, Inc., 180 N. Michigan Ave., Chicago, IL 60601

Reprint Reprint Co., P. O. Box 5401, 114 Hillcrest Offices, Spartanburg, SC 29304

Rinehart Predecessor of Holt, Rinehart & Winston (HR&W)

S G Phillips S. G. Phillips, Inc., 305 W. 86th St., New York, NY 10024

S Ill U Pr Southern Illinois Univ. Press, P. O. Box 3697, Carbondale, IL 62901

S&S Simon & Schuster, Inc., 1230 Ave. of the Americas, New York, NY 10020

Schol Bk Serv Scholastic Book Services, Div. of Scholastic Magazines. Orders to: 906 Sylvan Ave., Englewood Cliffs, NJ 07632

Scholarly Scholarly Press, 22929 Industrial Dr., E., Saint Clair Shores, MI 48080

Scribner Charles Scribner's Sons. Orders to: Shipping & Service Ctr., Vreeland Ave., Totowa, NJ 07512

Shoe String Shoe String Press, Inc., 995 Sherman Ave., Hamden, CT 06514

Stein & Day Stein & Day, 122 E. 42nd St., Suite 3602, New York, NY 10017

T Y Crowell Thomas Y. Crowell Co. Orders to: Harper & Row Pubs., Inc., Scranton, PA 18512

Tex Western Texas Western Press, Univ. of Texas, El Paso, TX 79968

Third Pr Third Press-Joseph Okpaku Publishing Co., Inc., 444 Central Park, W., New York, NY 10025

Third World Third World Press, 7524 S. Cottage Grove, Chicago, IL 60619

Time-Life Time-Life Books, Div. of Time, Inc. Dist. by: Little, Brown & Co., 34 Beacon St., Boston, MA 02106. Lib. & school orders to: Silver Burdette Co., Morristown, NJ 13664

Trident Trident Press, Div. of Simon & Schuster, Inc., 630 Fifth Ave., New York, NY 10020

Twayne Twayne Pubs., Div. of G. K. Hall. Dist. by: G. K. Hall & Co., 70 Lincoln St., Boston, MA 02111

U of Chicago Pr Univ. of Chicago Press. Orders to: 11030 S. Langley Ave., Chicago, IL 60628

U of Ill Pr Univ. of Illinois Press, Urbana, IL 61801

U of Mass Pr Univ. of Massachusetts Press, P. O. Box 429, Amherst, MA 01002

U of Mich Pr Univ. of Michigan Press, 615 E. University, Ann Arbor, MI 48106

U of NC Pr Univ. of North Carolina Press, P. O. Box 2288, Chapel Hill, NC 27514

U of Nebr Pr Univ. of Nebraska Press, 901 N. 17th St., Lincoln, NE 68588

U of Okla Pr Univ. of Oklahoma Press, 1005 Asp Ave., Norman, OK 73019

U of Pittsburgh Pr Univ. of Pittsburgh Press, 127 N. Bellefield Ave., Pittsburgh, PA 15260

U of Wis Pr Univ. of Wisconsin Press, P. O. Box 1379, Madison, WI 53701

U Pr of Miss Univ. Press of Mississippi, 3825 Ridgewood Rd., Jackson, MS 39211

Univ Pub & Dist Universal Publishing and Distributing Corp., 720 White Plains Rd., Scarsdale, NY 10583

Universal No business address available.

Vanguard Vanguard Press, Inc., 424 Madison Ave., New York, NY 10017

Viking Pr Viking Press, Inc., 625 Madison Ave., New York, NY 10022

Walker & Co Walker & Co., 720 Fifth Ave., New York, NY 10019

Warner Bks Warner Books, Inc. Orders to: Independent News Co., 75 Rockefeller Plaza, New York, NY 10019

Watts Franklin Watts, Inc., Subs. of Grolier Inc., 730 Fifth Ave., New York, NY 10019

Western Pub Western Publishing Co., Inc. Orders to: Dept. M, 1220 Mound Ave., Racine, WI 53404

WSP Washington Square Press, Inc., Div. of Simon & Schuster, Inc., 1230 Ave. of the Americas, New York, NY 10020

Yale U Pr Yale Univ. Press. Orders to: 92A Yale Sta., New Haven, CT 06520

Recording Companies

Buddah Records, 810 Seventh Ave., New York, NY 10019

Caedmon Records, 505 Eighth Ave., New York, NY 10018

CMS Records, 14 Warren St., New York, NY 10007

Douglas Records, 145 W. 55th St., New York, NY 10019

Folkways Records, 50 W. 44th St., New York, NY 10036

Nikton Records. Dist. by Atlantic Recording Corp., 1841 Broadway, New York, NY 10023

Right-On Records/Farem Productions, 408 W. 115th St., No. 2-W, New York, NY 10025

Strata-East Records, 463 West St., New York, NY 10014

United Artists, 6920 Sunset Blvd., Los Angeles, CA 90028

Author Index

Title Index

Authors

Barbara Dodds Stanford, an associate professor in the Teacher Education Program at Utica College of Syracuse University, is a graduate of the University of Illinois. She received her M.A. from Columbia University in 1966, and her Ph.D. in secondary education from the University of Colorado in 1973. Barbara Stanford's publications include *Theory and Practice in the Teaching of Literature of Afro-Americans*, of which she and Darwin Turner are coauthors; and *I, Too, Sing America: Black Voices in American Literature*, a textbook. In addition, she has edited world literature anthologies including *Small Planet* and *Flight Plan* in the Harcourt Brace Jovanovich Variations series. Her other books include *Peacemaking: A Guide to Conflict Resolution for Individuals, Groups, and Nations*, and *Myths and Modern Man*.

Karima Amin is a language arts teacher at the Academy for the Visual and Performing Arts, a new magnet school in the Buffalo City School District, New York. She grew up in Buffalo and, before assuming her Islamic name, was Carol Aiken Mingo. After earning her B.A. in English in 1969 at the State University of New York at Buffalo, she went on to complete her M.Ed. degree there, specializing in curriculum development for urban education. She has taught in secondary schools in the Buffalo system since 1969, and in 1977, received the Educator of the Year Award from the Black Educators' Association of Western New York "in recognition of distinguished and dedicated service to education." During the fall of 1977, she travelled on a sabbatical leave to study the programs, problems, and impact of black independent schools in six cities.

Northern Michigan University
3 1854 003 008 508
EZNO
Z1229 N39 S7
Black literature for high school student

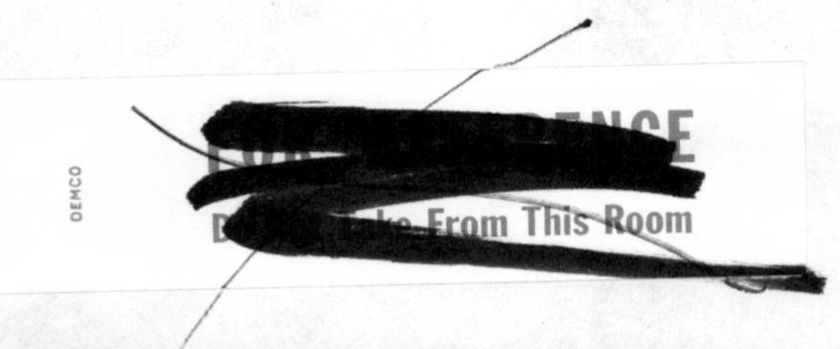
DEMCO
From This Room